PRENTICE-HALL
FOUNDATIONS OF MODERN SOCIOLOGY SERIES

PRENTICE-HALL
FOUNDATIONS OF MODERN SOCIOLOGY SERIES

Alex Inkeles, Editor

THE SCIENTIST'S ROLE IN SOCIETY
Joseph Ben-David

DEVIANCE AND CONTROL
Albert K. Cohen

MODERN ORGANIZATIONS
Amitai Etzioni

SOCIAL PROBLEMS
Amitai Etzioni

LAW AND SOCIETY: An Introduction
Lawrence M. Friedman

THE FAMILY
William J. Goode

SOCIETY AND POPULATION, Second Edition
David M. Heer

WHAT IS SOCIOLOGY? An Introduction to the Discipline and Profession
Alex Inkeles

THE SOCIOLOGY OF SMALL GROUPS
Theodore M. Mills

SOCIAL CHANGE, Second Edition
Wilbert E. Moore

THE SOCIOLOGY OF RELIGION
Thomas F. O'Dea

THE EVOLUTION OF SOCIETIES
Talcott Parsons

RURAL SOCIETY
Irwin T. Sanders

THE AMERICAN SCHOOL: A Sociological Analysis
Patricia C. Sexton

THE SOCIOLOGY OF ECONOMIC LIFE, Second Edition
Neil J. Smelser

FOUNDATIONS OF MODERN SOCIOLOGY
Metta Spencer

SOCIAL STRATIFICATION: The Forms and Functions of Inequality
Melvin M. Tumin

LAW AND SOCIETY:
AN INTRODUCTION

LAW
AND
SOCIETY
AN INTRODUCTION

LAWRENCE M. FRIEDMAN
Stanford University

Prentice-Hall, Inc., Englewood Cliffs, New Jersey 07632

Library of Congress Cataloging in Publication Data

Friedman, Lawrence Meir (date).
  Law and society.

  (Prentice-Hall foundations of modern sociology
series)
  Bibliography: p.
  Includes index.
  1. Sociological jurisprudence. 2. Law—
United States. I. Title.
K370.F7 1977   340.1'15   76–54180
ISBN 0–13–526616–5
ISBN 0–13–526608–4 pbk.

340
.115
F911L

Printed in the United States of America

10 9 8 7 6 5 4 3 2 1

Prentice-Hall International, Inc., London
Prentice-Hall of Australia Pty. Limited, Sydney
Prentice-Hall of Canada, Ltd., Toronto
Prentice-Hall of India Private Limited, New Delhi
Prentice-Hall of Japan, Inc., Tokyo
Prentice-Hall of Southeast Asia Pte. Ltd., Singapore
Whitehall Books Limited, Wellington, New Zealand

to **Leah, Jane,** and **Amy**

CONTENTS

PREFACE, *xiii*

CHAPTER 1

THE LEGAL SYSTEM:
An Introduction, *1*

Toward a Definition of Law, *3*
The Legal System, *5*
Legal Systems: Structure, Substance, and Culture, *6*

CHAPTER 2

THE FUNCTIONS AND METHODS OF LAW, *10*

Dysfunctions of Legal Process, *15*
Legal Systems and Allocative Systems, *16*

CHAPTER 3

THE PROFESSION OF LAW:
Lawyers, Judges, and Courts, *20*

The Professional Lawyer, *20*
Judges and Courts:
Third Party Settlement of Disputes, *27*

CHAPTER 4

ON THE ORIGIN AND HISTORY OF LAW, 35

The Emergence of Law, 35
A Thumbnail History of Law and Legal Thought, 38
Legal Thought in the Ancient World, 39
Post Classical Law, 40
On Legal Evolution, 42
On Legal Development, 45

CHAPTER 5

LAW AND LEGALITY IN THE MODERN WORLD, 48

The Subject Matter of the Law, 48
Late Modern Law:
The Impact of the Industrial Revolution, 51
Legal Thought in the Modern World:
Beyond the Code Napoleon, 53
Law in the Twentieth Century: Its Essential
Characteristics, 56
Freedom and Regulation in the Twentieth Century, 57
Law in the Twentieth Century:
What the Citizen Demands of the State, 59

CHAPTER 6

ON JUSTICE AND LAW, 61

Legal and Nonlegal Norms, 61
On Substantive Justice, 63
The Types and Sources of Bias, 65
Legal Ideology and Justice, 67

CHAPTER 7

ON SYSTEMS AND CULTURES OF LAW, 70

Legal Systems, National and Subnational, 70
On the Classification of Legal Systems, 72
The Theory of Legitimacy, 77

Classification by Internal Legal Culture:
Legal Reasoning, *78*
Types of Legal Logic, *86*
The Style of Appellate Courts, *86*
The Language of the Law, *88*

CHAPTER 8

EXPLAINING THE LAW:
Social Theories and their Rivals, 92

Internal Theories of Law, *93*
Mechanical Theories: Law as Technology, *93*
Law and Power, *99*
A Catalogue of Interests, *101*
The Disinterested: Interests and Reform, *102*
Judicial Behavior and the Social Theory, *105*

CHAPTER 9

THE MEDIUM AND THE MESSAGE:
Communication and Effect of Legal Rules, 111

Communication of Legal Acts, *111*
Legal Behavior, *115*
On Sanctions, *116*

CHAPTER 10

SOCIAL AND MORAL ROOTS OF LEGAL BEHAVIOR, 135

The Group Factor in Legal Behavior, *135*
Morality in Legal Behavior, *138*

CHAPTER 11

SOCIAL CHANGE THROUGH LAW, 156

Social Change Through Law: A Definition, *157*
Social Change and the Social Theory, *158*
The Independence of the Power of State and Law, *158*

On Public Reform,   *160*
Major Legal Change: On Planning and Veto,   *162*
Revolutionary Law,   *162*
Less Total Revolutions,   *163*
Social Change Through Law:
The Role of the Courts,   *164*
Social Change Through Law in a Non
Revolutionary State,   *165*
The Future of Legality,   *168*

SELECTED REFERENCES,   *169*

INDEX,   *173*

PREFACE

In this short book, I hope to make available to a general college audience some of the current thinking and research about the legal system —primarily the legal system of the United States, though I have tried to take account of research done in and about other societies. A good deal, necessarily, has to be left out. Law is a vast and important subsystem in society, but it has very indistinct boundaries; and the boundaries of what we might call the study of law and society are equally indistinct. I have drawn some rather arbitrary lines, much influenced no doubt by my own tastes and prejudices. But I think they help us get a handle on the subject.

I want to acknowledge, too, the help of a number of people and institutions. First of all, there is Professor Alex Inkeles, who enlisted me for this task, and whose comments on earlier drafts were invaluable. In writing the book, I have drawn rather freely on ideas expressed in my earlier book, *The Legal System: A Social Science Perspective*, published in 1975 by the Russell Sage Foundation. I wish to thank the Foundation, which sponsored and financed that book, and Stanton Wheeler, for his many acts of courtesy and aid. Among past and present colleagues from whom I have learned, I would like to single out two in particular: Jack Ladinsky and Stewart Macaulay, both of the University of Wisconsin. My secretary at the Stanford Law School, Mrs. Joy St. John, was totally indispensable to the work on the manuscript; and Jan Feldman helped me greatly in checking references and correcting errors. Finally, much of the writing was done when I was a fellow at the Center for Advanced Study in the Behavioral Sciences, during the academic year 1974–1975, and I want to thank the staff of the Center, one and all—well, for everything.

CHAPTER 1
THE LEGAL
SYSTEM

In Sivapur, a village in India, drums are beating. An offender is coming to justice. A messenger brings the news to elders of each caste in the village. Later, a trial takes place in the open, perhaps under a holy tree, before the people of the village.[1] On the same day, in Washington, D.C., the Supreme Court of the United States is about to go into session. The marshal announces the approach of the honorable justices. Nine men, in black robes, enter through red curtains; everyone rises.

Meanwhile, in Great Britain, the Speaker of the House of Commons announces the Queen's assent to an act of Parliament. Civil servants in the Home Office drafted the bill; the Prime Minister's party, with a majority in Parliament, dutifully enacted it. The Clerk of Parliament endorses the act; he uses a traditional formula, "a Reyne le veult," which means, in old-fashioned French, "the Queen so wishes." At this point, the bill, it is said, becomes "law."

These and other pictures crowd the mind when we think of law and legal process. Here is a comrade's court in Moscow. A man stands sheepishly before a judge. It is said he pilfered goods from his factory. He mumbles some excuse. The judge lectures him sternly about the duties of a Soviet citizen; he is sentenced to a year of "corrective" labor.

The Bible, too, tells a story of law. Moses leads the children of Israel to the foot of Mount Sinai. Dense smoke covers the peak; the Lord himself appears on the mountain. He issues his Ten Com-

---

1. See K. Ishawaran, "Customary Law in Village India." *International Journal of Comparative Sociology*, Vol. 5, pp. 228, 237–38 (1964).

mandments, and later, through Moses, a code of rules—for example, "whoever strikes his father or his mother shall be put to death." More prosaically, in Washington, D.C., the Federal Trade Commission discusses rules that might limit the claims aspirin companies can make on TV. In Chicago, Illinois, in the city-county building at 3:00 p.m. on a Monday, people stand in line, waiting to pay taxes, or to contest them; to settle their water bills; to buy hunting, dog, or marriage licenses; to adjust fines for overtime parking; to complain about the way their lot is "zoned;" to file a will, register a deed, or look up a record. Outside, the street is jammed with cars, buses, and taxis; a police officer directs traffic, blowing a whistle, motioning drivers with his hand.

All these images remind us, if we need reminding, that law is an important and ubiquitous presence in society. So many lives are touched by it each year. In 1969, in the United States alone, 485,000 people were arrested for seven major crimes (according to FBI statistics). There were perhaps 7,000,000 arrests for *all* criminal infractions, not counting traffic offenses. This is about one person out of 30 (no doubt some, during the year, were arrested more than once). If we add in traffic citations, and parking tickets, we include millions of people more. On the civil side, 715,000 couples went through the divorce court in 1969. In an average single year, 200,000 bankruptcies are filed, and about a million people sit on juries. Hundreds of thousands of civil suits are filed, settled, or threatened.[2]

The United States may be unusually litigious; yet, in every major country, there is a great mass of legal process. Notice that we have been talking only of judicial process, and moreover, only about ordinary cases, cases which do not make the newspapers. Newsworthy cases are infrequent; but they may have incalculable importance. Who can measure the impact on American society of the decision on "black Monday," in 1954—the decision that declared school segregation unlawful, thus setting in motion a chain of mighty events.[3] In June, 1975, a lower court in India declared the election of Indira Gandhi, the Prime Minister, illegal. Partly in reaction, Mrs. Gandhi proclaimed an emergency, arrested her opponents, and instituted censorship. (The Indian Parliament later passed a law, canceling the decision.) These are only two examples, out of many, of cases which shook their societies.

Courts, of course, are only one part of the story. They are the tip of an iceberg. Every citizen who fills out a tax return is responding to legislative behavior (the tax code is a statute) and to acts of other officials who

2. James Eisenstein, *Politics and the Legal Process*, New York: Harper and Row, 1973, pp. 206–10.

3. The decision was *Brown v. Board of Education*, 347 U.S. 483 (1954).

wrote the tax regulations, or who designed the forms that must be filled out. The whole vast regulatory apparatus of the modern state, including anti-trust policy, zoning ordinances, social security rules, food and drug law, and town planning, is in a sense part of the legal system. This gigantic edifice is part of our everyday environment; it envelops us like a cocoon. Society cannot survive—cannot eat, breathe, or walk (it seems)—without law.

But exactly what do we mean by "law"? "Law" is a common English word, so common that most people do not stop to consider what it means. Social scientists (and jurists), with a professional interest in the word, find it hard to capture the essence of law in simple language. In this regard, of course, the law has excellent company; many important social phenomena—the family, religion, education, the state—also are hard to define. In each case, there is perhaps a central core of meaning, surrounded by a hazy nebula, like the moons of Saturn. What is that central core?

TOWARD A DEFINITION OF LAW

There have been literally hundreds of attempts to define the law; more will no doubt be made. After all, "law" is not a tangible object of the real world, like a horse or a table. The word usually refers to a concept or process. No definition of law could satisfy everyone; no definition could be "true" or "false," except by some outside standard, based on an ethical feeling, or on experience. Definitions of law are, in short, conventional. They are good or bad, adequate or inadequate, depending on the *purpose* of the definition. The purpose of this book is to discuss how society and law (or legal process) are related; and to set out some of the work of social scientists who have studied the law (and legal process). We need to mark off the boundaries of the subject in some convenient way; to identify those events and processes which *conventionally* go by the name of law. "Law" for us, then, is what other people call by that name.

Other people, of course, are not of one mind. Sometimes the word "law" is used rather narrowly to mean a book of rules, or a set of norms. When lawyers say they must "look up the law," they mean that they intend to look in their books for some formal, written rule. This rule they think, would govern the case if it ever came before a judge or some other authority. When we say judges are bound to decide "according to the law," or that the French National Assembly has the power to make "laws," we use the word in a similar sense. We also use the word "law" to refer to processes and institutions, which carry out or enforce legal rules. When a person is caught or arrested, we sometimes say that person "fell into the hands of the law." The anthropologist, Hoebel, defines a norm as *legal* "if its neglect or infraction is regularly met, in threat or in fact, by the application of physical force by an individual or group possessing the socially recognized privilege of so acting."[4] Max Weber calls a rule (or order) *law* if "it is externally guaranteed by the probability that coercion (physical or psychological), to bring about conformity or avenge violation, will be applied by a *staff* of people holding themselves specially ready for that purpose."[5]

Perhaps there *is* a common core in these diverse definitions. At the heart of the law we find authoritative rules or norms, and institutions, processes, and people that deal with them—those who make rules, or give orders to other people, or interpret rules and norms, or try to carry them out. Not all rules and norms are the concern of (or part of) the law: only public, group, or authoritative norms are included. But if, as students of social science, we want to know what makes legal institutions work and how they affect the rest of the social order, we cannot overlook certain "private" behavior as well. When lawyers give advice to their clients in their offices, we have "private" behavior, but it is oriented toward, and influenced by, legal rules, processes, and institutions. If we want to understand the full *effect* of law and legal process, we will have to deal with behavior that is even more "private": for example, a man buys a printed form to use to draw up his will; a driver observes the speed limit for fear of arrest.

The world of law is the world of *authoritative* rules, the institutions that carry them out, and their impact on society. The rules are those having behind them, at least as a possibility, some chance of legitimate public sanction.[6] From this standpoint, the "house" rules and processes of General Motors or Royal Dutch Shell, large and powerful as these companies are, are not "law." For certain purposes, we might well compare the two organisms, corporation and country. The corporation too has a government, rules, and rulers. It prescribes norms and tries to enforce them. It has sanctions; it pays a bonus to employees who please or produce. It fines, demotes, or fires the deviant. From the standpoint of national law, these may be (largely) the company's private affairs. But we can, if we wish, study the company as a sort of society, and treat its procedures and rules as a kind of minilegal system. The point is, whatever the level of analysis we choose, law is part of the *public* or *group* or *governmental* aspect of that level. These metaphorical "legal systems"

4.   E. Adamson Hoebel, *The Law of Primitive Man, A Study in Comparative Legal Dynamics*, New York: Atheneum, 1954, p. 28.

5.   Max Rheinstein, ed., *Max Weber on Law in Economy and Society*, Cambridge: Harvard University Press, 1954, p. 5.

6.   Compare the definition of law in Leopold Pospisil, *Anthropology of Law: A Comparative Theory*, New York: Harper and Row, 1971, Chap. 3.

do not have to be terribly formal. A club or tribe can have law, provided it has norms, customs, or rules understood to be binding and provided violation does or can produce consequences—public disapproval, for example, to take the most informal type. Later on, we will discuss how and why informal systems stiffen up into something we can call more readily "law."

We have not, of course, given any strict definition of law. Nothing said aspires to universal validity or tries to explain what law "really" is. Our remarks are a guideline, nothing more. Sociologists of law take as their field of study certain activities that they find among governments, states, or authorities. They fix their eyes on norms or rules at this level: how they are made, applied, obeyed, disobeyed, or carried out; how they influence behavior. They are interested in the functions that these processes serve in society. For countries like Brazil, or the United States, the center of attention, naturally enough, is on courts, administrative agencies, police and legislatures, and how they work and behave; on lawyers, notaries and judges; and on ordinary citizens, as they relate in mind and deed to these officials and their labors.

THE LEGAL SYSTEM

Another way of summing up what we have said is to say that the focus of this book is not so much the law as the *legal system*. The legal system brings to mind not an abstract set of norms, but a working process, a breathing, active machine. The legal system is behavior, movement, demand, and response. Implicit in the way we talk and think about law is a general, rather abstract picture of the process. In our societies, we take for granted that there are definite legal roles and institutions. When someone sets the process in motion, we expect "the law" to react in a definite, patterned, nonrandom way. Two neighbors, Green and Brown, have an argument about a driveway that lies between their houses. Green says the driveway lies on *his* property; Brown denies this, and refuses to let Green use the driveway. Green and Brown both hire lawyers; attempts at settlement fail to budge Brown. Green and his lawyer go to court, file a complaint, and start a lawsuit. Brown's lawyer files an answer. These papers set a process in motion; eventually the matter will come to trial, if the parties still have not settled. In most countries, a judge or judges will hear and decide the case; in the United States, it is possible, though unlikely, that the case will go to a jury. Lawyers will argue facts and law, the judge will ponder (or instruct the jury); one way or another, a decision will be reached.

In this little tale, we have a life situation, a dispute, which turns into a *demand* for legal action; role players inside the legal system processed the demand, in their usual way and produced a legal output. The output is an order or judgment. It has "the force of law" behind it, meaning that the winner may force the loser to comply, if that proves necessary. Out of this situation may come other demands on the system. The loser may appeal, for example. In every use of legal process, in every use of a legal institution, there is demand, process, and response. People in a city become alarmed about air pollution. Their eyes begin to water, and they cough and wheeze. They demand that something be done, by Congress, perhaps, by their city council, by the state legislature, or by an Air Pollution Board. Each of these bodies may respond. Perhaps Congress acts; a bill is drafted, debated, and voted on. The President signs it into law. Perhaps the law sets up an agency to control industrial fumes. If the agency does too little, or too much, consumer groups, or companies, will make other demands. Perhaps a bill to control pollution is defeated. Inaction, too, is a kind of response. And it, too, may lead to further or different demands.

Every legal act, big or small, fits into this general pattern. Some acts, of course, are more formal than others. It is less formal to call the police than to draft a statute. And not all needs, desires, wants, and interests turn into demands on the legal system. People often swallow their anger or their hunger; some potential demands decay into apathy, or alienation; some take nonlegal or illegal forms—a riot, for example.

LEGAL SYSTEMS:
STRUCTURE, SUBSTANCE, AND CULTURE

For convenience, we can break down any legal system into the following (idealized) parts. Legal systems, first of all, have *structure*. They have form, patterns, and persistent style. Structure is the body, the framework, the long-lasting shape of the system: the way courts or police departments are organized, the lines of jurisdiction, the table of organization. One can describe a structure by drawing a picture of institutions: how they relate to each other, how many judges sit in a court, whether a legislature has one chamber or two, how many sections make up the Ministry of Agriculture. Structure is the legal system in cross section; it is what you see if you catch and freeze the system in a series of still photographs.

Substance is what we call the actual rules or norms used by institutions, (or as the case may be) the real, observable behavior patterns of actors within the system. Lawyers make a sharp distinction between two kinds of rules, rules of substance and rules of procedure. Rules of substance tell people how they must or may behave; for example, the law against embezzlement or rules for drawing up a contract or forming a corporation. Rules of procedure are either special rules for role-players inside the legal system or rules about how *outsiders* may approach and deal with these players. They include rules about how to file a lawsuit, how to appeal, how to pick a jury, and so on. For many purposes, it is useful to distinguish between these two kinds of rules. But in one important sense *all* legal rules are rules of procedure. A rule about how to behave "outside" the legal system has no meaning, unless it is coupled with rules (explicit or implicit) about how legal actors will or may react to such "outside" behavior. In other words, a "law" against embezzlement is not much of a legal rule unless it tells us what will or may take place if a bank teller is caught stealing money from the bank.

The legal system is part of society. By and large it does not move by itself. Outside pressures or demands set it in motion and keep it in motion. A court sits in its room, waiting for cases. If no one sues for slander, the court will never decide a case of slander. Besides *structure* and *substance,* then, there is a third and vital element of the legal system. It is the element of demand. What creates a demand? One factor, for want of a better term, we call the *legal culture.*[7] By this we mean ideas, attitudes, beliefs, expectations, and opinions about law. Let us think once again about our two neighbors, Brown and Green, squabbling over their driveway. They could resolve their quarrel in many different ways. One family could give way to the other. They could ask a friend, or a priest, to settle the matter. They could agree to toss a coin. They could go to court. The incident could turn into a blood feud. Obviously, there are many reasons why they might want or choose any of these alternatives. Take the court alternative: a lawsuit would cost money. *Structure* matters, too. Are courts easy to approach? Are they conveniently located? How long will a lawsuit take? The two sides might also consider *substance:* they consult a lawyer and find out that their chance of winning is large (or small) because of the state of the law. Each may also be affected by aspects of legal culture: is going to court a thing that people do (or do not do)? What would their other neighbors think about the lawsuit? Could they expect to get justice in court? Do they consider judges corrupt or stupid, or honest and impartial? Would they feel uncomfortable in court, embarrassed or exposed? What do they know about law, lawyers, and courts? What has been their prior experience with law? All these and other attitudes, values, and opinions make up the cultural element. Social forces do not "make" law directly. First they pass through the screen of legal culture. This is the vital screen of ideologies, beliefs, values, and opinions that takes interests and desires and determines their fate: whether to be turned onto the legal system in the form of demands, or to be shunted off onto another track, or to dribble off into oblivion.

7. Compare the concept of political culture, in Gabriel Almond and Sidney Verba, *The Civic Culture,* Princeton: Princeton University Press, 1963, p. 14.

This book is about the legal system. But there are many ways to talk about law and the legal system. Lawyers talk about law in one way, ordinary people in another, social scientists in still another. Lawyers earn their living from the law: their interests, basically, are practical. Most books about law are written by them and for them, which is only natural.

This book, in the main, looks on law from a different angle. It draws on work about law written by social scientists (or jurists who share their approach). This work is very different from work about law written for lawyers; just as the sociology of religion is very different from theology, devotional literature, prayer books, and so on. The sociology of religion studies how religion relates to society. This book is about society and law.

Each social science—sociology, anthropology, political science, psychology, economics—has its own perspective on law. We cannot cover everything or use every perspective. The legal system touches life at almost every point; hence many social sciences deal with it. Divorce is a legal institution, which figures in the sociology of the family; the law of church and state is part of the sociology of religion; inheritance and income taxation bear on the economics of public finance. Social study of law can be thought of as containing two kingdoms. One is general; it concerns ideas, processes, and institutions fairly specific to law and the legal system (for example, judicial procedure). The other is less general and shares its phenomena with other social sciences and their subfields (for example, the social study of divorce). The line between the two domains is, naturally, quite fuzzy. For reasons of convenience, to avoid trespassing on other books in this series, and to keep out subject within reasonable bounds, we will confine ourselves mostly to the *general* branch of our subject, dealing with particular branches only in passing and as they relate to themes more properly part of our venture.

Our subject is vast; we can only scratch the surface. First, in Chapter 2, we will look at the *functions* of law—what it does and how, in general, it does it. Having discussed *what*, we will turn in Chapter 3 to the *who*, casting our eye on legal professionals: lawyers, and judges, and the institution of courts. Then in Chapters 4 through 7, we will focus on the law itself. First we will cover its origins, history, development, and evolution. Then, we will take a closer look at law in the modern world: the subjects it deals with, the tension between freedom and regulation, and the problem of justice and fairness. We will conclude this part with some remarks on modern legal thought.

We will turn to legal cultures in Chapter 7. What *types* of legal system are there in the world, and how do these types relate to their social background? In exploring legal cultures, we will pay particular attention to categories of legal reasoning, and to the way in which jurists use language.

Up to this point, we have been painting with broad historical and comparative strokes. In the next part of the book we will look at theories and research that bear on the microsociology of law. What forces explain (in general) how particular legal acts (statutes, court decisions) come into existence? Why do judges decide as they do? Why do legislatures act as they do? Chapter 9 discusses two rival theories that try to explain how the legal system behaves. Chapters 10 and 11 pursue the question of behavior, but on the level of the citizen. What makes *him* or *her* obey or disobey the law? In these chapters, we will discuss such topics as sanctions and deterrence, the group factor in legal behavior, and the influence of conscience and the sense of legitimacy. Finally, in Chapter 12, we will discuss the concept of social change through law and its prospects for the future.

CHAPTER 2
THE FUNCTIONS
AND METHODS
OF LAW

Every day, thousands of concrete acts—orders, rules, decisions, bits of behavior—pour out of the legal system. In a broad sense, these acts are the *function* of the legal system, that is, what it does or what it accomplishes. But the word *function* has another meaning, too: not what a system does, but what it is supposed to do. The legal system is part of the broader social system. It has a function or functions within that system. It is like a subordinate officer, charged with certain tasks on behalf of the larger society. But what are those tasks? This chapter will list the major social functions of law, discuss them briefly, and then briefly describe the *methods* legal systems use, in the attempt to carry out their functions.

Functions, according to Robert Merton, can be *manifest* or *latent*. A manifest function is open and intended. However, an act can produce a result that no one consciously intends. This is its latent function. Merton uses as an example the rain ceremony of the Hopi Indians. The Hopi live in an arid climate. They often need rain. The rain ceremony has the manifest function of causing rain. But it has a latent function, too; it helps mold the Hopi into a single, united people. This latent function is accomplished whether or not a drop of rain ever falls and whether or not the Hopi themselves are aware of the latent function.[1]

A legal system, too, has both manifest and latent functions, intended and unintended goals—what people think the system should do,

1. Robert K. Merton, *Social Theory and Social Structure*, New York: Free Press, 1968, p. 118.

and what it actually does. We will list a few of these functions. All are real; all are also functions that at least some people *expect* of the system. They are thus both manifest and latent—or can be.

The first, and in some ways most obvious, is *social control*. This means, essentially, that the system enforces rules of right conduct. Every society defines some behavior as deviant.[2] Every society has ideas about good and bad behavior. All societies, even those where we would be hard pressed to find a "legal system," take some steps to encourage good behavior and to control or punish bad behavior. Encouragement and control can be subtle and informal—the merest raising of an eyebrow. Informal means of social control are by no means neglected in a complex modern system: a police officer yells at a driver; the President praises companies that hold the line on their prices. But the state also makes heavy use of formal sanctions: arrest, imprisonment, fines, and civil penalties.

Legal institutions are an important cog in the machinery of social control. In the first place, legal institutions are responsible for the making, care and preservation of those rules and norms which define deviant behavior; they announce (in a penal code, for example) which acts may be officially punished and how and which ones may not be punished at all. In the second place, the legal system carries out many rules of social control. Police arrest burglars, prosecutors prosecute them, juries convict them, judges sentence them, prison-guards watch them, and parole boards release them.

The legal system, to be sure, has no monopoly on social control. In every complex society, many "deviants" do not run afoul of the law at all: people who are rude to pedestrians, who have wretched table manners, who refuse to give to charity, are "deviants" in a sense; but the state lets them alone, officially at least. A night watchman found sleeping on his job will probably be fired. This is a terrible sanction; but it is not (except in a strained and artificial sense) a legal one.[3]

---

2. Is there behavior that *every* culture considers deviant? Yes and no. It is hard to find a society with no concept of murder as an evil. But what is murder? Murder is deviant or unlawful killing. An act which is murder in one society, may be self-defense, or justifiable revenge, in another. Homicide (to use a more neutral word) is certainly not universally condemned. Hardly any society disapproves absolutely and entirely of homicide (killing). Quite the opposite: almost every society allows life to be taken under certain circumstances—in self-defense, as punishment, on the battlefield, and so on.

3. Of course, the law, openly or by implication, may give or allow the owner of a business the right to fire a guard who sleeps on the job. We can, if we wish, conceive of the law as a gapless whole; every situation must be "covered" by some rule of law, if only by the (imaginary) rule that everything not forbidden is allowed. In this sense, the business executive *is* applying an authorized sanction when he or she fires the guard. But we generally use the word "law" in a narrower, less far-fetched way.

In other words, there are many patterns of authority within society. Authority will always try to control in some way behavior in the group which is under it. Parents, teachers, employers—leaders of all sorts—exercise social control, along with, and sometimes competing with, the law.

Dispute settlement is a second broad function of law. A *dispute* is the public assertion of inconsistent claims over something of value.[4] Disputes can be dangerous; they may degenerate into fights, or worse. Two people quarrel about an issue. If the people who are quarreling are blood relations, their dispute may split apart the family. If they are in business together, the dispute may ruin their company. We usually speak of *dispute settlement* when we have in mind small-scale quarrels or disagreements: a broken contract, a failed marriage, a contested will, a fuzzy boundary-line between two plots of land. The phrase *conflict resolution* usually refers to bigger and broader disagreements between groups or classes: farm owners against farm workers, industrial laborers against management, or the like.

Organized communities may provide many sorts of mechanisms for settling disputes or resolving conflicts. Institutions doing this work come in many forms and styles. One institution that immediately leaps to mind, is the *court*; but there are many others (arbitration boards, grievance committees, and ombudsmen, for example). Many of these institutions do more than settle disputes; at times they also resolve conflicts. In a sense, so does the legislature when it hammers out a new law by finding some middle ground or compromise among the babel of contending voices.[5]

Every society needs social control and dispute settlement. Law also can have a *redistributive* or *innovative* function. At any point in time, a legal system enforces two types of rules of behavior. One type consists of basic rules that people are familiar with and which change very slowly, if at all. These include, for example, rules about killing and robbery. Other rules of law, particularly in modern societies, are much more volatile. There is constant tinkering with traffic codes. Many changes in law are the end product of jockeying for power among interest groups. The

---

4. Richard L. Abel, "A Comparative Theory of Dispute Institutions in Society," *Law and Society Review*, Vol. 8, pp. 217, 227, (1973). Abel distinguishes disputes from disagreements about mere facts (for example, in what year did Marco Polo reach China?)

5. Torstein Eckhoff in his article, "The Mediator, the Judge and the Administrator in Conflict-Resolution," *Acta Sociologica*, Vol. 10, 1–2, p. 148 (1967), distinguishes between the mediator (see below, p. 28), the judge, and the *administrator*. The administrator, according to Eckhoff, also decides cases, but "in contrast to the judge, who merely pretends to determine what already *is* right," the administrator "establishes an arrangement which has the character of being new."

process of accommodating interest groups is a kind of conflict resolution; but other changes merit a rather different category, which we could call *social engineering*, that is, planned change directed from above. To draft a five-year plan for Poland or Hungary is social engineering. When a Food and Drug Commission draws up a code to regulate food colors and additives, or when the city fathers of London or Rome specify rules about parking and traffic, these too may be forms of social engineering. Traffic and food colors have their pressure groups; nevertheless a branch of the state has seized the initiative, has taken over an architectural role. The difference between dispute settlement and social engineering is roughly the difference between a private lawsuit, in which neighbors complain about a noisy night club, and a zoning ordinance, forbidding night clubs on residential streets.

Social control means control by rulers over those who are ruled. In many societies, the law, or part of it, is supposed to keep an eye on the rulers themselves. This is the function of the Scandinavian *ombudsman*. It is one of the ideas behind judicial review—the right of courts to judge whether acts of government agencies are legal or not. Closely related are proceedings we may call *claims of right*: a wounded veteran lays claim to a pension in court or before a tribunal; a mother demands her family allowance, a taxpayer his rightful refund. Suits by private parties against the government help control abuse of power, but their primary aim is to redress some particular wrong.

Discussions of law tend to emphasize the repressive side of law: rules of criminal law, and other "thou-shalt-nots." But many important norms aim to *allow*, not prevent: religious freedom, for example, or foreign travel. Many rules and orders try to make some conduct easier or more productive, or to encourage people to carry on certain work. Consider, for example, the law of wills, the law of contracts, or the laws which allow merchants to form partnerships and tell them how to do it. These laws are, in a way, like a bridge over a river. The bridge, it is true, *controls* traffic; it confines it to a definite lane or path. But without the bridge, how could the river be crossed? People would have to detour, use a ferry, or, if necessary, swim. The bridge guides people and goods across the river—but in a facilitative way. In a similar fashion, law specifies a form or formality so that people may reach their goal without danger of mistake or invalidity. Do it this way, make out this kind of will, and your estate will pass on as you wish, trouble-free. Legal forms and institutions are like standardized goods—cans of soup in a super market. No one *has* to buy soup, but if one wants to, a ready-made product is available, uniform in quality, with standardized ingredients.

Legal systems also handle much of the drudge-work of modern civilization. They store information; they register status and change of status; they legitimate claims. The state keeps track of births, marriages, and deaths. People sell and buy houses, and the deeds are recorded. Heirs probate wills. A modern society produces and consumes a staggering number of pieces of paper each day. Much of this is legal documentation: deeds, mortgages, contracts, articles of incorporation. *Notaries* in civil law countries draft many of these legal documents. Courts, too, have an important share of this humdrum but necessary business. People go to court to change their names or to get an (uncontested) divorce. The court merely rubber-stamps what parties have already agreed to; its role in the average divorce case is not much different from the role of a registry in accepting and recording a deed.[6]

Another legal function might be called *secondary social control*. A thief brought before a court is not only punished or controlled, he is also (one hopes) taught a lesson. Legal process aspires to be a kind of teacher, reformer, or parent. The law does more than *state* the norms; it tries to spread the word, explain the norms, convince its public to follow them. In many societies, trials are open to the public; people flock in to observe and absorb. In this way, they learn for themselves what is right and what is wrong behavior. In simple societies, everyone knows the basic rules; teaching goes on subtly, automatically. In complex societies there are so many norms and rules that knowledge of law can almost never be taken for granted. The system must devote great energy to teaching and persuading, that is, to secondary social control.[7]

The various functions of law can perhaps all be reduced to a single function: *social control*. Even dispute settlement is, in a way, a kind of social control. When a representative of society settles a dispute, norms and rules are imposed on the parties; in this way bad conduct is discouraged and good conduct fostered. Even so, it is useful to distinguish among the functions. One should also remember that there are many kinds of legal institutions; some perform one function, some perform others. Courts may or may not be instruments of social engineering or of claims of right. They will have different functions in different societies.

6. See Lawrence M. Friedman and Robert V. Percival, "A Tale of Two Courts," *Law and Society Review*, Vol. 10, p. 267 (1976).

7. Some social scientists feel that there are still other latent functions of law. For example, the punishment of criminals may act as a kind of catharsis, a release of aggression. Not everyone agrees; other social scientists insist that punishment has harmful side effects and, if anything, foments aggression. Albert Bandura, *Aggression: A Social Learning Analysis*, Englewood Cliffs, N.J.: Prentice-Hall, 1973, pp. 225–27. Depending on which side is right, hanging criminals in public, once a common practice, might be good (or bad) for society.

Neil Vidmar asked those Canadian adults who favored the death penalty why they felt as they did. About a third mentioned "retribution, vengeance, or punishment" as their reasons. Many people think law should make bad people suffer, or give murderers "what they deserve," or simply allow for revenge. These are reasons beyond the ordinary meaning of social control. The survey is reported in Neil Vidmar, "Retributive and Utilitarian Motives and Other Correlates of Canadian Attitudes toward the Death Penalty," *Canadian Psychologist*, Vol. 15, p. 337 (1974).

DYSFUNCTIONS OF LEGAL PROCESS

The functions have all been discussed in fairly positive terms; we have assumed that performing them is good for society, or at least a necessary evil. But institutions charged with these functions are certainly not universally good. (The Gestapo, Hitler's dreaded secret police, was an implement of social control.) Nor do legal institutions necessarily do their jobs well. From many cultures, we hear about courts that bungle the job of settling disputes or exacerbate conflict. Medieval litigation could, and often did, stretch on for years, entangled in endless formality. Charles Dickens, in *Bleak House,* drew a picture of English chancery courts in colors so dismal it has become proverbial. Robert L. Kidder describes a modern *Bleak House* in Bangalore, India:

> A well-known case involved two neighbours who had been fighting each other for twenty-five years over a strip of dirt three feet wide which ran between two houses. . . . The twenty-five year figure . . . did not seem unusual. When I expressed surprise during one conversation about an eight-year delay experienced by one aged litigant over repayment of a loan, I was told of a case he was still involved in which had begun in 1921. The 85-year-old 'court bird' seemed to delight in the fact that all of his original opponents and their lawyers were no longer even living.[8]

There are societies where litigation seems to serve mainly as an outlet for vindictiveness. It almost becomes a ritual means of "war" between families or neighbors. This use of litigation is not possible unless the court system lends itself to delay, unless it is prone to red tape or technicality. Still, why would a society allow its courts to degenerate so? Does the endless litigation have some redeeming social value? The English legal historian, William Holdsworth, observing the quarrelsome lawsuits of medieval England, felt that law had substituted for private war. The courts were "besieged with angry litigants" who fought their lawsuits "with the same spirit as they would have fought their private or family feuds."[9] People had transferred their "unscrupulousness and trickery" from war to litigation.

Sometimes, it is suggested, the sick court system is a kind of tumor, or alien growth, to be blamed on outside influence. This is how Bernard Cohn explains the endless, pointless lawsuits of India. The British

8. Robert L. Kidder, "Courts and Conflict in an Indian City: A Study in Legal Impact," *Journal of Commonwealth Political Studies,* Vol. 11, No. 2, pp. 121, 128, (1973).

9. William S. Holdsworth, *A History of English Law,* Vol. 3, London: Methuen & Co., 1923, p. 395.

imposed foreign procedures and concepts on the native population. The Indians, in response, "thought only of manipulating the new situation"; they "did not use the courts to settle disputes but only to further them."[10] In some places, too, official law is used as an escape hatch, a way to avoid or nullify the norms of local courts. In Zinacantan, Mexico, for example, witchcraft carries severe penalties in the local (Indian) communities. Persons accused of witchcraft sometimes try to evade these punishments by appealing to Mexican authorities, who regard witchcraft as superstitious nonsense.[11] In general, the Indians play off one form of law against the other.

Not *all* pathologies can be explained, however, either as the product of a mismatch between two legal traditions (one rooted in custom, the other formalistic and foreign), or as substitutes for the feud. Manipulative, hostile use of litigation is far too widespread. Litigation can be an instrument of ordinary political and economic struggle. This was its use in the small county of San Benito, California, in 1890—not "as an efficient, ethical tool for resolving disruptive disputes, as an agent of social harmony and peace," but rather as "an extension of physical and social stuggle." The law protected property against "aggressive attack," "exerted control over underlings and undesirables," and gave people weapons for use in the tough life-struggle for power and wealth.[12] In general, where law is technical, full of "tricks," and detached from everyday ideas of right and wrong, it can serve as a weapon of revenge or attack; as a source of unreasonable defense, as a means for delay and frustration of legitimate claims. If efficiency or harmony are the lodestars of the system, this use of legal institutions is much less likely to occur.

LEGAL SYSTEMS AS ALLOCATIVE SYSTEMS

In a brief and general way, we have described what the social functions of the legal system are. In this section, we will deal with the *methods* used by legal systems in performing their functions, that is, the techniques which a system of authoritative rules may employ to reach its decisions, and to carry them into effect.

Legal acts are, in an important sense, economic. They either dis-

10. Bernard S. Cohn, "Some Notes on Law and Change in North India," in Paul Bohannan, ed., *Law and Warfare*, Garden City, New York: Doubleday, 1967, pp. 139, 155.

11. Jane Collier, *Law and Social Change in Zinacantan*, Stanford, Cal: Stanford University Press, 1973, p. 147.

12. Lawrence M. Friedman, "San Benito 1890: Legal Snapshot of a County," *Stanford Law Review*, **27:** 687, 697 (1975).

tribute scarce goods and services within a society or tell others how to distribute them. This, in the most general way, is the method by which law carries out its function. In other words, the legal system can be compared to a kind of rationing board. It issues commands, gives benefits and takes them away, tells people what they can or cannot do, and enforces its own rulings. All this has the effect of deciding who gets what, or who keeps what. For example, the system deals with transfer and inheritance of property. Law and legal process make it possible for people to leave part of their wealth to their families when they die. The state may, however, tax some of the wealth away and redistribute it. Even more fundamentally, law and legal process define what is meant by property (Is slavery legal? Private ownership of land?); rules and institutions maintain the existing distribution of property, settle disputes that arise within it, keep deviance in line, protect the rights of property (by punishing theft, for example), and, when occasion arises, permit orderly change.

How does the legal system carry out these functions? One way is through *rewards and punishments.* Subsidies give funds to some people; fines take money from others. The *market* itself is a means of allocation. Legal rules and institutions create, define, and maintain the market, that is, the domain of free bargaining or contract. Some kinds of agreements are forbidden. (People cannot sell themselves into slavery in modern societies. A contract that tends to create a monopoly is also illegal.) Rules about private property, banks, money, and stock markets are important for a market system. Criminal justice, as we have seen, acts as a watchdog, guarding property against embezzlement, violence, and theft.

But there are many other ways to distribute values or rights, and each of them, even *chance,* has at least some basis in law. People in doubt about personal decisions sometimes let fortune decide; they may for example, toss a coin. Torstein Eckhoff cites a ninstance in which courts of law followed this path in a matter of life and death. In Sweden and Finland, in the eighteenth and nineteenth centuries, chance was given an official role in cases of murder where two or more people were known to be involved, but it was not clear which one had delivered the fatal blow. The judge could decide by a toss of the dice which person would die, while the others suffered lesser punishments. The sense of the community was that someone had to die to atone, by law, for the victim's death. To kill the whole group was unjust. There was no way, rationally, to choose among the defendants. Only chance could end the uncertainty: "this way of settling the matter served to exempt the judge from taking responsibility for the fateful choice, and at the same time it made manifest that no partiality was involved."[13]

13. Torstein Eckhoff, "Impartiality, Separation of Powers, and Judicial Independence," *Scandinavian Studies in Law,* Vol. 9, pp. 9, 16–17 (1965).

The *lottery* is another way to make decisions at random. In a lottery, every ticket has the same chance to win. During the war in Vietnam, the United States government chose men to serve in the army in an order that was fixed by lottery.[14] In old Albania, village elders used to divide a dead man's property among his sons, using pieces of paper (with or without holes) or beans of different colors, or other tokens to determine who got what.[15]

A lottery gives equal chances, but it produces unequal results. Goods can also be allocated *per capita* (by the head); here the outcome or result is perfectly equal. This method is common in rationing schemes (one pound of sugar per family, for example). The right to vote is also given out *per capita;* each registered voter has one vote, and only one. *Merit* is still another way of allocating. Any agreed upon standard can be used to measure merit. The state may allocate jobs in the civil service, for example, to those who score highest on standard tests. *Need* is another criterion. It too can be variously defined. Medical care is given to the sick; the wealthy (those with negative need) pay the highest taxes. Other criteria are *ascriptive* (based on status or birth)—the right to inherit from one's father, for example, or the rights of bastards and adopted children.

For any given situation, there are many ways that might be used to allocate. During wartime, rationing (in the literal sense) is used for scarce goods. They are handed out according to some principle—merit or need or simply in equal shares. If gasoline were tight, the state could allot it to those who deserved it most (by some standard), to those who needed it most, or by the head (5 gallons per person per week). The state could also allow the market to do its work; the price would rise and act as a kind of automatic rationing scheme. Or the state could fix a price and announce that the gas would be given out (in 20 gallon units, say) every Monday at noon, first-come-first-served. When supplies ran out, there would be no more gas for the week. Some people will get in line on Sunday and wait all night, to be sure of a good place in line. This too is a kind of market in which some people can be easily "priced out." There are those who cannot "afford" to wait in line. Some may not have the time. Some are too old or too sick. Some have small children they must care for. Others are able to make the effort but do not want to; they would rather take a bus than stand in line for gas.

When goods have no price, or a fixed price (and a limited supply), queuing (the time-and-effort market) takes over. Court services are an

14.   Proclamation No. 3945, Nov. 28, 1969, 34 F.R. 19017, "Random Selection for Military Service." The order depended on a man's birthday. The days of the year were picked at random, ranked from 1 to 365, and men were drafted in that order.

15.   Margaret Hasluck, *The Unwritten Law in Albania*, Cambridge: Cambridge University Press, 1954, pp. 68–69.

example. The judge's time is "free;" but only so many judges sit. Litigants must therefore queue up; in some places trials are delayed, and a serious backlog results. Legal rules that set up or imply a time-and-effort system shift resources from people with money to people with patience or time. This is a frequent result when goods and processes are "socialized." In socialist countries there are constant complaints about shortages and long lines. These may be the "price" of cheap goods in effort and time.

How does society choose its schemes of legal allocation? Social structure, history, tradition, and ideology all enter in. Culture plays a vital role. Why is *chance*—in many ways so fair a method—rarely used by the law? It lacks cultural support, in short, legitimacy. A judge who decided lawsuits by a flip of a coin would be driven from the bench. Only "principle" is legitimate here.

Choices between markets (say) and a pure rationing system, or between merit, need, and the market are among the most fundamental a society can make. Indeed, we characterize societies (as socialist, liberal, and so on) by means of what we consider to be the *basic* allocative choices made within the legal system. The overall functions—such as social control—are fairly universal, but the mix of techniques for achieving the functions is as distinctive to a society as a fingerprint.

CHAPTER 3
THE PROFESSION
OF LAW

Law in its broadest sense takes many hands to implement—the police-man on the corner, directing traffic; the clerk who records marriages; a tax accountant in a business firm. But in a special way law belongs to its *professionals*, the lawyers and trained judges. In the popular mind, the essential arena of law is not the legislature, not the office of lawyer or administrator, but the courtroom. Here it is that the legal system is most vividly represented. This chapter deals with the professionals, and with their instrument, the court.

THE PROFESSIONAL LAWYER

Most societies in human history (the overwhelming majority, in fact) have had no lawyers, no legal profession.[1] In only a few societies have there been people who work at law for a living—who go to court, advise clients, and interpret "legal" texts for money.[2] Lawyers are not found in societies without a written language, but advanced ancient

1. Richard D. Schwartz and James C. Miller, "Legal Evolution and Societal Complexity," *American Journal of Sociology*, Vol. 70, p. 159 (1964).

2. Dietrich Rueschemeyer lists three "core characteristics" of the lawyer's role: "(1) specialized knowledge of legal rules, (2) partisan advice to clients not related by kinship, and (3) representation of clients in relation both to other parties and to legal authorities." *Lawyers and Their Society*, Cambridge, Mass.: Harvard University Press, 1973, p. 1.

societies—the Greeks, the Hebrews—also did not know the lawyer as such.

As long as it does not distinguish between the "legal" and nonlegal world, a society will not need lawyers. A society must separate law from custom, ethics, and rules of courtesy and good behavior before it will feel a need for lawyers; and even then, it will feel the need only if "legal" materials are dense enough, or tricky enough, so that people are willing to pay for skill or expert advice. Many simple societies have courts and judges, but no lawyers. Custom and law coincide. The stock of norms is not divided into legal and ethical norms. Everyman is his own lawyer, and everyone more or less knows the law. Of course, some people are wiser than others, more skilled in social affairs. But this skill is not considered *legal* skill. In sacred law systems, the "law" is the word of God, or derived from it. Priests, rabbis, imams, and wise men, may be specially trained in "the law," specially skilled at handling "legal" materials. They perform some of the functions that lawyers perform in modern, secular societies. But the modern legal profession is essentially different. It is organized. It is lucrative. It is closed except to those who have undergone training or apprenticeship. It holds a monopoly of courtroom work and the giving of "legal" advice.

Even in lawyerless societies, a glib tongue or a good head will certainly help a person in court. Some societies let the less surefooted litigant bring in some help at the trial. In ancient Athens, for example, if a litigant was ill, a relative or friend could appear and plead his cause. The word "attorney" originally meant an agent, a person who acts or appears on behalf of someone else. Halfway between lawyerless societies and fully professionalized societies are those societies which allow and use these helpers; such societies, with their specialized orators and court helpers, were found in Medieval Europe as well as in the ancient world.

The Rise of the Lawyer. A legal *profession* first developed in Rome. Initially, Rome too had only orators, those with the skill to argue cases on behalf of others and trained, if at all, in schools of rhetoric. A law enacted in 204 B.C. forbade orators to take fees. By Cicero's time, there were jurists as well—men learned in the law, rather than gifted with their tongues. People went to these men for legal opinions because they were wise in the law (*juris prudentes*). The *juris prudentes* did not yet constitute a profession. They were members of the upper class, and they were strictly amateurs.[3] During the Imperial Period lawyers began to practice law for a living and professional schools of law emerged. By this time the law of Rome was exceedingly complex, the law of a mighty empire. The developed legal profession arose together with sophisticated

---

3. John Crook, *Law and Life of Rome*, Ithaca, New York: Cornell University Press, 1967, p. 89.

—and specifically legal—thought. The complexity of law made the Roman lawyer indispensable.

Lawyers are indispensable, too, in the modern industrial world. The rise of capitalism gave the legal profession a tremendous shot in the arm. Business requires planning; it requires efficiency and standardization. Lawyers have become useful, even essential, in buying and selling land, in finance and commerce, in business planning, and in the disposition of property at death. Certainly in socialist countries attorneys play a more restricted role. Still, the economies of socialist countries are vast and complex and their criminal codes are in full force; there is plenty of room for specialists in law. After an initial period of fervor, when lawyers were banned, the Soviet Union brought lawyers back, though as tame employees of the state, organized in "colleges of advocates," rather than in private law firms.

Indispensable people are not always popular. We must have lawyers, because the law is baffling, complex, and incomprehensible. Yet, to the lay person it may seem as if lawyers make up as many riddles as they solve. Lawyers have come to represent prevailing injustice—the pervasive mumbo-jumbo of law. They are seen, then, as shysters, charlatans, and tricksters—sinister tools of special interests. Some societies have tried to stamp out lawyers or to drive them out of business. Usually—as in Soviet Russia—the lawyers come back.

The Lawyer as a Professional. The lawyer in Rome, as we mentioned, was originally an amateur of high status who practiced oratory. The English barrister, too, has long clung to the pleasant fiction that, as a gentleman, he charges no fee. What he collects is an "honorarium," a gratuity from a grateful client. In fact, the modern barrister is as rapacious as the next man or woman and the client pays "not what he regards as . . . appropriate," but "what he is charged." A few relics of the old concept survive; technically the barrister cannot sue a client for the fee, if the client fails to pay.[4]

Like many fictions, this one has some purpose. Lawyers earn their bread by practicing law, but they insist that they are not "mere" business executives. Their usual claim is to *professional* status. This means that lawyers, in their view at least, are experts, doing work beyond the layman's power; since the work requires skill one cannot master it without long and arduous study. A profession (according to its members) has rules and standards. It has its "ethics" and a mandate from society to perform some socially useful role in a responsible way. At least, this is the theory.

---

4. Michael Zander, *Lawyers and the Public Interest, A Study in Restrictive Practices,* London: Weidenfeld and Nicolson, 1968, pp. 1–2.

Modern societies grant their professions a monopoly over work which "belongs" to that corner of knowledge or skill. Only a licensed doctor may remove a gall bladder; it is a crime for someone else to try. Only a lawyer can practice law. Restrictions on practice are supposed to protect the public against quacks and imposters, but the profession gains as well, because it has a monopoly. In fact, all sorts of things that lawyers (and doctors) do could be done just as well by cheaper help, by "para-professionals." The cost of using lawyers has been rising over the last century. High costs mean that some jobs will not get done, or will be done only for the rich, or that some shadowy half-profession will grow up to do law jobs at a cut-rate price. Indeed, this phenomenon is reported in a number of countries. In India there are the so-called "sea lawyers" and in Indonesia "bush lawyers" who have no law degrees, but who actually ply their trade in the courts.[5]

Certainly, many jobs that lawyers do could be done just as well by clever laymen. One of the lawyer's important jobs, in many societies, is simply to know the way around government and the legal system. Lawyers are experts in knowing who to see. They have friends in city hall, at the provincial capitals, in the agencies of government. They unravel red tape. This makes the lawyer valuable to clients who must cope (as so many must) with bureaucracy. In this regard, the lawyer merges with the "bush lawyers" and "sea lawyers," who do lawyer's work without formal training. Indeed, in some societies, one finds "underground lawyers," who also lack diplomas or certificates, but who know their way around. In Brazil, they are called *despachantes* (expediters). Though not professionals, people could not manage without them. The yellow pages of Rio's phone book, we are told, in recent years listed over 300 *despachantes*.[6]

The Size of the Bar.   Countries vary greatly in the sheer number of lawyers per head. The United States has an enormous array of lawyers—far more than other countries more or less on the same plane of development. In 1970, there were over 350,000 lawyers in the United States.[7] If we subtract retired lawyers, inactive lawyers, lawyers on the bench, or occupying other legal roles, we are still left with about 300,000 lawyers. By way of contrast, the British have one tenth the lawyers at most, serving a population about one quarter as large. In Germany, in 1970, there were 22,800 lawyers in practice; the population, at 60 million, was larger than

5. Charles Morrison, "Clerks and Clients; Paraprofessional Roles and Cultural Identities in Indian Litigation," *Law and Society Review*, Vol. 9, pp. 39, 54 (1974).

6. Keith S. Rosenn, "The Jeito, Brazil's Institutional Bypass of the Formal Legal System and Its Developmental Implications." *American Journal of Comparative Law*, Vol. 19, pp. 514, 536 (1971).

7. American Bar Foundation, *The 1971 Lawyer Statistical Report*, p. 5.

Great Britain's. Even more extreme is the case of Japan. In 1960, there were 9,114 Japanese lawyers, for a population of 93,000,000.[8] In general, in the Far East, tradition downgrades "law" in the formal sense, and treats lawyers with fairly intense suspicion. There are only a few thousand lawyers in Maoist China, organized in *legal advisory offices*, and working on a salaried basis.[9]

Clearly, the *number* of lawyers in any given society is a function of the social role assigned to lawyers. That role is by no means static. Vilhelm Aubert, basing his conclusions on the Norwegian experience, thinks that lawyers are most important in the early stages of industrial society. At that point, lawyers, as generalists, are particularly useful, because "specialization is poorly developed, and . . . it is difficult to foresee and satisfy demands for highly specialized expertise."[10] The role of the lawyer shifts with industrial maturity. Economists, business specialists, engineers, indeed, professionals of all sorts, take over many jobs that lawyers once performed.

The bar *is* declining in size in Scandinavia. In other countries, the bar is growing, but legal education, once the dominant form of university study, has lost its position relative to other courses of study. In Germany, in 1830, 29 percent of all university students were studying law; this dropped to 21 percent in 1910, 16 percent in 1950, and by 1965 was less than 10 percent. In Switzerland the absolute number of law students dropped 25 percent between 1936 and 1958, while the number of university students rose by some 20 percent.[11] In Spain, there was an "avalanche of law students" as late as 1945—30 percent of all university students; by 1970 the percentage of students had fallen to 12.5 percent. The number of lawyers actually in practice, however, rose from less than 6,000 to 15,875 in 1969.[12] In Germany, too, the bar rose from 4,000 in 1880 to almost 23,000 in 1970.

The Bar in the United States. Not only is the American bar im-

8. Richard W. Rabinowitz, "Law and the Social Process in Japan," *Transactions of the Asiatic Society of Japan*, 3rd Series, Vol. X, Tokyo: p. 46. The German figures are from Holger Volks, *Anwaltliche Berufsrollen und Anwltliche Berufsarbeit in der Industriegesellschaft*, Hanover: Arbeitskreis für Rechtssoziologie, 1975, p. 386.

9. Shao-Chuan Leng, *Justice in Communist China*, Dobbs Ferry, N.Y.: Oceana, 1967, pp. 127–46.

10. Vilhelm Aubert, "Law as a Way of Resolving Conflicts: The Case of a Small Industrialized Society," in Laura Nader, ed., *Law in Culture and Society*, Chicago: Aldine, 1969, pp. 282, 301n.

11. See Wolfgang Kaupen, "Uber die Bedeutung des Rechts und der Juristen in der Modernen Gesellschaft," in Günter Albrecht et al., editors, *Soziologie: Sprache, Bezug zur Praxis, Verhältnis zu anderen Wissenschaften*, Opladen: Westdeutscher Verlag, 1973, p. 376.

12. José-Juan Toharia, *El Juez Español, Un Analisis Sociologico*, Madrid: Editorial Tecnos, 1975, pp. 79–80.

mense in size; it is also rapidly growing. About 33,000 students a year graduate from American law schools. New law schools have opened up in recent years because of the demand for legal education. (If jobs grow scarcer, this demand may ease off.) Compared to other professions, and to the bar in other countries, the American profession has also been quite open-ended. Until the late nineteenth century, one trained for the bar through apprenticeship. It was fairly easy to become a lawyer. Harvard Law School opened its doors in the early nineteenth century, and it had many competitors by 1900; yet law school was not demanding in either its entrances or exits. By the turn of the century there were also dozens of part-time and night-time law schools. Even today, especially in California, there are many marginal, profit-making law schools, where students have at least an outside chance in the lottery of bar examinations.

A century ago, in the United States, American lawyers spent much of their professional time checking tangled real estate records, dealing in land, and collecting debts. They also litigated a lot. The lawyer was par excellence a courtroom specialist. The most revered lawyer was the spellbinding orator. When Daniel Webster argued a case before the Supreme Court—he could go on for hours, even days—the galleries would be packed with spectators, and a good speech might wring tears from the ladies' eyes.

Historically, the profession has been exceptionally nimble in finding new jobs as old ones disappear or fill up. In this regard, the American bar may differ greatly from the Scandinavian bar. Most title and debt work has been lost to title companies and collection agencies. Workmen's compensation and, now, no-fault auto insurance eliminate much personal injury work. But lawyers have found other roles—in government service, in land use planning, in tax consulting, and the like.

In general, the center of gravity of law has moved from the courtroom to the office. Many lawyers who work for large law firms never see the inside of a courtroom. Their work is business and legal planning; they are quiet, discreet people who never make headlines, and who would pass by unrecognized on the streets. The criminal lawyer tends to be more flamboyant. But even in the criminal justice system, the lawyers, prosecutors, and judges are less courtroom actors than before. Up until (say) the late nineteenth century, the trial played a vital role in screening out the innocent from the guilty. The lawyer's job was to marshal arguments and evidence to convince a jury that the defendant should go free. "Police science" is relatively recent. Before the middle of the nineteenth century, there were few professional police, and no finger-printing, radar, breathalysers, walkie-talkies, blood tests; no FBI, no Interpol, no computers with data on crime and criminals. Bad luck, suspicion, or rumor often led to arrest. Judge and jury sifted the evidence, mainly using common sense. The lawyers tried to persuade. Of those arrested in (say) 1850, more were brought to trial, and a higher proportion found innocent than today—possibly because they *were* innocent. Now, in criminal justice, most of the crucial work goes on outside the courtroom. Police, detectives, and prosecutors filter out the most obviously innocent; for most defendants, the lawyer's job is to strike a good bargain. In the life-cycle of a case, the trial has become much less common, and the function of the criminal lawyer has correspondingly changed.

Stratification and the Divided Bar.　It is wrong, of course, to think of "the bar" or "the legal profession" as a monolith. The American bar is quite stratified. Some lawyers work in large "factories" of 100 lawyers or more, on Wall Street and in the financial districts of other cities. Others are sole practitioners. Some specialize in divorce law, criminal law, or patents.[13] There is a big distance, socially and economically, between the senior partner of a Wall Street law firm, and the small town general practitioner. The majority of lawyers are white males of middle class background; but the ethnic bar (Polish, Italian, Jewish, and so on) has been significant since about 1900. A trickle of blacks (since the mid-nineteenth century) and women (since the late nineteenth century) has leavened the bar, recently at an accelerated pace.

In some countries, the bar is officially divided into classes. In England,[14] the bar is split between *barristers* and *solicitors*. Only barristers argue cases in the higher courts. Barristers have no direct relationship with clients; clients work through solicitors, who refer litigation to barristers. Solicitors do not appear in the higher courts, but they perform the office work and business planning that big firm lawyers perform in the United States. There are more than ten times as many solicitors as barristers; in 1960, there were less than 2,000 barristers and 22,000 solicitors. High court judges are appointed only from the ranks of the barristers. Practically speaking, the two segments are hermetically sealed from each other; it is not possible to move from branch to branch.

Until 1971, there was also a divided profession in France. The *avocat* was roughly the equivalent of an English barrister; the *avoué* prepared the pleadings, but did not argue the case. In 1971, the two were merged into a single profession, and the office of the *avoué* essentially abolished.

Lawyers in Politics.　In the United States, the lawyer's role spills

---

13.　Sociological studies of the bar in the United States include Jerome Carlin, *Lawyers on Their Own*, Rutgers, New Jersey: Rutgers University Press, 1962; Arthur Lewis Wood, *Criminal Lawyer*, New Haven, Conn.: College & University Press, 1967; Erwin O. Smigel, *The Wall Street Lawyer*, Bloomington, Indiana: Indiana University Press, 1964; Joel Handler, *The Lawyer and His Community: The Practicing Bar in a Middle-Sized City*, Madison, Wisconsin: University of Wisconsin Press, 1967.

14.　For a sharp critique of the British divided profession, see Michael Zander, *Lawyers and the Public Interest, a Study in Restrictive Practices*, London: Weidenfeld and Nicolson, 1968. See also Brian Abel-Smith and Robert Stevens, *Lawyers and the Courts, A Sociological Study of the English Legal System 1750–1965*, Cambridge: Harvard University Press, 1967.

over into arenas which are not strictly "legal." Lawyers have a prominent place in the ranks of corporate executives. It is not rare for the company lawyer, after thirty years with the firm, to attain the president's chair; the company doctor, accountant, or engineer is much less likely to rise to the top. The more doctors specialize, the more they gain prestige; for lawyers this is not the case. Doctors who are elected to the legislature must leave their practices behind; lawyers, on the contrary, find clients more eager than ever to have them. Moreover, for lawyers, the legislature is a stepping-stone to good public jobs. Many of these jobs (judgeships, for example) are set aside for lawyers only.[15]

In the United States, lawyers scramble all over the political scene. Roughly three out of four United States senators are lawyers. Presidents, governors, and representatives in Congress are also likely to be lawyers. Actually in almost every country, lawyers are overrepresented in law-making bodies, that is, there are more lawyer-legislators than one would predict from their share of the general population. The exact percentage varies from country to country. Mogens Pedersen reports figures ranging from 56 percent (the United States House of Representatives in 1957) to 2 percent (lawyers in the lower house in Sweden, in 1964). One third of the members of the Canadian House of Commons in 1962 were lawyers, 28 percent of the Lebanese Chamber of Deputies (1960–64), 25 percent of the Indian House of the People in 1952, 11 percent of the Swiss National Council in 1959, 10 percent of the Israeli Knesset in 1957, 8 percent of the Japanese House of Representatives in 1963, and 4 percent of the Danish Folketing in 1969. Danish lawyers, according to Pedersen, mostly belong to conservative parties. In Denmark lawyers can not use the legislature as a stepping-stone to judicial careers; judges have a separate career line of their own.[16] (In the United States, political lawyers are in both major parties.) These differences help explain the wide disparity between the political role of the lawyer in these two countries.

JUDGES AND COURTS:
THIRD PARTY SETTLEMENT OF DISPUTES

Societies without lawyers are common; societies without judges and courts are much more rare. Institutions that resolve, or help resolve, disputes are ubiquitous; all but the very simplest societies have them. Per-

---

15.   Paul L. Hain and James E. Piereson, "Lawyers and Politics Revisited: Structural Advantages of Lawyer-Politicians." *American Journal of Political Science*, Vol. 19, p. 41 (1975).

16.   Mogens D. Pedersen, "Lawyers in Politics: The Danish Folketing and United States Legislatures," Chapter 2 of Samuel C. Patterson and John C. Wahlke, eds., *Comparative Legislative Behavior: Frontiers of Research*, New York: Wiley-Interscience, 1972.

haps the judge evolved from the *mediator*, that is, a third person who tries to help people iron out difficulties by themselves—a kind of go-between, without power to force the parties to settle. Some simple societies without judges have had such mediators, for example, the Nuer of the Sudan, where the "leopardskin chief" played this role.[17] We may call dispute-settlers *judges*, whenever they can back up their decisions with force. The word "judge" usually brings to mind the professional judge, trained in the law, earning a living as a judge, and deciding cases on the basis of "law." For modern societies, it is convenient to distinguish between the judge using the process of *adjudication* and the work of the arbitrator (*arbitration*). Arbitration, like adjudication, produces decisions that can be enforced; but the arbitrator need not be a trained and professional judge. In other words, the arbitrator is a judge in the broad but not the narrow sense of the word—a kind of temporary judge, frequently used in labor and commercial disputes.

Adjudication and Society. What is the relationship between the type of social system and the choice of a particular institution for third-party settlement of disputes? First of all, simple societies with simple economies and small populations living in tight face-to-face relationships, often lack "law" in the sense of organized institutions. These societies tend to mediate, not adjudicate. In a community where people live in close contact, force and formality may not be needed; people solve their problems and obey the rules without them. More complicated societies have judges and courts. But trials in many tribal societies seem quite unlike trials in modern Western societies. Max Gluckman, who studied the Barotse in what was then Northern Rhodesia, has given us one classic description. Among the Barotse, relationships were "multiplex." The parties to a dispute were neighbors and kinsmen, tied to each other in a number of interlocking relationships. (Litigants in modern nations are far more likely to have only one, rather impersonal relationship: two strangers whose cars collided, for example). Barotse judges were not bound by narrow rules of evidence; rather, they delved into the whole of a controversy, trying to seek out the root of the problem. Disputes were "inevitably very entangled. What appears to be a trifling dispute . . . over the neglect of a woman to give her father a cup of beer may bring to a head a long record of festering troubles and produce recitals by both parties of grievances exacerbated by smoldering irritations over points of fact."[18] The aim of a lawsuit, as far as the judges (and society) were concerned, was to bring the litigants back together, to solve the underlying problem,

17. E.E. Evans-Pritchard, *The Nuer*, Oxford: Clarendon Press, 1940, pp. 163–64.

18. Max Gluckman, *The Ideas in Barotse Jurisprudence*, New York: Barnes & Noble, 1965, p. 7.

to sew back together the ripped social fabric. Because relationships were "multiplex," nothing else would do. (Indeed, in these societies, Gluckman points out, one could say that, in a sense, disputes among kin were "never . . . finally settled.")

Courts in tribal societies are typically cheap, popular, and accessible. They do not use a specialized jargon. Everyone, or almost everyone, understands the norms and the rules. In formal courts of the West, on the other hand, justice is formal and expensive. Many students of courts have been struck by the contrast between the two types, which seem to be polar opposites. In general, anthropologists appear to admire the tribal courts. They feel that these courts work well. They settle disputes with efficiency, and restore social harmony. Social scientists who study the courts of the West take a far more jaundiced view of their subject. Western courts, they feel, are remote, class-biased, and technical; for one reason or another, they are virtually useless in settling the conflicts and disputes of ordinary people, or for that matter, helping out in the ordinary business dispute. The public seems to agree. A survey of French opinion confirms the negative image of Western justice. French respondents thought that judges, though honest, were distant and inaccessible. Legal process itself they described as complex, slow, and expensive, and not suited at all to their problems.[19]

The Function of Courts in the West. Why should this be so? It is possible, of course, that the studies of tribal courts err a bit on the romantic side, while studies of Western courts are a shade prejudiced against the courts, and public opinion a shade unfair. But the essential facts about Western courts remain true. Perhaps this is on the whole what we might expect in a system where "professionals" are in charge. "Professionals" have little to gain and a lot to lose from informality. If the word gets around that wisdom and common sense are all that is needed for giving advice or deciding cases, the professionals suffer.

But there must be a reason, deeper than professional self-interest, why society would tolerate these professional pretensions. It may be that societies in the West—complicated, individualistic—do not want or need careful excavation of disputes, in all their richness of context, as one finds it among the Barotse. If courts are expensive and technical, disputants will shun the courts. This may be essential for a market society that puts high value on freedom to buy and sell without friction and fuss. In the nineteenth century, as the economy rapidly expanded, new legal tools were needed to keep the market vigorous and healthy, that is, to foster free,

19. Yves Baraquin, *Les Justiciables face à la Justice Civile*, Paris: Centre de Recherche . . . sur la Consomation, Vol. 1, 1973, iv. Survey data from other countries —for example, Germany, Japan, and the United States—show similar views. (Survey conducted, 1974, under the auspices of the Youth Bureau, Prime Minister's Office, Japan.)

rapid, and voluminous trade. Law became streamlined. New business forms were devised—the check was one—that were standardized in their wording, appearance, and legal effect; rapid, routine, trouble-free exchange was the ideal. A vigorous market is one in which people absorb losses in the short run and continue to trade. They do not break off relationships in the middle of the competitive struggle, and they do not funnel transactions through courts. The market society seems to allow the cost of litigation to rise; it tolerates a system of formal, distant courts to discourage all disputes but the most intense, or those for the highest stakes.[20] What happens to the other disputes? Some simply disappear; people learn to "lump it;" they swallow their anger, ignore their claims, or work matters out somehow.[21]

The Decline of Litigation. That this is a plausible reason is suggested by an interesting fact, attested to in a number of countries. Litigation rates do not rise with industrial expansion; indeed, they remain static or even decline. In this sense, there is no "law explosion." This last is one of the messages of José Juan Toharia's remarkable study of Spanish courts in the twentieth century.[22] As Spain became an urban, industrial country, the volume of civil litigation, per 1,000 population, declined. On the other hand, the work of the notaries rose sharply. (Notaries in Spain prepare legal documents and do paper work necessary to form corporations.) This shows that *legal* activity was rising; but the new society was shunning the courts. The same decline in the use of formal courts has been reported in other countries, for example, Costa Rica, Denmark, Sweden, and Italy. In Norway, civil case loads for the last century have not kept pace with population growth.[23] In England, the United States, and West Germany,[24] too, the litigation rate has been relatively static.

Courts, of course, remain important. In some respects, they are more indispensable than ever, especially in countries like the United States, where courts have a great deal of independence and can exercise power over other branches of government without fear of reprisal. Their posi-

20. See Lawrence M. Friedman and Robert V. Percival, "A Tale of Two Courts: Litigation in Alameda and San Benito Counties," *Law and Society Review*, Vol. 10, p. 267 (1976).

21. William L. F. Felstiner, "Influences of Social Organization on Dispute Processing," *Law and Society Review*, Vol. 9, pp. 63, 81 (1974).

22. José Juan Toharia, *Cambio Social y Vida Juridica en España, 1900–1970*, Madrid: Edicusa, 1974.

23. Vilhelm Aubert, "The Changing Role of Law and Lawyers in Nineteenth and Twentieth Century Norwegian Society," *Juridicial Review*, Vol. 17, N.S., p. 97 (1972).

24. On Germany see, Erhard Blankenburg, "Studying the Frequency of Civil Litigation in Germany," *Law and Society Review*, Vol. 9, p. 307 (1975).

tion makes them good guardians of the rights of minorities. As they lose what was once their staple product (the resolution of ordinary disputes arising out of everyday life), their role as guardians of fundamental liberties (quantitatively unimportant, but politically vital) increases.

To remedy the lack of "people's courts," however, a number of devices have been tried. There are "small claims courts" in the United States. These courts are cheap, and people may present their claims without lawyers. The British created a network of county courts in the nineteenth century, also for small causes. From their very inception, both of these types turned out to be "people's courts" only in the sense that "the little man" was present as defendant. Small merchants collected debts from customers and tenants, tenants and working class customers rarely used the courts on their own. Only in the last few years have the two countries begun to worry about making these courts more responsive to the ordinary citizen.

Cheap, local, lay justice is a feature of the socialist countries—the Soviet Union, Eastern Europe, Cuba, as well as such countries as Tanzania and Burma.[25] The "people's courts," however, are also courts that help maintain tight social control. They are particularly useful in societies committed to discipline, to central planning and to developing a "socialist consciousness." They bring to bear on the deviants the force of their neighbors' disapproval. Typically, they dispense real punishments. According to a law of 1961, the chief task of the Soviet Comrade's Courts is to "prevent violations of law and misdemeanors detrimental to society, to educate people by persuasion and social influence, and to create an attitude of intolerance toward any antisocial acts."[26]

Arbitration. The decline of the formal courts is accompanied by the rise of arbitration. To be sure, there were arbitrators of private disputes in ancient Rome; private citizens used arbiters, for example, to settle their quarrels over disputed boundaries.[27] But arbitration is particularly important in modern society because of society's deep distrust of formal, traditional courts. In countries where the volume of litigation is static or declining—Sweden and Denmark, for example—business people, who avoid the courts, frequently arbitrate disputes over building construction.[28] Business people in the United States also tend to avoid litigation, if they possibly can; litigation is disruptive, and business people

25. See, on Burma, *New York Times*, Nov. 12, 1974, p. 16, col. 3.

26. Quoted in Harold Berman, *Justice in the USSR*, Cambridge: Harvard University Press, 1963, p. 289.

27. John A. Crook, *Law and Life of Rome*, Ithaca: Cornell University Press, 1967, pp. 78–79.

28. Britt-Mari P. Blegvad, P. O. Bolding, Ole Lando, *Arbitration as a Means of Solving Conflicts*, Copenhagen: Ronota, 1973.

are not comfortable with technical rules of law.[29] They have more confidence in arbitrators. The arbitrator uses business norms and common sense. Procedure is simple and straightforward. Technical rules of evidence are not adhered to. An arbitrator with a reputation for fairness and efficiency will be hired again and again. (Judges do not depend on the parties for their job, and they have less incentive to please them.)

The government, too, bypasses the courts. In every nation, administrative agencies and tribunals act as detours around the court system. These bodies decide disputes and regulate economic activity, free from the tradition and technicality of courts. They are not hamstrung by rules of evidence. The judges are left free to act as "legal" as they wish in a shrinking domain.

Professional and Lay Judges. It is only the modern, professional judge who faces this loss of a role. In traditional and early societies, the leader (king, chief, prophet) served as the judge; and the judge was king, chief, or prophet. The very name of the biblical Book of Judges recalls this fact. The kings who replaced the judges in Israel were themselves judges as well as kings; Solomon sat in judgment and was famous for his wisdom as a judge.

In Lesotho, in Southern Africa, "every chief had his own court. There was no distinction between what are now called 'administrative' and 'judicial' affairs." Judging was simply an aspect of ruling.[30] In medieval times, too, the king or lord was the highest judge in his domain. Judgeship was an attribute of lordship. Saint Louis, King of France, administered justice in person, with the aid of his council. This was by no means unusual behavior for medieval kings.[31] In sacred law systems, the judge was a religious figure—a rabbi, priest, or imam.[32] Wisdom and holiness made the judge, not special training in law.

The idea of a separation of powers—of an independent judiciary— is modern. Modern, too, is the concept of the professional judge, who is not merely a person of wisdom, or a charismatic or political leader, but someone trained in the law. In civil law countries, judgeship is a specific career. The future judges study law; then their training branches off from

29. See Stewart Macaulay, "Non-Contractual Relations in Business: A Preliminary Study," *American Sociological Review*, Vol. 28, p. 55 (1963).

30. Ian Hamnett, *Chieftainship and Legitimacy, An Anthropological Study of Executive Law in Lesotho*, London: Routledge & Kegan Paul, 1975, p. 90.

31. Jean Brissaud, *A History of French Public Law*, Boston: Little, Brown & Co., 1915, p. 428.

32. In sacred law systems, in general, the division between a "legal" and a religious issue is not sharp. A medieval rabbi, for example, was an expert in "law" as well as in religion; the rabbis "acted as judges in legal, civil, and monetary cases between individual members of the community." David M. Shohet, *The Jewish Court in the Middle Ages*, New York: Sepher-Hermon Press, Inc., 1974, pp. 166–67.

the training of lawyers. The judge is a civil servant. Higher judges assess lower judges, and promotion comes from within. However, even in the civil law world, professionalization is not complete: in Germany and in Scandinavia, layment sit on the bench in some courts, voting along with professional judges.[33]

In common law countries, the situation is somewhat complicated. There is a strong tradition of lay judgeship; in many American states, the judges of the bottom layer of courts (justices of the peace, for example) need not be lawyers. In 1975, only 433 out of 2,420 town and village justices in New York State were lawyers. The justices deal with petty crimes and minor civil matters. As of 1975, North Carolina did not formally require its judges to be trained in the law. A fire extinguisher salesman, with a high-school education, decided to run for Chief Justice of the State Supreme Court. He won nomination on the Republican ticket but lost to a lawyer in the general election.[34] As late as the end of the eighteenth century, lay judges sat on many high courts in the United States. By now, lawyers have a monopoly of judgeships in federal courts and high state courts. The lay judge is rapidly disappearing even from the lowest courts. In England, all high court judges are barristers, chosen from the ranks of "queen's counsel," a select group of barristers. In the United States, the President appoints federal judges (with the advice and consent of the Senate). For the most part, state court judges are elected. Judgeship can come to a lawyer at any stage of his or her life. Judges tend to be politically active lawyers. Many are appointed or elected to high judicial posts, with no court experience to speak of. There have been Supreme Court justices who, before their appointment, never judged a day in their life.

The Judge's Role: Active or Passive. "Judges" (in the narrow, formal sense) differ greatly from society to society in the way they are recruited, the training they receive, the procedures they follow, and the degree of control they exert over trials. This last is an important dimension. In the "inquisitorial" type of trial, the judge is an "activist", developing the facts independently, then reaching and announcing a conclusion. In the "adversary" system, the judge is "relatively passive"; the disputants control the proceedings, either personally or through advocates. The first is supposed to be the type used in French and German law, the second in Anglo-American law. In practice, to be sure, the distinction is far less pure.[35]

---

33. See, on this subject in general, John P. Dawson, *A History of Lay Judges,* Cambridge: Harvard University Press, 1960.

34. *New York Times,* June 2, 1975, p. 16, col. 3.

35. See John Thibaut, Laurens Walker, Stephen LaTour, Pauline Houlden, "Procedural Justice as Fairness," *Stanford Law Review* **26:** 1271, 1273–75 (1974), for an attempt to test differences between the two systems.

The term "active" can also be applied to another feature of judges and courts. An active judge or court is one willing to innovate. It was as an "activist" court that the United States Supreme Court overturned the abortion laws of almost all the states. A lower court, too, can be "active" in this sense. But opportunities for innovation are very limited at the trial court level; bold moves will only survive if higher courts ratify them. Activism, then, is mainly a feature of appeal courts. In style, if not in result, most courts are passive rather than active. They want to look as if they do no more than apply known rules of law. Courts in the United States—relatively passive in the conduct of trials—are much more active in law-making (or admit it more readily) than continental courts, which are more active in the conduct of trials. But even in the United States, it is the exceptional court, and the exceptional case, that evokes the active style.

Function also affects the *size* of the bench. Continental judges prepare cases for trial; they investigate facts and gather evidence. Their countries need more judges than common law countries, where more of the burden falls to lawyers. This helps explain why, for example, there are about 200 professional judges in England (the population is roughly 50,000,000) and about 10,000 in West Germany, whose population is about 20 percent higher.

Legal research has neglected the work of lower courts. American scholarship beams its spotlight mostly on appellate courts, and especially on the Supreme Court. High courts decide the most dramatic cases and publish written reports. Even here, scholarship rather naively tends to take what courts say at face value. Only in recent years has there been more of an effort to study the true process of decision. This is never easy. Judges deliberate in secret, are chary about giving interviews, and cloak their output in legal words and phrases.[36]

36. On judicial decision-making, see below, p. 104–10.

CHAPTER 4
ON THE ORIGIN
AND HISTORY
OF LAW

THE EMERGENCE OF LAW

In Chapter 1 we saw that the word "law" has many connotations. In one important and popular sense, law refers to certain definite *formal* institutions and their processes. It is "legal" to take a case to court; if a tribe or a union-management committee goes to a mediator, if husband and wife take their problems to a minister or marriage counsellor, they are not using "law" in this formal sense. One can ask, then, under what conditions, and when, will a society, or a part of society, decide to formalize dispute settlement and social control. The question can be asked in two ways. First, it can be asked as a historical or evolutionary question. It can also be asked in a second (and more general) form. When and why will a group, a family, a club, or any other system, large or small, decide that it should *formalize* its processes and institutions—that is, create a legal system for itself? In this chapter, we will look briefly at this general question; then we will sketch some of the main strands in the history of legal systems, and the question of legal evolution.

The beginnings of law, in the dim past, are beyond recall. Formal legal systems emerged long before the invention of writing. Law is not easily inferred from pottery shards or arrowheads. Anthropological study of simple societies does offer some clues. Many preliterate cultures have elaborate systems of law; others do not.

A study by Richard D. Schwartz gives us a glimpse of the conditions under which "law" bubbles up from amorphous social relations.[1] Schwartz compared two Israeli settlements. One of them was a *moshav* (a cooperative), the other a *kvutza* (a more sternly collective community). The *kvutza* had been founded on strict socialist principles. It did not recognize private property. Children were communally raised in the *kvutza*. Members ate their meals in a common dining hall. The *moshav* took a less extreme approach to group living. Each family— parents and children—had its own little bungalow, where they ate and slept by themselves.

The *moshav* had a formal legal structure; the *kvutza* did not. In the *moshav,* a special judicial committee settled disputes that arose among members. Informal pressures—words, gestures, expressions of disapproval or approval—enforced community standards in the *kvutza*. Informal controls had been tried, and abandoned, in the *moshav*. They were too weak to work. When a community, in other words, cannot "adequately" control its members' behavior, through informal group pressures, it will design for itself a system of formal controls.

But why is this so? We can, of course, turn the question around. When will a society be satisfied with informal controls? These controls are strong enough when members of the group generally agree about the rules (what they are) and about their duty to follow them. A society can rely on informal controls, too, when members share common views about the lines of authority. This second condition can sometimes take the place of the first, and vice versa. That is, a group need not agree about rules, if members agree about authority. And if there is strong agreement about rules, agreement about authority is not so vital.

A father, a teacher, a chief rules a family, classroom, or clan. No problem arises, and no one has any particular need for formal "law," so long as no one questions the right of the ruler to rule. Failing that, one would still not need formality—in the little world of the classroom, say— so long as the members agreed about the rules of right conduct. In that case, when someone strayed from the path, he or she might meet swift informal "punishment"—laughter, a sneer, perhaps a beating. E. A. Hoebel describes how Eskimos deal with killers.[2] There is no organized government, but a kind of consensus wells up from the group: the murderer must die. A civic-minded man undertakes the job of killing. No blood-feud follows, however, and the matter ends there. The system works, and without formal structures, because of general agreement about norms. Agreement ensures, first, that people can recognize a deviant; second, that the one who assumes the enforcer's role will find public approval and

1. Richard D. Schwartz, "Social Factors in the Development of Legal Control: A Case Study of Two Israeli Settlements," *Yale Law Journal,* **63:** 471 (1954).

2. E. Adamson Hoebel, *The Law of Primitive Man,* Cambridge: Harvard University Press, 1961, pp. 88–89.

public support. A family does not need formal law if its members agree about the rules. Nor do they need it if the children (say) accept father's (or mother's) word as final, that is, accept it as law.

These two conditions, however, imply a third. The informal sanctions must have *power*. That is why they work best in small societies, where people are in face-to-face contact. Disapproval, ostracism, and banishment do not pack enough muscle in a big, bustling society where people come and go, and there is much interaction among strangers. Small societies, where people rub elbows every day, make powerful use of shame. In the American colonies, lawbreaker were put in the pillory or stocks, so that every passerby could see them. Shame loses its force in societies too large for consensus. Informal sanctions only work in a society small and compact enough for these sanctions to sting.

About 250 people live on Tristan da Cunha, a small, barren island in the South Atlantic. They are almost totally cut off from the outside world. The islanders are descended from a handful of English sailors who took mulatto brides from the island of St. Helena. Nominally, the British own the island, but there is virtually no organized government. There are no courts, no "laws," and almost no deviance, as outsiders would understand it. A serious crime has never been committed on the island. There are informal sanctions—public teasing is one—and these sanctions, however mild, are devastating on an island where everyone knows everyone else, and where there is *absolutely no escape* from the neighbors. Tristan da Cunha is "transparent"—"every islander is aware that in all his doings and sayings he is under the Argus-eyed vigilance of the community."[3]

When members of a society cannot agree on essentials, or if they cannot or do not trust each other, they will put their rules and relationships in writing and make formal institutions for themselves. But the shift from informal to formal has many consequences. Formality changes the way laws are made, enforced, and applied; it can revolutionize the authority system. This happened, for example, in British India. According to Sir Henry Maine, writing in 1871, the British, when they established Courts of Justice, had not "the slightest design of altering the customary law of the country." But this change, which they made "without much idea of its importance" was unwittingly quite momentous. Before this, the "body of persons to whose memory the customs are committed" had "probably always been a quasi-legislative as well as a quasi-judicial body;" it had "always added to the stock of usage by tacitly inventing new rules."

3. Peter A. Munch, "Sociology of Tristan da Cunha," p. 305, in *Results of the Norwegian Scientific Expedition to Tristan da Cunha, 1937–1938*, ed., Erling Christopherson, Vol. 1, Oslo: Norske Videnskaps-Akademi, 1946. I am indebted to Professor Walter Weyrauch of the University of Florida for this reference, and for other materials on the informal legal system of the island.

Customary law, reduced to writing, formalized, and given over to Western-style courts to be administered, lost its subtle flexibility. Now, when new rules and doctrines were needed, they were brought in from outside—that is, from English law. Customary law was thereby eroded along with the social structure it implied.[4]

A THUMBNAIL HISTORY
OF LAW AND LEGAL THOUGHT

As we have said, the beginnings of law are lost beyond a trace. Countless societies came and went without any surviving evidence of legal life. Pottery fragments, old bones, and the like are not revealing. A few advanced societies—fairly recent, as evolutionary history goes—have left behind some fragments or texts, a clay table here and there, an inscription, a crumbling papyrus. Even the oldest of these is relatively young. In any period, the living law is hard to know. This is true today, and it was even truer in the past. Formal legal documents and codes are preserved; informal practices and customs pass away, without clear records.

Among the earliest legal texts known to scholars is the "code" of Hammurabi, King of Babylon (about 1800 B.C.).[5] When discovered, Hammurabi's code created a stir in the scholarly world. The code added much to our knowledge of the law of the ancient Near East, and it shed light on the (much later) codes preserved in the Old Testament. These codes were now seen as resting, in part, on older legal traditions. The codes of the ancient Near East seem in general to rest on a common fund of legal ideas. Ancient peoples probably borrowed from each other, but we would also expect a good deal of similarity, simply because ancient societies had many points in common.

In the ancient world, rules of law (or what we would now call rules of law) were intertwined with religious norms and taboos. The Hebrews, for example, drew no real distinction between religious and secular norms. The two types were formally identical. A society that believes *all* law comes from God will not treat murder or theft as different from witchcraft, blasphemy, or incest God has forbidden both kinds of acts. The book of Deuteronomy (mainly 7th century B.C.) prescribes death by stoning for those who worship the sun or the moon (Chap. 17); such rules mix freely with rules about buying and selling, and about ordinary crime (theft or murder). Moreover, political authority in the ancient

4. Sir Henry S. Maine, *Village Communities in the East and West*, 2nd ed., London: J. Murray, 1872, pp. 70, 71, 75.

5. On the nature of Hammurabi's laws see G. R. Driver and John C. Mills, *The Babylonian Laws*, Vol. 1, New York: Oxford University Press, 1952, p. 41.

world regarded itself as divine. God, not man, was the author of the law, which God handed down to his servant, Moses. Hammurabi announces in his code that the god Marduk commanded him "to give justice to the people of the land."

The law of Rome also begins with a "code," the so-called *Twelve Tables.* According to tradition, the *Tables* date from the fifth century B.C.; they were engraved on bronze tablets and stood on view in the Roman Forum.[6] Neither the Twelve Tables nor the other ancient law-texts were codes in the modern sense of the word. They were not systematic statements of the whole law, or even of whole branches of law. They could be understood only against the backdrop of customary norms, which they changed or added to in some particular way. Hammurabi considered himself a reformer, not a codifier. His "code" was a patchwork of laws on this or that subject; it spoke only where emphasis or amendment of the old law was needed.

LEGAL THOUGHT IN THE ANCIENT WORLD

In every society with a consciousness of law, people hold opinions about what law is and should be, where it comes from, and what makes it binding. For most people, these ideas are taken for granted. *Formal legal philosophy,* however, is far less general among societies than law itself. Ancient law, *except* for the Romans, "was law without legal science," as J. Walter Jones has put it. The Greeks, for example, had "little interest in legal questions, except when they were political and ethical questions as well."[7] This does not mean that the Greeks had no ideas about law, its nature, and its function; but they did not create a formal legal philosophy or write legal treatises, arranging the laws in some rational system of order.

Of course, formal legal thought—philosophy of law—is not independent of society. Common sense theories of law at large in society, and the nature of the legal profession, determine the nature of formal legal thought, if any.[8]

Without a self-conscious legal (or judicial) profession, a society will

6. The tablets were later destroyed, and no complete text has survived. But references to and quotations from the *Tables* are scattered about in works of Roman authors, so that quite a lot is known about their contents.

7. J. Walter Jones, *Historical Introduction to the Theory of Law,* Clifton, N.J.: Augustus M. Kelley, 1940, p. 1.

8. In totalitarian states, legal theory must follow the official ideology. Soviet jurists *must* be Marxists, and must follow the official line. Those who deviate do so at their peril. Some of the leading Soviet philosophers of law disappeared in the 1930's.

not develop legal theory, or legal science, in Jones's sense. There will be no learned treatises, no Blackstone, no Pothier, no Roscoe Pound, no Hans Kelsen.[9] Even without legal theory, however, a society will have theory about law. In fact, absence of legal theory is itself a theory of law; it is the theory that law cannot be separated from social, ethical, or religious life. A society that treats social norms as legal norms, or that does not divide its single mass of norms into legal and nonlegal norms (or religious and secular norms), will not have legal theory. In hindsight, we can analyze the norms of ancient societies, labeling these norms as legal, those as religious, these as ethical. But we are making a distinction never made by the people of those societies. Hammurabi had ideas about law, but no philosophy of law. Most preliterate societies, too, past and present, have undoubtedly lacked a full, formal theory of law.

In Rome, however, where a true legal profession gradually developed we find the first known books *about* law—the first legal treatises. During the Imperial Period, professional law schools were located at Rome, Constantinople, Alexandria, Athens, and Beirut. Roman jurists wrote text-books, commentaries on particular aspects of law, and also on the law in general. The jurists enjoyed working with legal concepts, analyzing them, and arranging them in a logical and systematic order. On the whole, they were practical-minded and concrete. Gaius (second century A.D.), in his *Institutes* was clearly writing law for those who wanted to solve legal problems, deducing propositions of law from known concepts and principles. Gaius' work is the one text of classical Roman law that has survived largely as written. No other ancient society had anything like it, as far as is known.

POST CLASSICAL LAW

Roman law was unique in its logic and order, and in its sway. Rome was mistress of a vast empire, which had swallowed up all of its rivals and conquered the civilized Western world. The western half of that empire collapsed in the fifth century A.D. In the sixth century, the Eastern emperor, Justinian, from his capital in Constantinople ordered a restatement and reform of the law. By 535, the *Codes of Justinian* had been completed. One part, the *Digest*, gathered together extracts from the works of classical jurists, discarding what was obsolete and unusable. Justinian also republished those older laws he intended to keep in force.

9.   Sir William Blackstone (1723–1780), author of *Commentaries on the Law of England;* Robert Joseph Pothier (1699–1772), an influential French jurist and author of treatises; Roscoe Pound (1870–1964), American law teacher and legal philosopher; Hans Kelsen (1881–1973), Austrian philosopher of law.

We owe most of our hard knowledge of classical Roman law to Justinian; the original sources, with rare exceptions (Gaius' *Institutes*) have been lost.

In the West, Germanic kingdoms sprang up on the corpse of Rome. They enacted their own codes of law; typically, these were a mélange of Roman and Germanic elements. The formal unity of classical law fell apart. In the Middle Ages, law was intensely local. Each little center of political power—each barony, each town—had its own legal system. Within a culture-area (say, Germany or France), the local legal systems tended to be similar, though not identical, just as today the laws of North and South Carolina are similar but by no means identical.

In the Middle Ages, too, the voice of the Church was a powerful one; medieval legal thought was the servant of the medieval (Christian) view of the world. The legal philosophy of St. Thomas Aquinas, for example, rested firmly on the teachings of the Church. St. Thomas developed the idea of a "natural law," implanted in human beings as part of their nature. This *lex naturae* (law of nature) was the participation of humanity as rational beings in the eternal laws of God.[10]

The outstanding event in medieval law—and in medieval legal thought—was the rediscovery and revival of Roman law as an object of study. This began in the Italian universities. It spread from there to centers of learning in other parts of Europe. Concepts and rules out of Justinian were "received" in most of Europe. (The major exception was England.) From the time of the "reception" on, European law took on a deeper coloration of Roman law, and European society grew accustomed to the idea that law was an object of scholarship, to be studied at universities and expounded by learned men. But the "reception" did not bring uniformity to European law. The law of France and Germany still lay shattered into fragments. The law of each area or principality was its own unique mixture of "custom" and Rome.

As the political, social, and economic underpinnings of medieval society changed, so did the structure, substance, and culture of its law. The old theories of "natural law" were based on the dogmas of a universal church. The jurists recast them in a more secular form after the Reformation. "Natural" principles of law were derived from innate human reason. This theory of law found it hard to account for, or justify, the localism and variability of legal systems. Human beings were everywhere the same, had the same mind, the same inborn rights, the same reasoning powers. There was no excuse then, for the quirks and foibles of local custom, or for the historical survivals that so strongly colored the various systems of law. Why should the law be so different in two towns a stone's

10. J. W. Jones, *Historical Introduction to the Theory of Law*, Clifton, N.J.: Augustus M. Kelley, 1940, p. 105.

throw away from each other? "Curious, that a river acts as the boundary of the law," said Pascal, "that what is truth on this side of the Pyrenees is error on that side."

Ultimately, the Age of Reason became the age of legal codification. What society needed was a single, rational code. In it, the lawmaker would set out, clearly and distinctly, principles of law flowing from human nature and the nature of life in society. Moreover, such a code would be uniform throughout the land. It can hardly be an accident that the codification movement went hand in hand with the rise of the unitary, powerful, absolutist nation-state. The Code Napoleon in France (1804) was the crowning achievement of the movement. Its influence was felt throughout the civil law world; no modern legal text ever won so great an empire, though the German civil code, adopted almost a century later, has been almost as influential in the twentieth century as the French code was in the nineteenth. Napoleon's armies spread his code, but the later conquests, spearheaded by French legal thought, were longer-lasting. European law today is codified law.

What do the codes contain? Basically, in Western Europe, they set out those principles that make up, in essence, the "lawyer's law" of their respective countries. Legal thought in Europe tends to agree that:

1. The codes are the highest, and in some ways the only valid sources of law; local custom and judicial decisions are second-best, or of no real validity.

2. The codes state *all* of the law. They are gapless—that is, every legal problem finds a solution somewhere in the text of the codes.

3. Law is a science; it is rational and systematic. Scholars develop and use rational principles to explain, correct, and apply the law. The law is certainly not frozen into some mystical and immutable form; on the other hand, it is emphatically not mere public opinion, not to mention naked expediency, interest or whim.

ON LEGAL EVOLUTION

Once a "legal system" exists, does it follow definite patterns of development or growth? Does law evolve? Are there "laws" of legal development? There are among the earliest questions taken up by social scientists looking at law. Evolution, as we normally use the term, means progress from a lower or less complex form to one that is (by some standard) higher, better, or more complex. "Legal evolution" means that legal systems, as they develop or change, pass through definite stages in some definite order. It does not mean that every system will necessarily move from stage 1 to (say) stage 4; after all, there are many "primitive" systems. But the idea means that a system must start at stage 1, and pass through 2 and 3 (in that order) before reaching 4.

Is there such a pattern of growth? Sir Henry Maine, in his brilliant book, *Ancient Law* (1861), thought he saw one. Early law was generally patriarchal. Individuals had few rights or obligations. The basic legal unit was the family, in which the father ruled. A person's rights and duties were more or less determined by status, and they were fixed by the facts of that person's birth. An eldest son, born into a Hindu caste, would grow up to have rights and duties distinctively different from those of a daughter or a member of another caste. Position at birth wrote a fixed and rigid program for many aspects of life. Modern law, on the other hand, is the law of free individuals; people shift in and out of legal relations, voluntarily, through bargain and agreement. In Maine's words, the "movement of the progressive societies has been uniform in one respect. Through all its course, it has been distinguished by the gradual dissolution of family dependency, and the growth of individual obligations in its place. The Individual is steadily substituted for the Family, as the unit of which civil laws take account. . . . We seem to have steadily moved toward a phase of social order in which . . . relations arise from the free agreement of Individuals. . . . The movement of the progressive societies has hitherto been a movement from Status to Contract."

Other social scientists and legal scholars have detected a somewhat similar pattern in history. Émile Durkheim (in his *Division of Labor in Society*), saw a movement from penal law, stressing punishment, to contract law, stressing restitution. Max Weber, too, found modern law distinctively *rational,* compared to older periods of law.[11]

Recently, some scholars have seen a kind of evolution in the way legal ideas develop among children. Children, according to these studies, develop stages of legal consciousness as they grow.[12] First, they feel they must obey rules because of fear of punishment. As they grow older, they learn that obedience to rules is necessary for social order. Still older children *may* come to understand "autonomous moral principles;" they judge rules one by one, testing them against ethical standards. Hence, some attitudes toward law are more childish or primitive than others. Perhaps, then, as humanity grows, its ideas about law change too, moving from lower to higher stages.

Child development, of course, is a complex subject. Scholars do not

11. Max Rheinstein, ed., *Max Weber on Law in Economy and Society,* Cambridge: Harvard University Press, 1954, pp. 61–64. Law making and law finding are "rational," when they follow general principles and rules; they are "irrational" when they depend on magic, oracular utterances, ordeals, or revelation, or when they are wholly based on hallowed tradition. Modern law is rational in authority, and rational in its methods.

12. June Tapp and Lawrence Kohlberg, "Developing Sense of Law and Legal Justice," *Journal of Social Issues,* Vol. 27, No. 2, p. 65 (1971); June Tapp and Felice Levin, "Legal Socialization: Strategies for an Ethical Legality," 27 *Stanford Law Review,* **27:** 1 (1974).

agree on whether there are stages of moral or legal development.[13] The studies are studies of attitudes, rather than behavior. Children, as they grow up, learn (among other things) how to express attitudes that society values. In some societies, children are *trained* to respect authority; no one reaches the "higher" stages. The stages, in short, may be learned and culture bound, rather than inborn and programmed.

Whatever the case, it would be rash to project these studies of children onto a broader canvas. Legal systems, to be sure, have changed greatly in historical times. But historical time is a mere speck of evolution. As far as we know, human nature has not changed in recorded history. The evolution of law has been rapid and recent (in evolutionary terms), while inborn structures turn by a much slower clock, whose beat is in millions of years.

Theories of Legal Evolution Assessed

Recent scholarship has been skeptical, too, about theories of legal evolution. Anthropology rejects Maine's "patriarchal" theory, that is, the idea that society was organized in independent households, in which all power was in the hands of one man, the father or grandfather.[14] Durkheim's idea—that early law was largely penal—is either wrong, or unverifiable, or needs to be radically restated; otherwise, it is simply out of line with the facts about preliterate society.[15] Preliterate society was, if anything, more "restitutive" than modern society; often it was possible to pay for a wrong, even murder, and the distinction between tort[16] and crime was blurred.[17] Is "legal evolution" a meaningful concept

13. The methodology of Lawrence Kohlberg (the leading exponent of this school) and his followers, has come under attack. William Kurtines and Esther B. Greif, "The Development of Moral Thought: Review and Evaluation of Kohlberg's Approach," *Psychological Bulletin*, **81:** p. 453 (1974).

14. See Robert Redfield, "Maine's *Ancient Law* in the Light of Primitive Societies," *Western Political Quarterly*, Vol. 3, p. 574 (1950). Redfield points out that Maine wrote before there were any sustained studies of primitive societies. Maine based his work on the early Greeks, Romans, Hebrews, and Hindus, whose societies were already quite advanced.

15. See Richard D. Schwartz and James C. Miller, "Legal Evolution and Societal Complexity," *American Journal of Sociology*, **70:** p. 159 (1964).

16. A "tort" is a wrong that gives rise to an action for damages, but is not necessarily a crime. If I carelessly run my car into yours, I will not be arrested (unless I was wantonly reckless, or drunk); but I may well be liable "in tort" for the damages I caused.

17. On this point, see Leon S. Sheleff, "From Restitutive Law to Repressive Law: Durkheim's *The Division of Labor in Society Revisited*," *Archives Européenes de Sociologie*, **16:** No. 1, p. 16 (1975).

at all? Legal systems are products of society. We expect them to change as society changes; unless we found a single path of evolution, for society in general, we should not expect to find such a path for *legal* evolution.

To be sure, there are fundamental differences between the law of modern nations, and the law of the Trobriand Islanders, or Cicero's Rome, or Charlemagne's France. Rome had no railroads, energy crises, sonic booms, fingerprinting, or computerized tax audits. New technology and new social conditions generate new needs and new problems; society fashions rules and institutions to cope. There is also a difference between the *culture* of modern and nonmodern law. Modern law holds firmly, in the main, to an *instrumental* theory. Ruling opinion, in almost every country, rejects the idea of law as divinely inspired, or based on natural law or immutable tradition. (A partial, striking exception is the hold of classical Islamic law on some conservative Moslem countries, such as Saudi Arabia.) Modern law is "rational" in Weber's sense. This does not mean that modern law is better at its job, or more "effective"[18] than other, older systems of law. But people today see law as a human product, not a product of God or tradition or nature. Law is a means to an end; it is something that society molds and shapes and shifts to suit its purposes. In this sense, law is rational indeed.

Legal evolution remains, in short, an open question. There may be definite patterns of change, as far as the content of law is concerned, or with regard to particular institutions. (A legal *profession,* we have noted, is a late and uncommon development.) Victorian England was capitalist; medieval Germany was feudal; the Soviet Union is socialist. No wonder contractual relations loomed so large in one legal system, status elements in the second, state planning in the third.[19] It is harder to find patterns among more *technical* elements of law, or in the short run, except at a level of abstraction so high as to almost lack meaning.

ON LEGAL DEVELOPMENT

One offshoot or relative of the concept of legal evolution is worth some further mention. This is "legal development." It is a subject of

18. To say that one legal system is more effective than another requires some test of effectiveness. But what would the standard of effectiveness be? It is not easy to see how one would decide that (for example) the law of modern Italy was more (or less) "effective" than the law of Caesar's Rome. Does it bring about more human happiness or satisfaction? Does it "fit" its society better? Is it better enforced?

19. See Robert B. Seidman, "Law and Development: A General Model," *Law and Society Review,* **6**: p. 311 (1972).

vigorous debate.[20] Since 1945, old empires have dissolved. Britain, France, Portugal, and other colonial powers have lost or given up their overseas possessions. A hundred or more new sovereignties have come into being. Most new countries have kept part or all of their colonial law. Almost every new country is poor and underdeveloped. Many of them, especially in Africa, have no national traditions. They owe their boundaries to colonial wars. They are a jumble of peoples and languages. Politically, they want national unity; economically, they want to break out of poverty. Everyone talks about economic development and political development. Why not legal development? The older law (colonial or indigenous) must have been somehow underdeveloped; it should be modernized, made more uniform, rational, systematic. To many leaders and scholars, this means stamping out customary law; in all cases, it means somehow leveling regional subcultures.

The basic idea behind legal development is not at all new. The Japanese in the nineteenth century were in a great hurry to catch up with the West in technology and armies. They borrowed great chunks of Western law, to replace their own "backward" system. In the 1930's, Ataturk imposed a new code of family law, mostly Swiss, on Turkey, as part of *his* plan of modernization. More recently, the Ethiopian government called on a French legal scholar, René David, to draft a code for that ancient land. He obliged, without once setting foot in the country. Naturally, his code was European to the core.[21] These instances of borrowings assume, first, that "law" is a kind of technology, second, that it is in essence culture-free, and that it improves or evolves, and third, that "modern" law must be better than "older" law, just as modern medicine is better than leeches and witchdoctors, and a Boeing 747 goes faster and carries more than an ox-cart. If these assumptions are true, then the latest product of France *will* be better for Ethiopian development than a code fashioned out of native traditions.

It is easy to understand why third world leaders want a single, uniform, modern system of law. It would serve as an instrument of unity, like a national language, or a single political party. "Modern" law—

20.   David M. Trubek, "Toward a Social Theory of Law: an Essay on the Study of Law and Development," *Yale Law Journal*, **82:** 1 (1972); David M. Trubek and Marc Galanter, "Scholars in Self-Estrangement; Some Reflections on the Crisis in Law and Development Studies in the United States," *Wisconsin Law Review,* **1974:** 1062 (1974); Lawrence M. Friedman, "On Legal Development," *Rutgers Law Review* **24:** 11 (1969).

21.   He sets forth his point of view in René David, "A Civil Code for Ethiopia: Considerations on the Codifications of the Civil Law in African Countries," *Tulane Law Review* **37:** 187 (1963). The code provided, in Article 3347(1), for the abolition of "all rules whether written or customary previously in force concerning matters provided for in this code." See Kenneth R. Redden, *The Legal System of Ethiopia*, Charlottesville, Virginia: Michie Co., 1968, p. 72.

from France, or England, or Belgium, or Portugal—looks rational, suitable, and scientific. It is free from the influence of local tribes. A single legal system, radiating from the capital might indeed change the life of the law. A legal order of this kind would push aside village elders and chiefs. They would lose their grasp of the law and their authority to govern.[22] Civil servants, or professional judges would replace them. This change in the power structure, however, would not depend on the *content* of the law; any new rules would do, just as any new typewriter keyboard would tend to make older typists obsolete.

The ideas and assumptions of "legal development" are by no means confined to the West.[23] Socialist jurists too are convinced that their law (not only what it *does*, but its techniques and its habits) are better and more scientific than the historical rubbish of old peoples. They agree with the West that there is value in "legal science," of the European type; that modern law will hasten social development. But the traits most admired by "legal science" (uniformity, order and system) are paper traits. They are, in particular, traits of the elegant codes of continental Europe. These codes have had more influence in the Third World than the common law has had, except where Great Britain or the United States actually ruled. The civil law is neat; it is compactly packaged for export. The common law is cumbersome, unsystematic; to import it, is like carrying groceries home in one's hands without a shopping bag or net. In fact, the Code Napoléon teaches us about as much of the living law of France as we learn about Egypt from *Aida*. But this fact is a well-kept secret. It takes enormous pains to find out how law really works in practice; legal scholarship has largely ignored empirical reality. The evidence that economic growth and social development needs "developed" law (in the lawyerly sense) is scanty, to say the least. Little is known about the role of borrowed law in everyday life, in the borrowing countries—or for that matter, in the source countries. What little there is suggests, not unexpectedly, that impact is variable and complex. We have barely begun to understand it.

22. On the relationship between the power of chiefs, and their control of legal authority, in one new nation, see Ian Hamnett, *Chieftainship and Legitimacy, An Anthropological Study of Executive Law in Lesotho*, London: Routledge & Kegan Paul, 1975, especially Chap. 5.

23. In socialist East Germany, for example, after a short period of iconoclasm, jurists turned once more to the familiar concepts of "legal science." See, in general, Inga Markovits, *Socialitisches und Bürgerliches Zivilrechtsdenken in der DDR*, Cologne: Verlag Wissenschaft und Politik, 1969.

CHAPTER 5
LAW
AND LEGALITY
IN THE MODERN
WORLD

It is a premise of this book that modern law and legal thought (roughly since 1800—since the beginning of the Industrial Revolution, in other words), differ from the law that came before. In this chapter, we will look at these differences, and in so doing, briefly describe characteristics of modern law. We will give some notion of the major fields of interest of modern law and show how they have responded to social change. We will also look at modern legal thought and the balance between freedom and regulation in a complex, highly legalized world.

THE SUBJECT MATTER OF THE LAW

Modern legal systems, are strikingly large and complex. There is an immense amount of raw material. Each self-conscious legal system develops some way to classify and analyze its substantive rules, its procedures, and its institutions. Each legal system regulates or treats some matters, and leaves other largely alone. Systems that share a legal culture will tend to divide and arrange legal materials in a more or less similar way. But the rises and falls of fields of law bear the unmistakable imprint of social and economic events, more than they reflect a *legal* tradition.

It is, of course, impossible to sum up in a few phrases differences among the *content* of various legal systems. What concerns one society does not concern another; if we described all those matters that law controls or affects, we would almost end up with a description of the whole society. Medieval law contained endless rules about landed estates; it had little or nothing to say about road accidents. In the Great Yasa, the law code of Genghis Khan, there were elaborate provisions for military organization; the code also dealt in detail with the hunt, which the Khan valued as a way to train warriors.[1] Law codes reflect social structure, economy, values, and taboos. In Mongol law, it was a heinous crime to urinate on a fire. The Biblical codes specified minutely which birds, animals, and fish were unclean and not to be eaten. They also regulated the treatment of slaves. The law of slavery figured prominently, too, in the code of Hammurabi, in ancient Rome, in eighteenth century Jamaica and Brazil, and in the American South before the Civil War. Legal concern with clean air and water, zoning and land use, and abortion and contraception reflect the bursting populations of the twentieth century, and the pressure of people and industry on precious resources.

The common law, as it developed in England, drew a sharp line between real property (meaning basically land), and personal property (everything else), If a landowner, in 1600, died without a will, his land passed to his eldest son. This was the principle of primogeniture. His personal property, on the other hand—money and goods—went to his children in equal shares. The ruling elite in England was a landed aristocracy. The law of property was, in many ways, odd and irrational, but the basic emphasis on land and the main outlines of land law made sense for a society with such a social system. Similarly, the law of torts (civil wrongs) was not very important in England before 1800. The major legal treatises dismiss it with a few short pages. In the nineteenth century, because of railroads and factories, the number of serious accidents to property and the body multiplied enormously. Meanwhile, the Industrial Revolution destroyed old kinship and authority relations. The first treatise in the English language on the law of torts was published in 1850. No field of law, in the late nineteenth century, grew faster or was the subject of more talk, writing, and litigation than the law of torts. It became one of the fundamental building blocks of legal study, along with contract.

Even more fundamental than the distinction between realty and personality, movables and immovables, is the distinction between *procedure* and *substance*. Rules of procedure are rules *about* rules: how to tell a good rule from a bad rule; how to go forward with a case; how to behave in the role of a judge, litigant, or lawyer. Rules of substance are rules of conduct. Law, according to H. L. A. Hart, is distinctive precisely because of this double stock of rules. Law is the union of primary rules (roughly substance) and secondary rules (roughly process). Many

---

1. George Vernadsky, "The Scope and Contents of Chingis Kahn's *Yasa*," *Harvard Journal of Asiatic Studies*, Vol. 3, p. 337 (1938).

social systems have rules of conduct, according to Hart, but only *law* has rules about rules.[2]

Modern law also draws a firm line between *civil* and *criminal* law. The distinction seems very natural to us, but it is far from universal, and it is by no means as sharply defined as many people think. A crime is an offense against the state, or the general public. Because crime (murder or robbery, for example) threatens and injures us all, the state takes over the job of catching, trying, and punishing the criminal. Yet it is quite a subtle matter to distinguish between private and public (collective) wrongs. In smaller and older societies, murder merely gave rise to a *private* right of revenge. Among the Eskimos, as Hoebel describes it, we see a kind of intermediate phase. When there is a dangerous killer in the community, people may get together, informally, and discuss the problem. If they decide that the killer must die, a public-spirited person will simply do away with the killer; and there will be no right of revenge.[3] Here it is hard to tell what is public and what is private, and conventional definitions of "crime" and "criminal law" break down.

Even in modern times, what is crime is not always crystal-clear. We recognize the presence of crime and punishment when a burglar is arrested, tried, convicted, and sent to jail. But there are doubtful situations: traffic fines, or administrative "punishments" (taking away a television franchise, for example). A person quarantined to prevent epidemic is confined to his house, but not by way of punishment. When someone is sent to a mental hospital, or a home for juvenile delinquents, the authorities strenuously insist that they are giving treatment, not punishment. But the *effect* of the process is a good deal like the effect of criminal justice, regardless of form. In other cases, such a minor traffic "crimes," the form is like criminal justice, but the effect is not.

Civil (noncriminal) law is conventionally divided into a number of "fields." Blackstone's *Commentaries* (late eighteenth century) nobly tried to set out in clear, simple language, a bird's-eye view of English law. Of the four volumes of the *Commentaries,* the fourth dealt with crimes ("public wrongs"). Blackstone drew a line between the civil law of "persons" and the law of "things." Marriage, the rights of women and children, the rights and powers of the king, were part of the law of persons. About a quarter of the book was devoted to land law; that, together with commercial law, made up most of the law of things.[4]

---

2. H. L. A. Hart, *The Concept of Law,* New York: Oxford University Press, 1961, pp. 91–92.

3. E. A. Hoebel, *The Law of Primitive Man,* Cambridge: Harvard University Press, 1961, pp. 88–89.

4. The third volume, on "private wrongs," mainly concerned procedure and forms of action in civil cases.

Blackstone derived his central dichotomy between the law of "persons" and "things" from late Roman law. This basic distinction also was followed by the continental codes, which, in general outline, tended to use the classifications current among jurists in the late Roman Empire. The continental systems also distinguish between "public" and "private" law. This distinction, too, was a product of late Roman law and was revived on the continent in the nineteenth century.[5] Private law, roughly, is made up of branches of law that regulate the rights of private persons (or businesses) in their relations with other private persons (or businesses) —contract, tort, and divorce law, among others. Constitutional law, state regulation of business, criminal law, tax law, and procedural law, are all part of public law. The continental systems also lump contract and tort together under the heading of "obligations"; I can owe an "obligation," either because I bound myself to you in a contract or because my car smashed yours on the highway.

LATE MODERN LAW:
THE IMPACT OF THE INDUSTRIAL REVOLUTION

Blackstone in the 1750's and the draftsmen of the French civil code two generations later arranged fields of law in a way they thought logical, rational, and normal. Their social background, and their legal training, shaped their notions of logic and normality. A century later, massive change had overtaken economy and society in England, Western Europe, and the United States. Commercial law had grown majestically in importance. Land had become less rigidly tied to birth and status; it could be bought and sold on the market, almost as if it were ordinary goods. The special rules of land law were either eroding or merging with rules in the growing field of contract. Industrial accidents, we have seen, created a new law of torts. Divorce became possible in England in 1857; by then it was no longer a rarity in the United States. And the law of business associations grew exponentially.

Blackstone had barely mentioned the corporation. It was tucked away in a corner of his book, as a side-issue of the law of "persons."[6]

---

5. See B. Rehfeldt, *Einführung in die Rechtswissenschaft*, 3rd edition, Manfred Rehbinder, ed., Berlin: Walter de Gruyter, 1973, p. 134.

6. Corporations were "artificial persons," that is, associations treated as if they were persons, in that they had some rights (to sue or be sued) which otherwise belonged only to "natural persons." Blackstone explains that "all personal rights die with the person;" since this was "very inconvenient" for continuing bodies, it was necessary "to constitute artificial persons, who may maintain a perpetual succession, and enjoy a kind of legal immortality." *Commentaries*, Vol. I, p. 467.

Before the nineteenth century, in the United States as elsewhere, corporations were uncommon. The legislature chartered them, one at a time. Most of the charters went to churches, municipalities, or charitable organizations. Less than 10 business corporations had been chartered in the colonies before 1776. But by 1870 corporation law had blossomed into a major field, the special charter system had been abolished, and the number of corporations established in any single year was greater than in all of the eighteenth century.

The influence of socioeconomic change on the continental codes is in some ways less obvious and less dramatic than changes in the common law. The texts of the codes change rather slowly. Yet behind and beneath the surface, the law was in rapid flux in the nineteenth century. Many of the changes ran parallel to changes in England and the United States. This, of course, is not surprising. France and Germany were also shedding their ancient order: cities were growing; old social patterns were dissolving; industry was crowding out agriculture. Whatever their technical starting point, industrial countries tended to reach similar legal results when the economy required it. France, in 1867, granted a general right to the public to form business corporations without special charter or authorization; the German code of commerce, in 1870, did the same. A corresponding development took place in common law countries at about the same time.

In every major country, nineteenth century law underwent massive change. These transformations, of course, were very complex. One clear theme stands out: the rise of an industrial economy meant that old restrictions on individual enterprise, land ownership, and freedom of contract had to be dismantled when they were clearly dysfunctional. Willard Hurst, studying the first half of the nineteenth century, sees the dominant value of American law as "the release of indivdual creative energy." The law was made over, in order to serve the economy, in order to act as an efficient tool of growth; law was "inextricably involved in the growth of [the] market." It was less interested in protecting "vested rights" than in protecting (and furthering) "ventures."[7] A similar process took place in other countries, at differing paces to be sure. In the twentieth century, even the sleepiest society, even countries in the remotest corner of the globe, even a Nepal, an Afghanistan, began to respond to the call of economic growth, and its laws accordingly entered an era of rapid transformation.

7. J. Willard Hurst, *Law and the Conditions of Freedom in the Nineteenth-Century United States,* Madison, Wis.: University of Wisconsin Press, 1956, pp. 7–8, 24; see also Harry N. Scheiber, "Property Law, Expropriation, and Resource Allocation by Government: the United States, 1789–1910," *Journal of Economic History,* Vol. 33, p. 232 (1973).

LEGAL THOUGHT IN THE MODERN WORLD:
BEYOND THE CODE NAPOLEON

The idea of a natural law of reason, so strong in the eighteenth century, was sharply challenged in the nineteenth. One challenge came from the so-called historical school. Its leader, the German jurist Friedrich Carl von Savigny (1770–1861), argued that law does and must grow out of folk-consciousness, out of the history and traditions of a nation. Codification, on the French model, is likely to be false to those traditions.[8]

The *utilitarians*, notably Jeremy Bentham (1748–1842) in England, stressed the social consequences of legal acts. Bentham despised the common law, which he felt was hidebound and feudal. Law was, or should be, a means to an end. We have called this general idea the *instrumental theory* of law. It stands in sharp contrast to the notion that law is or can be the product of pure reason, or that law is timeless, divine, or transcendental. Instrumental and utilitarian ideas rose to prominence with the rise of modern industrial society; they put law at the service of state and economy.[9] With instrumentalism went the concept of *legal positivism,* that is, in essence, the idea that law is nothing more than its concrete manifestations—the statutes, cases and so on—discarding as ancient baggage any notions of innate ideas, eternal truths, and the like. Positivism implies that law is the product of somebody's very palpable decision, and that it is definitely changeable by some further decision. This attitude is appropriate to an age whose social life is extraordinarily complex, one in which people and groups face possibilities and choices incomparably vaster than before.[10]

Yet older legal ideas never totally died out. Indeed, one can argue that older natural law concepts are stronger than ever—especially ideas about the "rights of man," or the freedoms of the citizen. They are to be found at least in the constitutions of virtually every modern nation. Of

8. Surprisingly, Savigny himself turned to the study of Roman law, which he looked on as somehow the basic element of German legal culture. See Franz Wieacker, *Privatrechtsgeschichte der Neuzeit,* Gottingen: Vandenhoeck & Ruprecht, 1952, p. 235. William Graham Sumner, the American sociologist, shared Savigny's "juristic pessimism." To him, law evolved organically; attempts to change social customs or habits through hasty, radical legislation were, therefore, either useless or counterproductive. See also Geoffrey Sawer, *Law in Society,* Oxford: Oxford University Press, 1965, p. 172.

9. See Lawrence M. Friedman, "On Legal Development," *Rutgers Law Review,* **24:** 11 (1969).

10. Niklas Luhmann, *Rechtssoziologie,* Vol. 1, Reinbek bei Hamburg: Rowohlt, 1972, pp. 190–205.

course, those ideas are instrumentally very important. They are crucial tools in building arguments for *political* reform; they are the life blood of theories that have as their aim controlling the power of the state.

Among nineteenth century jurists, however, the chief rival of instrumentalism was *conceptual jurisprudence.* Conceptual jurisprudence is a system of thought that tries to treat law "as a closed system of definitions, rules of operation, and substantive major premises," within which "any specific legal problem can be solved by deductive reasoning from the propositional system so established." In its extreme form, it claims "that a mature legal system in a modern state can provide logically necessary solutions for all conceivable cases and one only 'correct' solution in each case."[11] It denies or ignores social forces, history, and tradition (except for legal tradition) as formative elements in the work of the law. The high-water mark of conceptual jurisprudence is, perhaps, to be found in the labors of German legal scholarship of the late nineteenth century. But it was a powerful force everywhere in continental Europe, and in the common law world as well. For the legal profession, conceptualism was and is exceedingly useful. It makes economic and political sense for lawyers and judges to argue that "law" is an independent, difficult, and noble science. Only they can master it; only they can apply it to concrete cases. Conceptualism, in other words, can enhance the prestige and professional status of judges and lawyers. This is no mean contribution.

Of course, counter-movements to this school of thought developed as well. In Germany at the turn of the century, the so-called "free law" school argued that the judge's role was, and ought to be, highly creative. The judge was, and should be, free to disregard strict logic and precedent, with the right and duty to adapt law to society's needs and to adjust rules to the needs of the particular case. The English judge was the model held up by writers of the free law school. (English judges, ironically, were by and large conceptualists themselves, denying their freedom.) In France, a group of magistrates went so far as to put free law ideas into action—creating new rights through loose reading of statutes and embellishing their opinions with radical talk. In Switzerland, free law ideas led to the adoption of Article I of the Civil Code of 1907. This famous article allows judges, in any case not "covered" by their texts, to make up rules on their own—rules which (they think) the legislature would enact, if it had the problem before it.[12]

In the United States, *legal realism* was more or less parallel to the free law movement. Its intellectual father, perhaps, was Justice Oliver

11. Sawer, *op. cit.,* p. 17.

12. Sawer, *op. cit.,* pp. 22, 23.

Wendell Holmes, Jr. A famous passage in *The Common Law* (1881) announced that the "life of the law" was not logic, but rather "experience." Legal realism burst onto the scene around 1920. The most prominent member of the school was Karl Llewellyn. In truth, realism was not so much a "school" as a set of attitudes, shared by a group of scholars and judges. The realists were skeptical of formal rules. The rules, they felt, as they appeared on paper, did not describe how judges actually handled their cases. Legal process was too subtle to be caged within dry, abstract formulas. Law was changeable, human, imperfect, and protean. Judges had, in fact, a good deal of freedom: discretion to pick among competing rules, to bend the facts of a case to fit this or that rule, to alter rules or ignore them. The world, thought the realists, would be better off if judges became aware of their power, and used it openly to make law more socially responsive. At the very least, judges should know what their values were, and be attentive to the way their decisions impacted on society.

Much realist thought has survived; indeed it has become tritely accepted. Although the realists were good critics, few of them went further, actually trying to *explore* the gap between law on the books and law in action. There is a difference between "sociological jurisprudence" ("speculations of . . . jurists who have . . . emphasized the social relations of law rather than its metaphysics or its formal logic")[13] and the social study of law, that is, actual investigation of legal phenomena. The two are, of course, obviously related. The Austrian scholar Eugen Ehrlich, who worked around the turn of the century, meticulously explored the "living law" of parts of his homeland. Around 1930, under the influence of legal realism, a few careful studies of the work of American courts appeared. But a social science of law hardly existed before the second World War, and it hardly constituted an intellectual rival to other modes of scholarship and legal thought.

Today much has changed. The social study of law is rapidly increasing. Its center of gravity lies, perhaps, in the United States, which leads in the social sciences, by virtue of its wealth, size, and power. Legal education is also somewhat less conceptual in the United States than in England or continental Europe. The balance of scholarship is, however, slowly shifting; there are important centers of work in Germany, Italy, Scandinavia, Poland, Holland, and Great Britain. After long neglect, every social science has begun to pay more attention to legal phenomena: anthropology, renewing itself with the work of Bronislaw Malinowski; political science, especially the behavioral study of courts; sociology, building partly on the great tradition of Max Weber, partly spurred by

---

13. Sawer, *op. cit.*, p. 16.

new empirical techniques; economics; and (somewhat belatedly) psychology. There seems little doubt that the social study of law will continue to expand. There is no *logical* inconsistency between empirical study of law and classical legal thought—a statistical study of a bankruptcy court will hardly contradict any of the great historical schools of jurisprudence. Still, in practice, empirical study of law jostles and squeezes other approaches. It demands the time and attention of scholars, not to mention a share of the money and status. Meanwhile, in many countries, both empirical and theroetical legal scholarship adapts itself to the demands of Marxist theory. This school of legal thought is important in numbers and influence. In the socialist countries, Marxist thought has a state monoply; in many other countries, it competes in the market place of ideas, and with considerable success.

LAW IN THE TWENTIETH CENTURY:
ITS ESSENTIAL CHARACTERISTICS

Social change in the twentieth century has been so massive and rapid that law, too, has had to be constantly transformed. Old categories have faded; new fields spring up like mushrooms. The main lines of development are familiar enough: administrative law, welfare law, regulation of business and the economy. New bodies of law have been created out of nothing, or almost nothing: antitrust law, social security law, environmental law, labor law, zoning and housing law, securities regulation, pure food and drug laws. As we have said, these developments are worldwide: virtually every country shares them. Many modern lawyers spend, perhaps, 80 percent or more of their time on fields of law that either did not exist before 1900, or are only dimly related to older law.

Obviously, it is impossible to sum up, in a single formula, the developments that set off modern law from the law of earlier eras. A few striking features can be mentioned.

1. An industrial society is light years away from the world of oxcarts and handicrafts; law, as a means of social control, struggles to regulate the vast machinery of economic life. This job is too much for traditional courts and legislatures. Day by day work falls to administrative bodies (agencies, ministries, boards, commissions). In some of their functions, they can be compared with legislatures (they make up rules and regulations), with the police (they inspect and enforce their rules), and with courts (they decide disputed cases). Some of the cases they decide begin in investigations conducted by the agency itself: did this company break the rules of the Securities and Exchange Commission, or did it not? Some are cases brought by one party against another—a union may complain of a company's "unfair labor practices" before the National Labor Relations Board.

Meanwhile, as we have seen, the formal courts have lost importance, in some countries at least, relative to other legal agencies (including administrative agencies). In particular, courts do not shoulder the main burden of social control and dispute settlement.

2.   The modern state tries to provide some minimum standard of living, and some minimum benefits, for everyone living within its borders. Welfare law has grown from a small, insignificant branch of the legal system to a mighty enterprise. A huge body of law deals with old age pensions, family allowances, medical care, unemployment benefits, workmen's compensation, free schooling, and so on. Some countries provide far more benefits than others, but the trend in all countries is unmistakable. Once welfare was distinctly a local function in the United States and Great Britain. United States President Pierce in 1854 vetoed a land grant for the benefit of the insane. The federal government, he said, could not act as "the great almoner of public charity, throughout the United States."[14] But in the twentieth century, welfare increasingly has moved from township, parish, and county to a more national or central level of responsibility.

3.   To pay for its multifarious activities, the state must levy and collect, in taxes, the ransom of a million kings. Leviathan has a greedy appetite; it must be fed. Hence, taxation is at the center of law and legal practice: who shall pay and what, how to plan business deals to the best tax advantage; levies on estates and inheritances; exemptions and deductions; tax evasion and avoidance, and so on.

FREEDOM AND REGULATION
IN THE TWENTIETH CENTURY

Compared to medieval societies, tribal societies, and ancient empires, the scope for individual self-expression in modern society is vast. Personal freedom, self-government, and parliamentary democracy are ideals which, though hardly brand-new (the concept of democracy is as old as ancient Greece), are peculiarly associated with the modern, industrial world. As world economies expanded in the nineteenth century, so too did the franchise. Country after country gave the right to vote to more and more people; property qualifications were dropped; regimes opened new channels for political and legal participation, though never for everyone, and not all at once. (Women, for example, did not vote in the United States before the twentieth century, and a stubborn male electorate in Switzerland prevented them from voting in federal elections and from holding federal office until 1971.)

By almost any measure, the parliamentary regimes of Europe, along with the United States, Canada, Australia, New Zealand, Israel, Japan, and a scattering of other nations, provide their citizens with more personal freedom and individual choice than was dreamt of in the past.

14.   Quoted in Lawrence M. Friedman, *A History of American Law*, New York: Simon & Schuster, 1973, p. 188.

This may also be true of some aspects of life, and some strata of society, in the socialist countries, even though they pay less heed to the "bourgeois" freedoms. On the other hand, the overwhelming majority of nations today are one-party states, and the ruthlessness and tyranny of twentieth century totalitarianism can put older despots to shame. The technical instruments of oppression (from wire-tapping to the giant labor camp) have been perfected to an alarming degree. Solzhenitsyn reminds us that Stalin's terror was much worse than that of the Czar; probably not because the Czar was nobler, but his regime was that much less efficient. "Bourgeois democracy" has never had a foothold in Russsia. Other countries have slid in and out of totalitarianism. No one who contemplates the recent history of such countries as Uruguay, India, and Chile can glibly state that the future belongs to human rights.

Moreover, the relationship among freedom, individual choice, and law (regulation) is by no means simple in modern society. In an urban, industrial world, freedom itself, paradoxically, gives rise to regulation, and individual choice creates conditions that demand a great deal of law. Traffic rules are largely unnecessary in a society of peasants tied to the soil. Freedom to travel, however, leads to rules to control, channel, and restrict the freedom and manner of travel.

It would be an interesting exercise to follow the legal consequences of this single freedom. People move from place to place by bus, train, airplane, and car. The freedom to travel means that diseases, insects, and exotic plants move easily from country to country; nations now must guard themselves as never before against plant pests, infectious diseases, smuggling of drugs, and so on. The tiny new country of Western Samoa thus feels obliged to impose restrictions on imports of animals, cooked meat, and grain, except under heavy safeguard; to require every captain of a ship arriving in Western Samoa to "put a rat guard on each line mooring the ship to any wharf;" and to force the arriving traveler to "walk, in his ordinary footgear, if any," through a "footbath containing a four per centum solution of sodium carbonate."[15] Travel by modern conveyance means the possibility of serious accidents. Safety becomes an issue. This alone accounts for tons of rules—about airplane safety, train and bus safety, safe driving, manufacture of safe automobiles. Airports, depots, and highways have to be built and maintained, leading to thousands more rules. An immense body of tort law grew up around the railroad accident in the nineteenth century and the automobile accident in the twentieth. Insurance, no-fault, seat-belts, the Warsaw convention, passport regulations, customs regulations—one could go on almost endlessly, mentioning areas of law that flow, more or less, from the chain of events freedom to travel sets in motion.

15. Western Samoa, Animal Diseases Prevention Regulation, 1968, paragraphs 4, 5, 6, 8, and 10.

None of these rules about travel and transportation is "necessary," in the sense of inevitable; none can be deduced or predicted in exact detail, directly from the freedom to travel. There are always choices and subsidiary decisions. Some of these secondary decisions depend on balancing the social demand for safety against freedom or efficiency of travel. Shall we inspect baggage for bombs, for example? One basic point, however, seems clear: in a complex, crowded world, freedom itself produces a great gaping need for law; without law, the freedom is empty, or frustrated, or unstable. Of course, each society will deal with travel according to its own light. In Maoist China there are virtually no private cars; and the Chinese may not travel freely abroad. Freedom of travel meant one thing in the horse-and-buggy world, quite another in the age of cars and jets.

LAW IN THE TWENTIETH CENTURY:
WHAT THE CITIZEN DEMANDS OF THE STATE

We have seen that the demand for freedom, for personal choice, gives rise to conditions that make regulation necessary. As government grows, moreover, government is able (or seems able) to accomplish more —both because it is bigger and richer and because tasks that were not possible before seem technically feasible (control of the money supply; sending up satellites). The level of demands on government rises accordingly. The growth of Leviathan is not spontaneous, is not foreordained; big government is a genie summoned from its bottle by the public itself.

In the twentieth century, as far as one can tell, demands on government, demands for law, have increased even more sharply than in the century before. People expect change; they expect government (and law) to stand at the center of change. This flows, first, from a cultural mood— from what we have called the instrumental theory of law.[16] The instrumental theory is not a philosophy of law, in any systematic sense. It is a popular idea about law. Ordinary people believe in it, as well as professional scholars. Wherever this theory has a strong grip on people's minds, there is no obvious limit to the demands they can make on law, or through law. Law is a tool; why not use it? The only limit is itself cultural: first, some demands are not "right" ethically—it would be wrong to tax or seize the money or goods of one group and give it to another;[17] and some demands (people think) would do more harm than good— price controls, perhaps, if they create a black market. Some people oppose

---

16. See supra, p. 45.

17. Such ideas of course are constantly changing; a good part of the population of the United States saw nothing wrong with seizing land from the Indians, in the nineteenth century; and the recent plunder of Asians in Uganda was apparently popular in that country. Other examples, alas, are all too common.

laws against drunkenness, gambling, and sexual deviance, because they think law should not meddle in people's lives; others oppose these laws because they think they cannot be enforced without intolerable snooping and oppression.

In premodern times, people expected or wanted much less from the state. They had tight ideas about the limits of law, compared to today. Today, government is pervasive. People do not feel that law is sacred and unmoving; it is human and must work as their servant. Doubts about the *effectiveness* of law have also ebbed. In the socialist countries, the sphere of the state has crowded out much of the space that is "private" in capitalist countries. But in "capitalist" countries, too, the state is bloated far beyond the worst nightmares of a nineteenth century liberal. State and private enterprise are often in such intimate partnership that the lines of demarcation blur. In the United States, the banks are private, but heavily regulated. In France, the largest banks are government owned, but "function exactly now as they did before nationalization."[18] Public and private are intertwined.

But if so, less and less is purely private. People decry "big government" yet they expect and demand state action. Not even natural disasters are treated as private. Once the only collective reaction to plague, earthquake, flood, or other "acts of God" (the term is significant), was fasting, prayer, and resignation. In the nineteenth century an earthquake or other disaster might be followed by appeals for private charity. There might be some small public aid, but the stricken community was expected to roll up its sleeves and rebuild by itself. Today the state must intervene. We expect the President to declare a disaster, offer words of cheer, perhaps to fly over the scene in a helicopter; and we also expect soft loans, special programs of relief, and so on. If the President fails to do enough, he will shoulder some of the blame; he, or the government, will be called to account. Indeed, the disaster itself is more likely than before to be blamed on the state. Why was this dam not properly inspected? Why were earthquake regulations not complied with? Why were there no fire-retarding walls in the factory? Why was the mine not properly inspected? And so on. Thus a cycle of demand and response sets in. Demands lead to new programs, which set up fresh expectations. In theory, a negative cycle is also possible: A chain of disillusionments sets up demands that government dismantle itself, that it self-destruct. Anarchists dream of this, politicians promise it (a little), currently (1976) the idea seems to be gaining in appeal; but it remains to be seen whether smaller government is anything but a forlorn and foolish hope.

18. Anthony King, "Ideas, Institutions and the Policies of Governments: a Comparative Analysis: Parts I and II," *British Journal of Political Science*, Vol. 3, pp. 291, 295 (1973).

CHAPTER 6
ON JUSTICE
AND
LAW

In the last chapter we noted the growth of instrumental demands on government, demands, that is, for law. But ideas of the proper, legitimate way to approach the legal system decisively influence the forms and techniques in which many of these demands are cast. A letter to a legislator is legitimate, a bribe is not. Some *outcomes,* too, are legitimate, while some are not. Ideas about fairness and justice influence attitudes and behavior about law; people are continually measuring performance of a legal system against their ideas of justice. This chapter discusses the ways in which societies assess fairness, justice, and bias in their legal systems.

LEGAL AND NONLEGAL NORMS

Modern systems draw a sharp distinction between legal and nonlegal norms. This means that there is a "legal" solution to many problems, which is different from the common sense solution, the moral solution, or even the (scientifically) rational solution. Suppose a woman enters an apartment building, at night, and trips and falls on the stairway. The stairway was dark and unlit. Should the landlord pay for the victim's medical expenses? For her pain and suffering? People can argue whether the landlord "should" pay—was it (morally) his fault? Perhaps the visitor was to blame; she might have paid more attention and been less careless. We can argue about "rational" solutions: if we made landlords pay in this type of case, what social consequences would follow? Will rents go up? Will the accident rate go down? We might bring in data (if we had any) about these effects. At any rate, our "social" answer might well be different from the "legal" or "ethical" answer. We find the "legal" answer by looking up "the law." It tells us what "the law" requires, that is, how such a case would be decided in court. We expect a lawyer (or judge) to know how to find the law—how to dredge up cases and statutes that "cover" the situation. The lawyer (or judge) knows how to gauge legal materials, how to measure them, understand them, and use them. The ordinary citizen does not.

But the difference between "legal," "social" and "moral" solutions presents us with a kind of paradox. We recall that law, in modern society, is basically instrumental. It must *work*, and it must bring about some sensible end. We know, or think we know, that some "legal" answers are not rational (or instrumental); they are not the same as the best moral answers, or the best economic answers, or the answers most in accord with common sense. In some deeper sense, the solutions may be the optimum answer, or they may represent the best solution to a problem, given opposing interests and demands. But on the *surface,* we find that the law wears technical clothes, and it hides any deeper underlying reasons; the law appears to be radically distinct from other forms of social logic.

This deep division may sour people on law; indeed, surveys report the common attitude that law is slow, technical, hidebound—even foolish. Strict "legality" strikes many people as empty ritual or mumbo-jumbo. The workings of the law appear mysterious to some; to others, they conceal class bias (more on this later). If there is no social or ethical purpose to some particular aspect of law, why adhere to it? Law may be valued for its own sake—as is true in traditional and sacred societies. In instrumental societies, the law is subject to strict tests of utility, or morality; the older, more formal, parts of it increasingly fail the tests. This, we have seen, is one reason why ordinary "legal" business shifts to administrators and other experts.

Justifying the Norms. Even in an instrumental era, then, the traditional legal institutions (and in particular the courts) must justify themselves. First, the justification may rest on the *origin* of the rules, or on their *substance*; that is that they represent the will of the people in some cases and in other cases, morality, ethics, good sense, or social justice. Secondly, the justification may be *procedural*: the rules are carried out farily and impartially by honest people using honest means.

Judges, administrators, police officers and others are, in theory, bound to obey the law—that is, to follow the rules and to administer them in valid, impartial ways. But one can ask whether this ideal corresponds with social reality. Legal materials are dense, numerous, and often ambiguous. In many cases, this leaves judges and administrators real discretion to pick and choose among competing outcomes, even when "the law" does not admit that they have legitimate discretion. Leeways may be inevitable in the law, but insofar as they are visible, they call in question the ideal expressed in the phrase: "a government of laws, not of men."

This phrase has a procedural meaning, too. It means that rules should not only be fair and impartial, they should also be carried out honestly, in accord with standards of "due process," and without regard to race, class, or position. One can build different models of an ideal legal system, of course, by starting from other axioms. Socialist systems, especially in their militant phases, *demand* a brand of justice that shows open awareness of the class background of litigants. But "legality" and impartial justice are important standards, and most countries pay at least lip service to them as ideals.

We can ask: are these standards possible? Are they adhered to? And are they desirable at all? The ideal, it must be recalled, is really a double one: fair norms, and fair application of norms. These need not coincide. Some German judges, during the Third Reich, applied the vicious laws against Jews and "traitors" with what appeared to be the same flat, neutral techniques used for laws about overdue promissory notes. We will begin with the first consideration: the fairness of standards and norms.

ON SUBSTANTIVE JUSTICE

In one sense, legal norms cannot be truly "neutral." It is not even easy to tell what a "neutral" norm would be. Certainly, in every system, the norms fit the structure of that system. Even assuming that there are such things as eternal rules of justice or morality, no legal system can be made up *only* of these jewels. One cannot build a legal system solely from ethical traditions or common sense. An income tax code has to be put together from coarser stuff; this is true for Saudi Arabia, with a legal system based on the sacred law of Islam, the United States with its eighteenth century Bill of Rights, as well as for every other modern nation. Legal systems today must contain many purely instrumental rules (some would say all), and these rules necessarily make choices; they lean toward this or that group—favoring children over adults, pedestrians over drivers, employers over workers, druggists over customers, and so on, for the sake of expediency or policy. What people really mean when they say that norms are "neutral" or "fair," is neutral or fair *within* some value conception, or measured against some standard.

That moves us one step forward. When people ask if the laws of (say) Italy are "fair," they mean: do these laws conform to certain largely formal ideals, which most Italians are supposed to share, which are sung about, taught in schools, and which are somewhere expressed as goals (in a constitution, for example, or as part of a code of laws or as the "spirit" underlying the laws)? These ideals might include the notion of equal justice for all—meaning that a poor person accused of crime should be treated no worse (or better) than a rich person. Equal justice also means that people should not be oppressed merely because they hold unpopular opinions; that no one should be punished without committing a crime, because of the whim of some official; that, on the other hand, people with relatives or friends in high places, or with money and prestige, should not enjoy privileges which are denied to the ordinary person. "Fairness" is a mosaic of such ideas, in a particular society.

Some of these ideas are procedural, some are substantive. In people's minds, procedural norms and substantive norms are much mixed together. Among legal scholars and legal thinkers, however, particularly heavy stress is laid on procedural justice—on due process. This is, perhaps, because procedures are the lawyers' stock-in-trade; procedure is most exclusively the lawyer's domain. Due process is of course a noble ideal; the right to fair trial is worth struggling for, even dying for. But the ultimate test of a legal system is what it does, not how it does it or through whom—substance, not procedure or form. It would be cold comfort to an innocent man to know that the trial that sent him to the gallows was scrupulously fair. If the substantive rules are unfair, or misguided, to apply them fairly is little help.

Procedure, then, is only a means to an end; the end is whatever collective problem society means to attack. Procedure follows substance; substance tells us which areas of procedure will become important. The United States Bill of Rights forbids "unreasonable" searches and seizures. Today, this is a particularly lively area of constitutional law. More "law" has been made on the subject in the last decade or two than in the whole nineteenth century. Why this outburst of interest and controversy? It began with Prohibition, and it was nurtured by the drug laws. These are laws that cannot be enforced at all, without searches and seizures. Hence the right became very salient and very much disputed. There is a great deal of new law, too, about "class actions"—lawsuits brought in the name of whole categories of litigants. This, too, is a procedural device made salient by social change and change in substance. The new field of environmental law has been responsible for much of the boom in class action suits—lawsuits about air and water pollution, or about protection of wildlife and natural beauty, which are begun by clubs and groups speaking in the name of a diffuse "class" of citizens.

There is a large, rather unsystematic literature, which tries to assess the *substance* of the norms. Marxists point out, on the whole correctly, that the law in bourgeois societies presupposes bourgeois property systems; the modern state is "nothing but a committee for managing the common affairs of the entire bourgeois class."[1] Indeed, legal institutions maintain and strengthen the existing system of property and wealth. This is only natural. In the United States, France, or Japan private persons own land, goods, money, and corporate securities. They buy and sell; they make out wills and leave their estates to their children, or to relatives or friends; they give and take. The law controls and regulates, but it also supports this state of affairs. To this extent, law is not and cannot be "fair," cannot be neutral, between classes and strata in the population. It favors those who have, even when it does nothing more than let them keep what they have. If we analyzed *any* body of law, the socioeconomic system would, subtly or blatantly, show through the folds of the garment.

But the attack from the left goes further. The left is skeptical about rules and procedures which are, on the surface, neutral and free of class bias: for example, the right to own property, the right of free speech, or the right to fair trial. Two charges are levied: first, some rights and freedoms are meaningless to the poor (the right to own a steel mill, or to publish a newspaper); others, like the right to a day in court, are hollow, since in actual practice the "haves" will come out ahead.[2]

THE TYPES AND SOURCES OF BIAS

The second charge is sociologically more interesting and opens the door to an immense body of research. The basis of the charge is: how rights operate *in fact*. The state promises a minimum amount of access to law, a floor under powerlessness, even in a society where people are very unequal in money and power. Are these promises kept? Or, to copy Orwell, are some pigs more equal than other pigs?

We hear about three kinds of bias:

1. *Random bias.* Perhaps a better word is unfairness. The law sets up, or tolerates, a system in which there is very wide discretion. People in equal positions can be, and are, treated quite differently. A good example is the judge's discretion in sentencing. Two men, both 25 years old, both with a minor criminal record, both black, both from poor families in Detroit, are convicted of armed robbery. A judge sentences the first to ten years in prison. A second judge grants the other probation. It depends, apparently, on the luck of the draw—what judge one appears before, what his or her mood is, his or her general philosophy of sentencing, who came up for sentencing immediately before, and so on.

2. *Social bias.* This often accompanies random bias and is probably more

1. *The Communist Manifesto* (1847), quoted in Carl J. Friedrich, *Philosophy of Law in Historical Perspective*, Revised Edition, Chicago: University of Chicago Press, 1963, pp. 144–45.

2. See Marc Galanter, "Why the 'Haves' Come Out Ahead: Speculations on the Limits of Legal Change," *Law and Society Review*, Vol. 9, p. 95 (1974).

serious. Certain groups (blacks, the poor, the mentally ill, the ugly)[3] fare worse at the law than others. They get worse lawyers, or no lawyers. They receive poor treatment from judges or juries. They suffer stiffer sentences. They are harassed by the police, while, on the other hand, they receive worse protection from police. Their civil cases are dismissed. Their rights are ignored by bureaucrats. Discretion hides the patterns. Each *individual* decision is legitimate; the cumulation is unfair.

3. *Fat-cat bias.* In some totalitarian societies, it is not the poor (or the poor alone) who are exposed to bad treatment. Where wealth is divorced from political power, the rich, too, may be fleeced, almost at the whim of the rulers. This was the position of rich Jews in the Middle Ages and at the start of Hitler's regime. It was the fate of the Church during the reign of Henry VIII, of landlords and merchants during early stages of the revolution in Poland, Cuba, Bulgaria, and other "peoples' democracies." Elliott Currie has pointed out a related phenomenon in the history of witchcraft. In Continental Europe, there was a regular "industry" of unmasking witches. Many of those accused of black magic were well-off. Officials grew rich by plundering the wealth of convicted witches.[4] Another example is the special vulnerability of intellectuals in the Soviet Union. In that nation, it can be dangerous to be prominent in the arts, or in the military; during the terror of the 1930's, thousands of writers, officials, plant managers, and army officers were arrested, imprisoned, or murdered.

Social bias is the key form of bias in Western societies. How widespread is it? Surprisingly little research (as opposed to polemics) has gone into the problem. The results, too, have been rather meager. Attempts to show that blacks do worse than whites in court, in the United States, holding all else constant, have been somewhat inconclusive and inconsistent. The poor (black or white) fare less well in court than the rich, the powerful, and the articulate. But studies of sentencing do not agree on how much injustice there is, and why. Sentencing, it appears, is a complex "human" process; many variables are required to explain it.[5] (Of course, there may be social bias—class or racial—at other stages of criminal process; for example, blacks may run more risk of arrest than whites, for the same general offense.)

3. Simulated jury studies find that people tend to be harsher to defendants who are physically unattractive—though not uniformly: the beautiful swindler was treated worse than the nonbeautiful, as reported in Harold Sigall and Nancy Ostrove, "Beautiful but Dangerous: Effects of Offender Attractiveness and Nature of the Crime on Juridic Judgment," *Journal of Personality and Social Psychology*, Vol. 31, p. 410 (1975).

4. Elliott Currie, "Crimes without Criminals: Witchcraft and Its Control in Renaissance Europe, *Law and Society Review*, Vol. 3, pp. 7, 22–23 (1968).

5. John Hogarth, *Sentencing as a Human Process*, Toronto: University of Toronto Press, 1971 (study of sentencing in Ontario, Canada); Beverly Blair Cook, "Sentencing Behavior of Federal Judges: Draft Cases—1972," *University of Cincinnati Law Review*, 42: 597 (1973).

We can distinguish between two meanings of justice. Justice can mean a guarantee of equal treatment; justice in this sense is impossible in any known society. As long as *other* goods are not distributed in equal shares, there is no way to distribute equal shares of justice. The rich can buy the best lawyers so long as there are lawyers for sale. Lawyers are not for sale in the Soviet Union; but power is as unequally distributed there as money is in American society; people "in the know," or with powerful friends, make their influence felt. Perhaps they can avoid harsh treatment far better than the ordinary citizen, even though, during periods of terror, they may have a special vulnerability.

Justice, however, may have another meaning. A society can define for itself a minimum ration of justice (just as it can define a minimum income, minimum health care, and so on); the ideal then is to provide this minimum for everyone. The minimum can be defined in terms of basic rights, fair redress of grievances, adherence to rational standards, and so on. The question is, whether justice defined even in this second sense has been achieved in the United States or in other countries. The evidence suggests that it has not, even when the minimum share of justice is modest indeed. The gap varies among nations, and it is probably less than some of the bitterest critics would concede.

LEGAL IDEOLOGY AND JUSTICE

What seems important is that in substance at least *some* norms (those dealing with the minimum ration) must be "fair," and they must be carried out fairly. The ideal is decidedly attainable. Even a society full of gross inequalities can try to narrow the gap between the minimum ideals and the way they are implemented. In this task, ideology plays, or can play, a useful role. If people believe society is and ought to be "fair," that justice should be done, though the heavens shake, that a government of laws is better than a government of men, the force of their conscience and opinions *may* bend the behavior of the legal system toward the ideal. This belief can be especially useful for legal actors—lawyers, judges, administrators. We often hear that these beliefs are really only "myths"; if so, they are healthy, perhaps indispensable myths. The myths, and their supporting propaganda, can coax society to move toward its noblest ideals, to creep inch by inch toward a genuine legality. Whether any particular society is traveling this path is a difficult question. But it seems at least plausible to guess that constitutional ideals have *some* impact on the behavior of the legal system in a number of nations.

The gap between legal ideal and legal reality may, on the other hand, come to play a sinister role in society. Teachers and professors preach and teach the ideals as articles of faith, almost as incantations. In practice, the system falls far short of fulfilling its promises. While part of the public is deceived, the rest become helpless to resist evil done in the name of the state. Thus ideology can paper over gross injustices and unfairness. The history of modern Germany illustrates this danger. After Germany was defeated in the First World War, the so-called Weimar Republic was established. Most of the judges were left over from the Kaiser's autocratic regime. They were intensely conservative and had no sympathy for liberal thought and the Weimar government. In court, right-wing agitators were treated with kid gloves, but judges "threw the book" at leftists accused of political agitation. A screen of impersonal legality disguised the most blatant unfairness.

When Hitler came to power, in 1933, the regime dropped much of this pretense. The Nazis had no use for such old-fashioned notions as equality before the law or abstract legality. The Nazi theory was frankly instrumental: "What benefits the nation is law." Indeed, more than one recent jurist, in Germany, has accused the instrumental theory of paving the way for the Nazis and their abominable crimes.[6] And yet, the Weimar judges who, in their own way, helped ruin Germany's experiment in democracy, were also bitterly opposed to the instrumental theory. Their misdeeds were hidden behind that very "legality" which was missing after 1933, as German justice sank into barbarism.

The world is full of injustice, and members of an unjust society naturally come to loathe the legal ideology that excuses or supports injustice. Soviet dissidents, appalled by the history of Stalin's mass arrests, deportations, and murders, long for a return to strict legality. They have seen what happens when the end is allowed to justify the means, when law turns into an instrument of naked policy. They prefer an independent judiciary, and a dry, technical, "correct" approach to law. In the United States in the 1930's, progressives felt the very opposite pull. They wanted to strip judges of their power and tilt the balance in favor of administrators, experts, and elected officials who would carry out policy openly and instrumentally. This was precisely because the judiciary (they felt) was too strong, too independent, and was blocking progress by declaring social legislation void, in the name of adherence to law. At this writing (1976), progressives are rethinking their premises once more. Indeed, the struggle between instrumentalism and "law" (meaning the ideology of a neutral, impartial, nonpolitical justice) seems to go on eternally; any solution is provisional. What a society needs, or thinks it needs, depends on how it assesses its problems, and what form of law-making and law-applying will, in its judgment, help solve those problems.

The myth of law, the legitimacy of law, have a broader scope than

6. See Ilise Staff, ed., *Justiz im Dritten Reich*, Frankfurt am Main: Fischer Bücherei, 1964, pp. 11–16.

as protective camouflage for judges. Adherence to order can be a matter of life and death to society. Respect for law sustains the status quo, with all its faults, but it also sustains the very foundations of social existence. In the short run, in most societies, order and tranquility are almost universally beneficial. Wars, revolutions, and riots destroy homes, ruin the economy, paint the streets with blood. And struggle leads to counter-struggle; blood on the right leads to blood on the left. "Like law itself," Alexander Bickel has written, "civil disobedience is habit-forming, and the habit it forms is destructive of the legal order. Disobedience, even if legitimate in every other way, must not be allowed to become epidemic." Individuals, Bickel feels, therefore, have a "duty" to "ration" their disobedience. Disobedience "is attended by the overhanging threat of anarchy."[7]

The main point can be conceded; but it is by no means clear exactly *how* habit-forming disobedience is. In many cases, for many people and groups, it is worth the price, despite the "overhanging threat of anarchy." Bickel's argument flows most easily from the lips of the sleek and the comfortable. Besides, there is disobedience and disobedience. On the one hand, there is Gandhi's *satyagraha*, nonviolent, ethically charged disobedience, and the disobedience of Southern blacks, boycotting buses and "sitting in" at lunch counters, for the sake of racial equality. On the other hand, there are the deadly skyjackers, and the murderous snipers and bombers of Belfast and Beirut. Both anarchy and progress often result from the work of people whose consciences tell them: this you must do. Conscience has never been an easy matter.

7. Alexander M. Bickel, "Watergate and the Legal Order," *Commentary*, **57**: 1, pp. 19, 24 (Jan. 1974).

CHAPTER 7
ON SYSTEMS
AND CULTURES
OF LAW

This chapter describes various types of national (and subnational) legal systems, and how they are classified. It asks how conventional classifications relate to types of *legal culture*. It also explores how culture and structure are related in legal systems, using as examples types of legal reasoning and styles of legal discourse. The chapter ends with a note on the language of the law.

LEGAL SYSTEMS, NATIONAL AND SUBNATIONAL

Whatever else it is, a legal system is a means of social control, an aspect of *government* or authority. Every state contains or implies a legal system. Each sovereign nation has at least one legal system. A conventional, if narrow view, equates the legal system with the official system, which is an adjunct of political sovereignty. Thus one speaks of the French legal system, the Peruvian legal system, and so on—as many legal systems in the world as there are national, self-governing, or sovereign entities. We can also use the term "legal system" in various broader senses, so that every factory, school, or club—every structure with authority—has a "legal system" of its own. Any large society will have great numbers of such legal systems inside it.

However, even by more or less conventional reckoning, many countries have more than one legal system. Sovereignty itself can be subdivided. There may be local legal systems besides the national one.

In the United States, each of the fifty states has a good deal of legal independence. Each has its own divorce law, for example, at least slightly different from the laws of the other states. Court structures and procedures of each state are also distinctive. Superimposed on the state systems is a federal (national) system, partly overlapping, partly complementary. As it happens, there is no federal law of divorce. But it is a "federal question" whether New York must recognize as valid a divorce which a New York woman procured in Reno, Nevada. Constitutional law, antitrust law, admiralty, bankruptcy, and many other fields are federal.[1]

Pluralism. A legal system is *pluralistic* when there is more than one legal sovereignty inside a single nation, state, or other political entity. (The second, third, fourth and *n*th system will, of course, have limited sovereignty.) Legal pluralism comes in a number of forms. In *horizontal* pluralism, the subsystems have equal status, like children of one set of parents. In vertical pluralism, the systems are arranged in some sort of order, one on top of the other.

In *horizontal* pluralism, the dividing line between systems can be cultural, political, or social. The Ottoman Empire was a case of *cultural federalism*. Within the Empire, Mohammedans, Jews, and Christians ran their own courts, applying distinctive laws of marriage, divorce, and related matters. This kind of cultural federalism survives to some extent in Israel and other countries of the Near East.

In *political pluralism,* each subsystem is a territorial, political entity. The United States, Canada, Australia, and Switzerland, among others, are politically federal states. The various states or provinces may, of course, be culturally different; and cultural pluralism is sometimes the excuse for politcal federalism. This is true in Canada, if we think of the boundary between Quebec and Ontario; but it is not true of the lines between Manitoba, Alberta, and Saskatchewan. Examples of pluralism where the line is drawn according to socioeconomic status, or class, are harder to find. Such lines—caste distinctions in India, for instance—usually have a strongly vertical flavor. But in medieval England, there were special courts for merchants—the "court of dusty feet" (piepowder), for one, which was "incident to every fair or market," and supposedly earned its name because its justice was as swift "as the dust can fall from the foot."[2] Meanwhile, the royal courts served the needs of the gentry and nobility. The system, to an extent, was one of horizontal pluralism.

Vertical pluralism can also be divided into three types. The first is cultural. Colonial systems were strongly vertical. In most African colonies, European settlers brought and used the law of their mother country.

---

1. They may have state counterparts, too.

2. Sir Edward Coke, *Institutes of the Laws of England, Part Four* (1628), p. 272.

This law had its sphere of influence in the capital and major cities, wherever Europeans lived and Western culture was strong. Native populations in the countryside lived by traditional laws. Western law was dominant, however; and it prevailed in case of conflict.[3] Colonial law, then, was a cultural form of vertical pluralism.

Second, vertical pluralism also has a political form. In the United States, the states are equal in sovereignty; but federal law overrides the law of the states, whenever the two levels conflict. Third, vertical pluralism based on socio-economic distinctions was, as we mentioned, common in medieval law. In some societies, law may be different—and harsher— for those without money and power. This "dual system"—one law for the rich and one for the poor[4]—is not technically pluralism, because separate sovereignties are not involved. But where it exists, it is an important social fact. We have discussed the related question of bias in Chap. 6.

ON THE CLASSIFICATION OF LEGAL SYSTEMS

We have seen that there are at least as many legal systems as there are countries; and, in an important sense, many more. Every self-governing entity or society has a legal system. No two are exactly the same. There are many similarities between the law of North Dakota and the law of South Dakota; a lawyer from one state could easily learn to practice in the other. Still, there are literally thousands of differences, big and small, between the law of these two jurisdictions. No two cultures are the same; yet some pairs or groups of societies or cultures have close affinities, in language, economy, politics, or tradition. We expect Honduras and Nicaragua to be more alike in culture (and law) than Afghanistan and France.

Can we group legal systems into classes or types, according to some sensible standard of affinity? Scholars tend to agree on a basic scheme.[5]

3. The French pursued a policy of assimilation in their African colonies. They wanted to replace native law, in the long run. This policy was "based on the double postulate that all men were of equal worth and that the European civilization was superior to the African. . . . Assimilation was considered the normal result of the civilizing policy, upon the mother countries taking the administration of the country into hand." René David and John E. C. Brierley, *Major Legal Systems in the World Today,* New York: Free Press, 1968, p. 467. The English in their colonies made much less of an effort to supersede native law, which they left free to operate—in its place.

4. See Joel F. Handler, ed., *Family Law and the Poor, Essays by Jacobus Ten-Broek,* Westport, Conn.: Greenwood Press. 1971.

5. See Konrad Zweigert and Hein Kötz, *Einführung in die Rechtsvergleichung,* Vol. I, Tübingen: J. C. B. Mohr (Paul Siebeck), 1971.

Legal systems fall into clusters, often called "families." Members of a family share a common "parent" system or have borrowed from a common source. So, English settlers brought English law to Canada, Australia, and New Zealand. Australian law is by now quite distinctive (as is Australian English). But it is closely related to the English system, as child to parent; and Canada and New Zealand are like brother or sister systems.

The largest and most important family is the so-called *civil law* family; its exact membership is, however, subject to quibble, and it has been called by many other names.[6] Members of this family owe a common debt to Roman law, which, as we saw, was rediscovered in the medieval universities and "received" in most of Europe. Western Europe is still civil law territory today: France, Germany, Italy, Spain, Portugal, the Low Countries. Through Spain and Portugal, the civil law traveled to Latin America. The French brought it to their colonies in Africa, the Belgians to Zaire. Strong elements of civil law color the legal systems of Scotland, Louisiana, and Quebec. The Scandinavian countries underwent a rather distinctive mode of development, but they have enough in common with other civil law countries to be usually assigned to this family. Civil law systems are, in the main, *codified* systems. Their basic law is found in their codes—orderly, logical statements of enacted law. This is, as history goes, a fairly recent development. The Prussian code, the *Allgemeines Landrecht*, dates from 1794; the civil code of France, the Code Napoleon, was promulgated in 1804.

One European country managed to resist the "reception" of Roman law. That was England. The English kept their native system—the so-called *common law*. Many ideas and terms from Roman law and the continent did, to be sure, creep in; but English law kept stubbornly to its ancient ways. It also resisted codification, despite complaints from an occasional intellectual like Jeremy Bentham, who saw the common law as chaotic, unwieldy, and archaic. The common law glories in its case-law, in the law built up by judges in concrete cases. The doctrine of *precedent* is a common-law doctrine. Institutionally, too, the common-law is distinctive. The jury and the adversary system both are features of the common law. Its substantive law, too, has many idosyncracies, such as the law of *trusts*, which developed out of the oddities of the English court system and English land law in the Middle Ages.

The common law was originally the law of one small country. But England became an empire, and the common law spread throughout the world. The countries in the common law family were once colonies of Great Britain, or, in some cases, colonies of colonies; they include, among others, the United States, Canada, Australia, New Zealand, Jamaica,

---

6. David and Brierly, *op. cit.* supra, n. 3, refer to it as the Romano-Germanic family.

Trinidad, Barbados, and Guyana. The common law is important, too, in former British colonies in Africa: Gambia, Tanzania, and Ghana, for example. It is dominant in Liberia, ruled by descendants of American slaves. It has influenced the law of India, Pakistan, Malaysia, and the Philippines.

Some scholars set apart, as a separate family, the socialist countries of Eastern Europe. Of these, the Soviet Union has been the most influential. Before the revolution, Russian law had close ties with the civil law family. Many habits and features of civil law remain; and some scholars still consider the Soviet Union, the people's republics of Eastern Europe, and Castro's Cuba as merely a subgroup of the civil law family. But jurists in the socialist countries insist that they stand by themselves. Obviously, Polish law will have a good deal in common with, say, Bulgarian law, and less with, say, Belgian law, since the state controls so much of the Polish and Bulgarian economies, and there are institutions (collective farms) that have no counterpart in Belgium or in Belgian law. Marxist ideology and a socialized legal profession generate still other differences. Whether these differences justify a separate "family" for socialist law is a question of taste. Within "families" there can be great differences. The living law of Haiti and the living law of France (however close they may look on paper) *must* be light years apart, since a vast economic, social, and political gulf divides these two countries, which are members of a single "family."

We have mentioned the two (or three) most notable groups. Other systems, living or dead, are more difficult to assemble into families. Far Eastern societies—Japan, Korea, China—in the past have had a more or less similar legal tradition. They also adopted Western codes wholesale, after exposure to the West in the late nineteenth century. China under Mao has swung off in a radically different direction. The *sacred law* systems have great historical interest, and in some cases, practical significance. Jewish law produced an enormous literature; the Bible embodies several codes of law, and the Talmud is, among other things, a book of law. It remains an influence in Israel. Moslem law, too, has a distinguished literature, and it is very much alive in some quarters today. In Saudi Arabia, classical Moslem law is at least nominally in force, modified to be sure by local custom and modern necessity; in Afghanistan, the Constitution of 1964 (Art. 102) directs the courts to use "the basic principles of the Hanafi Jurisprudence of the Shariaat of Islam," wherever the Constitution or laws do not specifically cover the case. Classical Hindu law, perhaps the oldest continuous legal tradition, still plays a role in the law of India.

In addition, every people or society—in Africa, Asia, Europe, and the Americas—has or has had a legal system of more or less complexity. The only exceptions are certain simple societies with no real "government," but even this point can be argued, since some anthropologists find "law" among these peoples too. Many native legal systems are of great interest. A number have been carefully studied by anthropologists—for example, the law of the Cheyenne, the Barotse, and the Tiv.[7] Some of these systems are already extinct; it is a question whether any will survive the twentieth century. They will die, not because they are "primitive," or incapable of adjusting to new circumstances (both Roman law and the common law were once "primitive" themselves), but because political and cultural conditions on which they depend are rapidly evolving to their detriment.

For example, many Indian communities in Mexico live by their own customs, languages, and laws. The customary laws, their local norms, have no official standing. Gradually, the Mexican government extends its influence. "Civilization" creeps along the roads, ending the isolation of the villages. Native languages and customs retreat. The central government is opposed to pluralism, both cultural and legal. If it could, it would bring in civil servants, trained in official law, to replace the old village leaders. The situation in Africa has points of similarity. The new countries are, on the whole, anxious to get rid of customary law. In the first place, the leaders look on native law as backward.[8] Whether radical or conservative, most of the new elite were trained abroad—in London, or Moscow, or Paris. They learned to look on more "modern" laws as models. In the second place, customary laws are local laws, laws of a single people or tribe. It is easy to feel that national unity must mean the demise of customary law. Some countries (the Ivory Coast, for example) have tried to abolish it completely.

Classification Schemes and Legal Culture. The notion that legal systems within a "family" closely resemble each other, that is, have traits in common, and that these traits sharply divide the members of a family from members of a "different" family is implicit within the conventional classification scheme. Some of the traits are structural (for example, does the system use a jury?); others are substantive (the trust as a means of "tying up" property is native only to common law countries). A few are cultural (Marxist ideology versus "bourgeois" ideology).

Every legal system has many, many characteristics of structure, substance, and culture. The classifiers single out a few of these and use them for diagnosis. The traits commonly used tend to be historical, that

---

7. Karl Llewellyn and E. A. Hoebel, *The Cheyenne Way*, Norman, Okla.: University of Oklahoma Press, 1941; Max Gluckman, *The Judicial Process Among the Barotse of Northern Rhodesia*, Atlantic Highlands, N.J.: Humanities, 1955; Paul Bohannon, *Justice and Judgment Among the Tiv*, New York: Oxford University Press, 1957.

8. "To the majority of Sudanese [the disappearance of customary law] is only a matter of time, and the shorter the time, the better." Francis Mading Deng, *Tradition and Modernization, a Challenge for Law Among the Dinka of the Sudan*, New Haven, Conn.: Yale University Press, 1971, p. 376. In the case of the Sudan, it is Islamic law rather than Western law which is looked on as the vehicle of national unity.

is, based on the origins and ancestry of the system. They also tend to be drawn from the most technical or "legal" parts of the system, those stressed in the training of lawyers, and those which form part of what we might call lawyer's law. Louisiana is supposed to be a cousin of France, legally speaking; this is certainly not because the traffic laws of Orleans and New Orleans are connected; or because of the way the tax codes of France and Louisiana treat capital gains.

The traditional classification is helpful in many ways. But it hardly seems adequate for studying law and society. It does not illuminate the way a legal system really works in a society, what impact it has, what forces mold it. The traditonal classification makes Haiti and France close kin, and France and England unrelated. One wonders how true a picture this gives of legal life, in the broadest sense, within these countries.

Without some knowledge or understanding of *legal culture,* structure and substance are, in a sense, lifeless artifacts. We define legal culture to mean attitudes, values, and opinions held in society, with regard to law, the legal system, and its various parts. So defined, it is the legal culture which determines when, why, and where people use law, legal institutions, or legal process; and when they use other institutions, or do nothing. In other words, cultural factors are an essential ingredient in turning a static structure and a static collection of norms into a body of living law. Adding the legal culture to the picture is like winding up a clock or plugging in a machine. It sets everything in motion.

In theory, one ought to be able to classify and compare legal systems by means of their cultures. This would be more meaningful for the social study of law than the conventional method of classification. But the study of legal culture, as such, is in its infancy. Until it grows stronger, it is hardly adequate to this task.

Basically, legal culture refers to two rather different sets of attitudes and values: that of the general public (we can call this *lay* legal culture), and that of lawyers, judges, and other professionals (we can call this *internal* legal culture). *Lay* legal culture can exist on many levels. It is possible to speak of the legal culture of France or Nigeria as a whole (attitudes and values which, on the whole are characteristic of Frenchmen or Nigerians). There are also regional, local, or group attitudes and values about law: those of the Yoruba, or Jews, or Britons, or plumbers, cab drivers, big business executives.

Lay legal culture, then, is far from uniform. And it is common for distinct cultures to coexist in a single political community. Most countries have more or less artificial boundaries; more than one language, race, or culture group are caught within the lines. In extreme cases—India, for example—there are dozens of language and culture groups in a single country. Often, no doubt, there are as many *legal* cultures as there are culture groups, not to mention the cultures of class.

In recent years, a growing amount of research has dealt with lay legal culture—knowledge and attitudes toward law. The research turns up striking national variations. For example, people have been asked whether they feel they should always obey the law. According to one study, more Germans answered "yes" to the question than did Dutchmen and Poles.[9] There have also been studies—relatively few in number—about public attitudes toward this or that particular field of law or legal issue: capital punishment, for example; or studies which combine investigation of knowledge and attitudes about law, for example, divorce law in Italy.[10] Of course, there is the nagging question about the way attitudes translate into behavior. But it is reasonable to expect *some* relationship. Theory suggests that attitudes toward law affect the use that people make of law; knowledge of law is thus certainly relevant. Hence the subject is a promising one.

THE THEORY OF LEGITIMACY

One particularly important aspect of lay legal culture is the theory of legitimacy that prevails within a particular group. *Legitimacy* is an attitude of respect or approval for law and legal process; a sense that law as a whole, or some parts, structures or processes, is or are valid. (The concept is further defined in Chap. 10.) Every legal system contains within it principles of legitimacy. There is some way to tell "valid" from "invalid" law. In the first instance, this is a matter of official norms. Second, it is a matter of the internal legal culture. Third, and most important, the principles, in order to survive, must command respect or approval from some part of the public, specifically, the people who matter—the ruling class, the elite, the articulate middle-class, or whoever holds power and wealth.

In short, a theory of legitimacy is an idea held by some group about the elements and processes that validate law. "Majority rule" is such a theory; so was the "Führerprinzip" (the will of the leader) in Hitler's Germany. There are many theories of legitimacy, and they change over time. When the basic principles of legitimacy change, the legal system is apt to change along with it. Revolution often brings about a transformation in *official* theory, as in Russia in 1917, or France during its

9. Wolfgang Kaupen, "Public Opinion of the Law in a Democratic Society," in Adam Podgorecki et al. *Knowledge and Opinion about Law,* London: M. Robertson, 1973, pp. 43, 46. There are, of course, serious problems of reliability. In another study, two-thirds of a sample of Germans stated that it was sometimes all right to disobey the law, for a good cause. This study was conducted in 1974 by the Youth Bureau, Prime Minister's Office, Japan, under the direction of Tamotsu Sengoku, in Japan, Germany, and the United States.

10. Amedeo Cottino, "Un Sondaggio sulla Conosenza della Legge sul Divorzio Nell'area Piemontese," *Sociologia del Diritto.* No. 1, p. 127 (1974).

Revolution, or when Augustus Caesar took power in Rome. Often, of course, underground *unofficial* change in theory paves the way for revolution, which overthrows a regime and its official theories with it.

There are many theories of legitimacy. Max Weber distinguished between three kinds of legitimate authority: Traditional, charismatic, and rational (or legal).[11] The pillar of legitimacy shifted from traditional (and charismatic) to rational authority at about the time of the Industrial Revolution. In traditional systems—in the ancient world, and in most tribal societies—people thought of law as divine, or transcendental, or holy because it was old; alternative world-views were simply unthinkable. Essentially, law was timeless and metahuman. People believed either that God or gods made law, or that the law embodied in itself a holy wisdom. In most traditional systems, deliberate, man-made change in the law was not a normal, every-day event. Change was the marvelous, the magical, the extraordinary. Change was the word of a chief, or the king in Parliament, or a fiery presence on Mount Sinai.

Modern law turns this presumption on its head. The manufacture of law is normal; it is churned out in great quantitties as needed. Law is a tool or instrument. Law and the laws are, essentially, man-made; they are constantly changing. People and governments make, unmake, and remake law to get their work or the world's work done. Ordinary people use law, and so do groups, special interests, and the state. The basic theory of legitimacy is that legal acts are valid if they follow valid procedures, if they conform to the rules of the game. *Content* does not affect legitimacy—at least not obviously. Legal acts are not sacred. The way is always open to change them, but for the sake of society, and for stability, change should be orderly, should use rational procedures, and should play by the rules.[12]

CLASSIFICATION BY INTERNAL LEGAL CULTURE: LEGAL REASONING

The study of internal legal culture is, in some ways, more advanced than the study of lay legal culture. Legal scholars, after all, have been

11. Traditional authority is, for example, the authority of a patriarch or a chief. Charisma is "actual revelation or grace resting in . . . a person as a savior, a prophet, or a hero." One obeys rational authority, on the other hand, because its norms represent the "law." One respects the norms rather than the person; the process, rather than the content. Max Rheinstein, ed., *Max Weber on Law in Economy and Society*, Cambridge: Harvard University Press, 1954, p. 336.

12. Roberto M. Unger, in *Law in Modern Society, Toward a Criticism of Social Theory*, New York: Free Press, 1976, pp. 50–52, distinguishes between "bureaucratic or regulatory law," which consists of "explicit rules established and enforced by an identifiable government," and the "legal order," which is "committed to being general and autonomous as well as public and positive." This corresponds roughly to the line between "lawyers' law" and the rest of the modern legal system. "Bureaucratic" law is more frankly instrumental, of course, though both types are, in terms of legal culture, rational and modern.

interested in the attitudes and behavior of judges for a long time. They usually have not looked at these attitudes and behaviors systematically or scientifically; but this, too, is beginning to alter.

Internal legal culture, in many ways, reflects the main traits of lay legal culture, or at least the legal culture of the movers and shakers in society. Its characteristics, behind the technical, traditional mask, cannot wander too far from what society demands. It is one thing to wear eighteenth century wigs, as the English barristers and judges do; it is quite another thing to try to impose eighteenth century legal habits on a twentieth century society.

We will discuss the relationship between societies and internal legal culture through one illustrative case: legal reasoning.[13]

A striking feature of the work of appellate courts, in Western countries, is the opinions they publish. In these opinions, courts announce their decisions, together with supporting reasons. These may or may not be the court's real reasons for its decision. In either event, the opinions are important, because they make law, or explain law, or interpret law. The opinion is that part of the decision most likely to carry a message beyond the original parties.

We use the term "legal reasoning" here in a special sense. Legal reasoning is the *formal* presentation of reasons for a particular legal act. Legal reasoning also must be *authoritative*. In our legal system, a scholar who writes a learned treatise or essay is *not* authoritative; the scholar's arguments, then, are not legal reasoning, under our definition. If a legal system treated a text book as "authority," then the arguments in the book *would* be reasoning, under our definition.

It is interesting that some legal actors use reasoning (in our sense), while others do not. Consider how a statute is made. There may be vigorous debate on the floor. There may be committee reports, research, staff memoranda. Or there may not be. Most statutes enter the world unburdened with any statement of reasons. They simply lay down new rules or remove old ones. A law is a law, even without explanation, and without debates or hearings or reports. Appellate courts, on the other hand, *must* reason.[14]

Why are some legal actors under an obligation to "reason," while others are not? One must look, first of all, to the theory of legitimacy in the society. We can distinguish two kinds of legitimacy in a legal system. *Primary legitimacy* is the legitimacy of ultimate authority. A person, institution, or process has primary legitimacy when it has the right and

---

13. See Lawrence M. Friedman, "On Legalistic Reasoning: A Footnote to Weber," *Wisconsin Law Review*, 1966: p. 148.

14. Short *per curiam* decisions—unsigned, laconic—are common in many courts. But the bulk of the work, and all important cases, carry full opinions.

power to make or change law on its own. In a parliamentary democracy, parliament has this authority. In an absolute monarchy, the monarch has it. In some societies, no worldly authority has primary legitimacy. It belongs to a sacred book or code, to God or tradition. Holders of primary legitimacy do not have to give reasons. This is especially true of charismatic authority. In the Bible, for example, God's revelation makes law; no further reasons are needed. And laws can be changed by revelation. The Book of Numbers (Chap. 27) tells the story of the daughters of a man named Zelophehad. Zelophehad died without sons. His daughters came to Moses and asked for the right to inherit. Moses "brought their cause before the Lord"; God, speaking through Moses, granted them their right. A new rule was laid down; when a man dies without sons, his daughters may inherit. Later, members of Zelophehad's tribe came to Moses and complained about this rule. They were afraid that when a daughter married, land would pass out of the tribe. Moses then modified the earlier rule, "according to the word of the Lord"; now any daughter who inherited must marry within her father's tribe (Chap. 36).

The rules here described were quite sensible, and they have parallels in many legal systems. The Bible, however, does not justify them on social or economic grounds. It ascribes them literally to God. And God alone had primary legitimacy. In most societies, primary legitimacy is human, but one can find some authority high enough to make, unmake, or remake laws, without elaborate reasons. Presidents who rule by decree do not need to give reasons, nor does the British Parliament.

All other legal actors, who have *derivative* legitimacy, must justify what they do. They hold their rights by delegation. They have to link their decisions to higher authority, or higher legitimacy. Essentially, there are two kinds of link: general and specific. A police woman, for example, wears a uniform and a badge; when making an arrest, she presents a warrant, signed by a judge. The uniform, warrant, and badge are all devices or signs of legitimate authority. The badge and the uniform are signs of general authority; they state that this person is an officer of the law. The warrant gives authority for a particular act. Legal reasoning, too, is a device of specific legitimacy. It shows the link between the judges' decision, and a body of rules or authority of higher legitimacy.

Four Types of Reasoning.   Legal reasoning, like all forms of reasoning, can be broken down into sentences and propositions. Some propositions are used as premises; some are used as conclusions. In many legal systems, it is possible to divide all possible propositions into two sorts. One sort consists of propositions defined as "legal"; these are the only propositions, strictly speaking, that can be used, as of right, as premises of legal reasoning. All other propositions are not "legal," and they cannot serve as legal premises. For example, a French court, deciding a contract case, may cite propositions from the Civil Code, from other statutes, or from the body of principles ordinarily used by the courts; it would be improper to quote from a column in *Le Monde,* however well-reasoned or persuasive. We can call a system that draws this line between legal and nonlegal propositions a *closed* system. A system that does not draw the line can be called *open.* Some societies, too, regard propositions of law as fixed and timeless. Others accept change as normal; they expect legal premises to be born, to grow, and to die. Combining these two distinctions, we derive four types of legal systems. We will look at each of them in turn.

1. Type 1: Sacred Law and Other Closed Systems

Some legal systems are closed and do not accept the idea of change. The best example of this type would be one of the sacred law systems, if it focused on a single holy book, did not believe in new revelation, and insisted each decision must be linked to some passage, word, or line in the holy text.

Classical Islam and Judaism show some of these traits. In Judaism, God's word is law, and it is embodied in the sacred book, the Torah. The Old Testament contains a great deal of legal material—the codes in Deuteronomy, for example. The Koran is much less explicitly a book of law. But Moslems believe it, too, is divine, and they look to it as a source of law.[15] In both religions, the words of the holy book were thought to be pregnant with secret meaning. In both, sacred texts were the highest possible source of law, though both recognized custom and the opinions of the sages as parallel sources of law. At one point, in both religions there was a closing of the canon; afterwards, new premises could not explicitly) arise. This happened in Islam in the early tenth century. After this, jurists could no longer reason independently; they were utterly bound by the doctrines of their predecessors. Of course, life never stood still, even when revelation dried up. New problems constantly arose; new social conditions appeared. The texts became more and more out of date. This placed a heavy burden on legal reasoning. The links stretched thinner and thinner.

Whenever this occurs, sacred law systems turn to legal fictions, legalism, hair-splitting, and analogy. This is a tendency of all closed systems. In addition, since the sources of law in sacred systems were holy texts, one could extract endless meaning from the texts, and this was a valid pursuit, regardless of practical consequences. Therefore, sacred law systems often ruled on questions that did not occur in real life. Thus Islamic jurists solemnly held "that melted butter, into which a mouse

15. See S. G. Vesey-Fitzgerald, "Nature and Sources of the Shari'a," in Majid Khadduri and Herbert J. Liebesny, eds., *Law in the Middle East,* Vol. I, *Origin and Development of Islamic Law,* Washington: Middle East Institute, 1955, pp. 85, 87.

had fallen and drowned, could not be used as fuel for lamps, because the air would be thus polluted by the impurity of the flesh of a dead animal"; they debated when one might begin to process the estate of a man turned to stone by the devil.[16]

At first blush, it might seem odd to put the common law in this category. The work of English judges seems totally unlike that of rabbis and imams. Yet the common law, too, on the whole, denied innovation. Common law principles and doctrines were the only valid premises (aside from statutes). "Precedents and rules must be followed, unless flatly absurd or unjust," wrote Blackstone in the eighteenth century (*Commentaries*, Vol. I, p. 89). The doctrine of precedent, or *stare decisis*, became even more rigid in the nineteenth century, when the canon of premises was (in theory) closed. Courts had no right to "make law"; they had to follow decided cases. These cases were a rich body of premises. Also, they had more capacity to grow than the words of a holy book. Still, situations constantly arose in which it was hard to squeeze a solution out of past doctrine. For this reason, legalism, hair-splitting, and a rather exuberant use of analogy flourished in the classic common law.

Legal Fictions.   In closed systems, we are likely to find that curious beast, the so-called *legal fiction*. A fiction is the practice of announcing some fact or situation as true, or real, when it is obviously false or unreal. There were fictions in Roman law, in the sacred laws systems, and in the common law. In England, common law courts used legal fictions to extend their jurisdiction. In cases that arose out of contracts drawn up overseas, the plaintiff would swear that his contract was executed, say, in Paris, but that Paris was really in England, "to wit, in the parish of St. Mary le Bow in the Ward of Cheap." If the defendant tried to remind the court that Paris was actually in France, and *not* in the middle of London, the court would simply close its ears.[17] In Jewish law, travel on the Sabbath was forbidden; people might walk 2,000 cubits from their towns, but no more. If a person needed to go a bit further, however, he or she could deposit some food at a place at the limit. The Rabbis treated this cache as a "temporary home," giving the person the right to go another 2,000 cubits.[18] A fiction, as Sir Henry Maine pointed out, "conceals . . . the fact that a rule of law has undergone alteration, its letter remaining unchanged, its operation being modified."[19] Its utility in a closed system, then, is obvious.

16.   N. J. Coulson, *A History of Islamic Law*, Chicago: Aldine, 1964, p. 81.

17.   William S. Holdsworth, *History of English Law*, Vol. V, London: Methuen & Co., 1924, p. 140.

18.   Herbert Danby, *The Mishnah*, New York: Oxford University Press, 1933, p. 793.

19.   Henry Maine, *Ancient Law*, London: J. Murray, 1861, p. 26.

2. Type 2: Legal Science

The second type is a system where the body of premises is fixed and closed, but which accepts innovation. This seems, on the surface, contradictory. If a fixed set of legal propositions exists, how, in the normal course of events, do we derive any new ones?[20] For one answer, we turn to the idea of science. In the popular mind, "science" is cumulative; knowledge moves onward and upward. Scientists constantly "discover" new facts about the world. The "discovery" of the cell ultimately leads to discovery of the genetic code and the double helix. But what is found out are truths of the real world. They were always there; only humanity did not know them. Especially in the nineteenth century, as we have seen, some jurists thought of law as a science. Using its raw materials—statutes, principles, cases—one could abstract broader and broader principles, and ultimately construct a truer, more sophisticated theory of law. Jurists played the role, in legal science, that biologists did in biological science; they discovered, perfected, and analyzed new facts and propositions about law. The propositions of law would, therefore, change, but not because of politics, policy, or whim. They would change as science advanced. A rule of law is "worked out . . . by developing the wider principles that it presupposes." The process "by means of which principles are discovered . . . may be compared to the analytical methods of chemistry." These words were spoken by a German scholar, Rudolph Sohm;[21] Germany was among the civil law countries where the idea of legal science was strongest and most affected the style of the courts.

3. Type 3: Customary Law

In the third type, the premises of reasoning are open, but the system does not accept legal change. Traditional or customary systems fall more or less into this category. These systems, as we have pointed out, have no norms of decision which they define as specifically *legal*. Judges draw on

20. We say "normal course of events" to exclude extraordinary situations—a charismatic leader, a conquering enemy, a parliament that stands above the courts and sometimes changes the code. Even sacred law systems recognize the need for some change, some accommodation to the secular world, which can be accomplished by decree; hence, the so-called Prosbol of Rabbi Hillel (1st century, B.C.), which significantly altered Biblical law on creditor's rights in a more or less legislative way. In modern time, the kings of Saudi Arabia have promulgated, by decree, a vehicle code, tax, corporation, and company codes, along with regulations concerning labor, mining, and foreign investment.

21. Quoted in John Henry Merryman, *The Civil Law Tradition*, Stanford, Cal.: Stanford University Press, 1969, pp. 66, 71.

common sense, custom, and the traditions of the people; they use accepted patterns of behavior as the starting point for their reasoning. Jan Vansina has described such a system among the Kuba in Africa; "legal norms," he writes, "are social norms, and nothing more."[22] At the same time, the societies accept the norms as given; they do not openly try to change them. Change takes place, to be sure, but the society is largely unaware of it.

4. Type 4: Revolutionary and Welfare Legality

The fourth type has an open canon and accepts innovation. Decisions under such a system are not tied to technical "legal" rules; judges are more or less free to change rules and add new ones, which they draw from sources outside of those composing their stock of past premises. Max Weber has spoken of *substantive rationality*. In a substantively rational system, the judge "accords predominance" to "ethical imperatives, utilitarian and other expediential rules, and political maxims," instead of norms "obtained through logical generalization of abstract interpretations of meaning."[23] In the real world, this fourth type can be divided into two subtypes. The first we can call *revolutionary legality*, using Russia in 1918 as an example. The triumphant Bolsheviks swept away the law of the Czars. They set up revolutionary tribunals, with party zealots as judges. These tribunals imposed swift revolutionary justice—new, informal, non-legalistic. Reasoning was short and to the point; it was not bound by old rules of law but drew on fresh and revolutionary principles, changing the rules as the situation warranted.[24]

The second subtype we can call *welfare legality*. In the United States, it is a style that arbitrators and a few appellate courts seem to follow, at least occasionally. Judges (or arbitrators) think of themselves as representing common sense and morality. Judges feel free to shift principles and rules about as the situation demands, or in accordance with the needs of the times or the case. They do not feel bound, then, to "follow the law" in the strict, traditional sense. Their reasoning is frank, open, and rational, not technical or legalistic. It calls on many sources, appeals to many criteria. If we look at a decision of the United States Supreme Court, in an important case, we find, of course, a great deal of

22. Jan Vansina, "A Traditional Legal System: the Kuba," in Hilda Kuper and Leo Kuper, eds., *African Law: Adaptation and Development*, Berkeley, Cal.: Univ. of California Press, 1965, pp. 97, 109.

23. Weber, *op. cit.*, pp. 63–64.

24. Harold J. Berman, *Justice in the U.S.S.R.*, New York: Vintage Books, 1963, pp 31–32; for the similar phase in Maoist China, see Shao-chuan Leng, *Justice in Communist China*, Dobbs Ferry, N.Y.: Oceana Publishing Co., 1967, pp. 27–32; Jerome A. Cohen, *The Criminal Process in the Peoples Republic of China, 1949–1963, an Introduction*, Cambridge: Harvard University Press, 1968, pp. 9–10.

"law"; but we might also find quotations from newspapers, social science surveys, and other material, and appeals to "policy," which are hardly traditonal sources of law. High courts in the United States (and elsewhere —for example, Sweden),[25] seem to be moving slowly toward this style.

We have talked about the four major *types* as characteristics of courts, and of whole systems of law. The labels can apply to parts of legal systems as well. Ordinary bureaucrats, in the immigration office, or the office of weights and measures, have very limited authority; whatever they do, they must try to link with some higher authority—a statute, a rule, the word of a superior. Notoriously, bureaucrats go "by the book." When forced to use formal reasoning, they tend to do so in a crabbed, legalistic way. In general, decision-makers in closed systems will act "legalistically." But closed subsystems may be parts of *open* systems; in fact, it is common to find open systems on top of closed subsystems. The legislature (or the king) can make law freely, using whatever premises it chooses (or no reasoning at all); the underlings have much narrower authority. A closed system, too, can have a more or less open subsystem—for example, the judges of juvenile courts inside the common law, were originally much freer, in theory, and had much more discretion than other judges within the system.

What lawyers call *legal reasoning* is confined, strictly speaking, to closed systems. The very idea of legal reasoning suggests that there is a closed set of premises, that there are two different kinds of propositions in the world, one legal and the other nonlegal. In an open system, we cannot tell legal and nonlegal propositions apart; in fact, the distinction is meaningless. These are societies or systems which do not have or use trained lawyers or professional judges. Actually, all legal propositions have some sort of social origin, just as legal words are drawn from ordinary speech (*tort* was just the French word for wrong), or are modified forms of ordinary words (*easement* is related to *ease*). Any proposition can become a legal proposition, so long as it is absorbed into the law. The only things different about legal propositions are their claims to be different, to be legitimate and authoritative, and, in complex societies, the idea (or fact) that only trained people can handle them properly.

A professional class of lawyers thrives only in systems that are more or less closed. No one else needs lawyers. Lawyers, then, have a personal stake in keeping a closed system closed. If common sense, ethics, wisdom, or native wit will make as good a judge, litigant, or lawyer as legal training will, then people with common sense, ethics, wisdom, or native wit might as well argue the law, act as judges, and assume legal control. Or if engineering, medical, or economic training leads to better solutions,

25. See Per Olof Bolding, "Reliance on Authorities or Open Debate? Two Models of Legal Argumentation," *Scandinavian Studies in Law*, Vol. 13, p. 59 (1969).

then let engineers, doctors, or economists decide. In a closed system, chances are that only people with specialized training can answer a legal question "correctly." This means lawyers or lawyer-judges, or in a sacred law system, priests, rabbis, or imams, those whose holiness sets them off from the laity.

TYPES OF LEGAL LOGIC

In some systems, there are special rules of legal logic and legal interpretation—ways to handle, manipulate, and construe rules of law and procedure. These sets of rules can also be classified as open or closed. In a *closed* system, rules for handling legal rules are set off from ordinary rules of logic or interpretation. Only a closed system of rules can have a closed system of rules of interpretation. Even in closed systems, legal logic is never *entirely* different from ordinary logic. But many closed systems develop special rules of logic, which they use along with ordinary rules. The sages of the Talmud, for example, worked out elaborate rules to squeeze extra meaning from the Bible. Some of these were plain rules of common sense—like the use of analogy. Ohters were of a more mystical nature. One technique, called *gematria,* depended on the fact that each letter of the Hebrew alphabet also stands for a number (the second letter, *beth,* stands for 2). Every word, then, has a number value as well as a meaning. This number value gave clues to hidden messages, locked in the holy book.[26]

THE STYLE OF APPELLATE COURTS

In all modern Western nations, there are appellate courts which prepare and publish written opinions. In all, the judicial systems are more or less closed. Courts are bound by "the law," though they may have greater leeway than (say) courts in sacred law systems. Despite overall similarities, court styles in the various countries are quite different in detail, as J. Gillis Wetter has shown.[27] The French *Cour de Cassation* writes in a curt, elliptical style. Syntactically, opinions consist of one monstrously long sentence in which the court strings together fairly abstract rules of law. The facts of the case barely appear. The style is

26.   Hermann L. Strack, *Introduction to the Talmud and Midrash,* New York: Atheneum, 1959, pp. 93–98.

27.   J. Gillis Wetter, *The Styles of Appellate Judicial Opinions, a Case Study in Comparative Law,* Leyden: A. W. Sythoff, 1960; Hein Kötz, "Uber den Stil Höchstrichterlicher Entscheidungen," *Rabels Zeitschrft für ausländisches und internationales Privatrecht,* Vol. 37, p. 245 (1973).

clipped and concise. Judges do not sign their opinions, and there are no dissents. The style is meant to impress the reader with the court's impartiality. Nothing is personal or political. The court quotes sections of the codes, and writes as if the decision follows mechanically from these sections. This is the style of a system that insists on legislative supremacy. Judges are as bound to the codes as robots to their masters. The principal purpose of an opinion is to show the world that the court "has arrogated nothing to itself and is merely enforcing the law. . . . It is the law that speaks." The process could be described as "extremely expert ventriloquism."[28]

The style of German courts is less impersonal, less mechanical. Their opinions are fully as "legal" as the French opinions. They also tend to slight the factual situation, but their discussion of legal principles is fuller, less barren and artificial. The judges give the impression of skilled professionals at work—judges carefully finding the right legal principles, and fitting them to the facts of the case. The methods are precise and scientific.

English and American judges write in a more conversational tone. American courts show more awareness, at least in big cases, that policies and premises do not fall from the trees; they have to be weighed and discussed. There is definite tension between the "rule of law" and the power of human beings. American theory has always been frank about the existence of the judge's power to create; in their decisions, judges can make, or find, new aspects of law. The United States Supreme Court (unlike the English House of Lords) has also come to see itself as a kind of council of elders—nine wise men who represent the "sober second thoughts" of the community.

Indeed, the court has moved far in this direction. And, more and more, it only hears hard cases, cases in which facts and issues are complicated, cases which are politically or socially delicate, cases fraught with dramatic consequence. This is the court that decides whether to outlaw capital punishment, desegregate schools, or order a President to give up his tapes and risk impeachment. The vast power of this court is not novel. The *Dred Scott* case,[29] decided in the 1850's, put the Court in the middle of the worst, most acid struggle of the day, the conflict over slavery. In the 1890's the court was once more in the eye of the hurricane, when it struck down the federal income tax law. In the 1930's, the Court slashed away at some fundamental parts of Franklin D. Roosevelt's New Deal. These cases aroused controversy, first of all, because of their dramatic results, and second, because of the path the judges were traveling. This path led to what we have called *welfare legality*. Some critics accused the

28. John Dawson, *The Oracles of the Law*, Ann Arbor: University of Michigan Law School, 1968, p. 411.

29. Dred Scott v. Sandford, 19 How. 393 (1857).

judges of abandoning their old and legitimate role. Some critics thought the court had become too obviously political. Judges, they believe, will lose their legitimacy, and, in the long run, their power, if the public sees them naked; they need to hide behind the myth of neutrality. But whether this loss of prestige will actually take place is pure speculation.

The Role of the Courts: What Judges Think. What do judges themselves think of their role? Most of the evidence is indirect. In the United States, there are signs that welfare legality has made some inroads on their minds. Compared to a century ago, judges seem more willing to dissent and put their own personal viewpoints forward. Judges cite more nonlegal materials than before (though not a great deal); they overrule prior cases more freely. Survey research sheds a certain amount of light on judicial roles. At least *some* judges say that "policy" is a factor in their decisons. John Wold interviewed judges on the highest courts of Delaware, Maryland, New York, and Virginia. He asked "[Should] appellate judges act as law interpreters or lawmakers?" Twelve (out of twenty-two) thought judges should restrict themselves to "interpreting" the law; only three (all from New York) asserted an activist ideology; the rest waffled somewhat, arguing that the role depended on the case.[30] Attitudes seem to vary from court to court. Another study found a hotbed of "realism" on the Supreme Court of New Jersey. The judges of Massachusetts, on the other hand, voice conservative attitudes.[31] One would expect civil law judges to be, on the whole, less "realist" than judges of the common law world. But Carlos-José Gutierrez, in a small study of Costa Rican judges, reports that six of sixteen saw the judge's role as that of "lawmaker." Six had a "mechanical conception" of the judge's function, and four had opinions that fell in between.[32]

THE LANGUAGE OF THE LAW[33]

Many cultures have words, phrases, and styles of language which they label as specifically legal. Obviously, these are societies with more

---

30. John T. Wold, "Political Orientations, Social Backgrounds and Role Perceptions of State Supreme Court Judges," *Western Political Quarterly*, Vol. 27, p. 239 (1974).

31. The study is Henry R. Glick, *Supreme Courts in State Politics: An Investigation of the Judicial Role*, New York: Basic Books, 1971.

32. Carlos José Gutierrez, "Los Jueces de Costa Rica," *Revista de Ciencias Juridicas*, No. 22 (1973), pp. 71, 79.

33. See David Mellinkoff, *The Language of the Law*, Boston: Little, Brown, 1963; Lawrence M. Friedman, "Law and Its Language," *George Washington Law Review*, **33**: 563 (1964).

or less closed systems of law. Only in such systems is there a legal profession, and only there does a technical language flower. In open systems, this is not the case. Where, as among the Soga of Uganda, litigants do their own pleading in court, and where "judging is only a part-time specialty, the barrier between the general culture and the legal subculture is thin. Competence in the legal subculture is widespread; the judges are only somewhat more expert in it than the litigants who come before them."[34] This is an open system, and it has no technical vocabulary of law, beyond the reach of the laity. There are words for court, judge, law, murder, and the like, but these words are in everyone's vocabulary.

In closed systems, however, especially those with legal professionals, we expect to find technical terms, for the sake of efficiency if nothing else. (This will be true of the sacred law systems, as well as such formal, legalistic systems as ancient Rome and the modern West). Technical words are of two types. Some are a form of shortcut; others describe concepts and processes not within the experience of the lay world. The lawyer's use of terms like "demurrer" or "habeas corpus" can be compared to the doctor's use of "nephritis," or the botanist's "monocotyledon." Any occupational group will make use of verbal shorthand; indeed, any group with shared experiences will do so. Lawyers share a common training, in law schools and universities. This gives them a common culture. Almost all American lawyers now practicing spent three years in law school; they all studied contract law in the first of those years. There they learned the so-called doctrine of consideration. Few lawyers ever meet this doctrine as a problem in practice. But lawyers can discuss the doctrine, joke about it to other lawyers, and resonate to the same remembered music. Words, phrases, and memories, drilled into lawyers' heads during training, unite the profession, link it to a shared tradition, mark it as a kind of brotherhood, separated from the layman's world.

Legal style also functions as *ritual*. The law is full of ringing phrases, such as "the truth, the whole truth, and nothing but the truth." In a society where no one knows how to read, sing-song or poetic phrases are especially useful. Poetic phrases are hardly mandated in the modern West; indeed, the culture admires law for justice and utility, not for poetry, magic, and tradition. Yet ritual language clings to a few outcroppings of the law—solemn and ceremonial acts, like the witness' oath, or the stock phrases in a person's last will. (These tend to come in clusters of threes— "I give, devise and bequeath . . . all the rest, residue, and remainder. . . .")

Hardly anyone admires the way lawyers handle language. Good professional writing is not common; a judge like Oliver Wendell Holmes, Jr., for example, known for his pungent style, is very much the exception.

34. Lloyd A. Fallers, *Law Without Precedent*, Chicago: University of Chicago Press, 1969, p. 66.

The Code Napoleon is said to be French style at its best. Stendhal, according to one story, sharpened his style by reading from its text. On the whole, however, lawyer-language is unloved. People indict it for a number of linguistic crimes. It is tricky, deceptive, unlovely, incomprehensible. Two sins are worth some brief comment. The first is vagueness—diffuse, windy language, whose meaning cannot be grasped; the second is verbosity, which also leads to poor communication.

Vagueness is common enough in legal writing. Sometimes it is quite deliberate. It may make sense to draft a statue vaguely; empty phrases can compromise, or paper over, irreconcilable differences, like the language of a diplomatic communique. Or vagueness may serve to pass some deliberate question on to another agency of government, or to buy time at the expense of precision. Vagueness can therefore be politically useful. For example, a bitter struggle took place in the days of the New Deal over the law to regulate Wall Street and the securities market. Early versions of the law were extremely detailed and precise. During the battle over passage, the bill became less and less specific. In the end, the law merely set up a Securities and Exhange Commission, giving it the vaguest, most general mandate. Thus the problem of regulating corporate securities was dumped in its lap. A lawyer who drafts a contract may also wish to leave some issues unresolved. This way the lawyer postpones or avoids a problem, which, chances are, will never come up in real life, and which might spoil the whole transaction once it is broached.[35]

Verbosity, too, is not merely accident or mistake or bad habit. Typically, English or American statutes were and are extremely wordy. Where one word would do, the drafters heaped on dozens of synonyms, one on top of the other. Here is one example; in it, the federal government tells the world that it is a crime to wreck a train:

> Whoever willfully derails, disables, or wrecks any train, engine, motor unit, or car used, operated, or employed in interstate or foreign commerce by any railroad; or
> Whoever willfully sets fire to, or places any explosive substance on or near, or undermines any tunnel, bridge, viaduct, trestle, track, signal, station, depot, warehouse, terminal, or any other way, structure, property, or appurtenance used in the operation of any such railroad in interstate or foreign commerce, or otherwise makes any such tunnel, bridge, viaduct, trestle, track, signal, station, depot, warehouse, terminal, or any other way, structure, property, or appurtenance unworkable or unusable or hazardous to work or use, with the intent to derail, disable, or wreck a train, engine, motor unit, or car used, operated, or employed in interstate or foreign commerce; or

35. See Stewart Macaulay, "Non-Contractual Relations in Business: A Preliminary Study," *American Sociological Review*, Vol. 28, p. 55 (1963).

Whoever willfully attempts to do any of the aforesaid acts or things—
Shall be fined not more than $10,000 or imprisoned not more than
twenty years, or both.[36]

To explain this habit, one must remember that, in the past, common
law judges treated statutes with something close to contempt. They
"construed" them very boldly. At times, they twisted an obvious meaning
out of shape. The judges did not regard statutes as part of the body of
basic law; they were intrusions, warts, excrescences. That day is largely
past. Today courts interpret statutes, on the whole, in a relatively reasonable manner.[37] Still, the right to interpret remains a powerful weapon.
Courts still use their power to stretch and shrink the meaning of words. In
theory, this is only the power to interpret; it is not the power to make
and unmake law. If a statute is really plain and explicit, even a cunning
court finds it hard to bend the words to its will. But the net of words
must be tightly drawn; otherwise the court may find some way to slip
through. In order to be safe, the drafter piles synonym on synonym,
hoping to plaster over each possible chink. In civil law countries, no one
questions the supremacy of the codes. The codes are statements of basic
principle. They are broad and flexible, but concise. Thus, they avoid the
wordiness that plagues the statutes of the common law. Ideas of legitimacy, and the relative power of legal institutions, put their stamp on
the very language of law.

36. United States Code Ann., Title 18, Sec. 1992.

37. Not in every field. In constitutional law, it is almost normal to stretch interpretation far beyond the wildest notion of the intention of the framers. The text of
the United States Constitution is very stable, very hard to amend. Like the holy
writs of sacred law systems, as it becomes out of date, it gives rise to more and
more flamboyant interpretation.

CHAPTER 8
EXPLAINING
THE LAW

We have discussed when and how a society or group will turn to formal law. We also have looked at legal evolution, legal development, and the growth of modern legal systems. These questions have been sketched on a broad canvas. At any slice in time, every day, every hour, legal systems are at work, producing decisions, rules, orders, and directives in countless multitudes. Most of the work of social scientists who are concerned with legal systems focuses on particular fields of law, in particular countries, or on particular legal events, looking for an explanation.

The legislature passes an abortion law; the court decides a case interpreting the banking code; a planning board publishes a plan to limit growth around the capital city. What factors explain why legislature, court, and board chose to act as they did? This chapter will take up the kinds of theories used to explain events in the law, and it will try to assess them. The main focus is on social theories of law. It will then examine in a bit more detail the relationships among the way the law operates, public opinion, power, and interest groups. It will then discuss theories of judicial behavior.

There are, of course many theories or kinds of explanation of legal behavior. We can group them, however, into a few main types. One type takes as the theoretical center of gravity the legal system itself and its parts; any member of this category we can call an *internal* theory of law. What unites internal theories is an emphasis on rules, processes, and structures inside the system itself, and a benign neglect of outside (social) forces. The second type of theory about what makes law looks outside the legal system for its fulcrum of explanation. Any such theory we can call a *social theory*, whether it stresses the general culture, economic forces, or other social causes of law.

Most theories today fall under these two heads. In the past, other kinds of theories of law have been important, but they have more or less fallen out of favor today. Sacred law systems ascribe supernatural origins to law. This remains true of the canon law of the Catholic Church and the law of a few conservative Moslem nations, notably Saudi Arabia. *Natural law* theories were prominent until the nineteenth century. Human reason, implanted by nature or God, was the source of human law. In traditional society, law meant right conduct; it was timeless, unyielding, and not the product of humans or their reason. Each type of theory fit a particular kind of society, and each contributed to social stability. We have discussed these theories in an earlier chapter. As we have shown, they are not by any means completely dead. The idea of natural law lives on in the form of "fundamental rights." Constitutional law and the law of civil liberties in many countries shows the influence of natural law ideas fairly strongly. But the main battle today is between *internal* and *social* theories of law.

INTERNAL THEORIES OF LAW

The dominant theory of law in legal scholarship, at least implicitly, is some form of internal theory. Jurists quite commonly, and naturally, assume that legal concepts, legal habits of thought, have a kind of life of their own. They believe that legal phenomena exist, in a sense, in the real world; there are legal "truths," or, at any rate, better (and worse) ways to formulate propositions of law. Each generation learns more about these propositions and concepts. As time goes on, our understanding of law becomes more and more precise. This is the theory of *legal science*, that is, the notion that legal scholars, when they write about the "correct" way to handle legal concepts, are like scientists in search of objective truth. The biologist builds on the work of earlier biologists; each generation adds to what we know about the science of life. Jurists, too, look for truth, using techniques that are appropriate to their own "science." The theory of legal science reached its peak in European thought in the nineteenth century. It is still important there today.

MECHANICAL THEORIES:
LAW AS TECHNOLOGY

The legal system, whatever else it is, is also a system. This means that, in a sense, it works like a gigantic machine. At one end, people file complaints and make requests or demands. The machine processes these demands and turns out answers or other products at the other end—a decision, a rule, an order, a verdict. "Mechanical jurisprudence" was a way of looking on law that took seriously the metaphor of a machine. It treated internal operations (mostly court decisions) as if they really were mechanical, that is there were "correct" answers to legal questions. Judges who were properly programmed and trained would find and emit these correct answers. Legal rules determined outputs. Mechanical jurisprudence rigorously predicted outcome on the basis of formal rules. "Mechanical jurisprudence," too, had its high point in the late nineteenth century and has never been wholly abandoned. Whenever judges insist that they have no personal choice or discretion, they are talking the language of mechanical jurisprudence. As we saw in the last chapter, the highest French court has adopted a style that mimics this theory of law.

No serious legal scholar today accepts the assumptions of mechanical jurisprudence, at least in their most extreme form. The analogy to a machine seems obviously wrong, certainly as a picture or model of the legal system over the long haul. A machine tooled to turn out little plastic cows cannot do anything else; the mold may wear out a bit, but the machine will never start to make plastic ships, not even by a process of gradual evolution. Yet this is exactly what courts seem to do, as they bend and shift doctrine over the centuries. Human systems change over time, and in ways that are (so far) impossible to predict.

To be sure, many legal acts *are* almost mechanical. If a man and woman, both over 21, take a blood test, fill out the forms, and offer the fee to the clerk in the marriage license bureau, except in the rarest of cases the clerk will surely give them the license. Much of the legal system not only can but does work mechanically. This is especially true of the lower rungs of bureaucracy. The bottom courts (traffic courts, for example) also process most cases more or less mechanically. The same can even be said of much of the work of ordinary trial courts. Indeed, these courts *must* act more or less mechanically; if every local judge felt free to weigh every little case against a personal sense of justice or social conscience, then any hope that law can be used to develop in a rational, orderly way flies out the window. But as a theory of the way appellate courts behave, or even trial courts in contested cases, mechanical jurisprudence cannot bear the weight of the evidence. Too many factors intervene between demand and response. There is the structure of the system (the way it is organized), the values, attitudes, and habits of the people who process and decide (judges, legislators), and the procedures used (trials, debates); traditions, customs and ideologies are also among the raw materials that go to make up a judge's decision. The free law and legal realist movements, which we have discussed earlier, arose in revolt against mechanical jurisprudence. These schools of thought insisted that judges had a great deal of leeway in fact; they were often, or always, able to shape legal doctrine to reach the result they desired.

SOCIAL THEORIES OF LAW

In contrast to internal theories, social theories look at law as a dependent variable, as an effect, a product, as a system molded by social forces, rather than as an isolated and insulated subsystem. The two types of theory stand in sharp opposition. Do legal systems grow and decay, according to their own internal rules? Or are they basically the creature of outside forces? If we want to explain "the law," where should we look? To what is going on in society, its events and ideas? Or to law, law books, and lawyers? Internal and social theories can be roughly compared to genetic and environmental theories of behavior. A baby grows inside its mother, following patterns coded into its system; the genes, not culture or environment, turn an embryo into a child. Obviously, a good environment is essential for proper development in life. Without food, water, and air, a creature dies. Both a horse and cow will eat grass, but the food becomes more horse in one case, more cow in the other.

We can use language as the competing analogy. A language—French, Swahili, Japanese—is tough and persistent. The vocabulary changes, to be sure; Swahili can borrow and invent new words to speak about television and quadratic equations, just as English or French did at an earlier time. Momentous change takes place among people who speak Swahili. They leave tribal society, they shake off colonial masters, they live in big, modern cities. Social and economic life is radically transformed, but the Swahili language stays essentially the same. The vast upheavals in Russia between 1914 and 1920 added a few words to the Russian language, altered syntax in some trivial ways, but did little else. In other words, language, compared to medicine, politics, or farming, is relatively autonomous.

Is law like language? Formal legal thought, in general, assumes that it is. But the example just given—the Russian Revolution—suggests the opposite. Law will be plastic and responsive to social force—most especially when people think so. People with power and wealth translate their demands into rules, doctrines, structures, and processes. A truly autonomous legal system would turn out results that rules would not want, results that went against their interests, or upset important social arrangements. Why would they let this happen? Much of the law is too important to leave to the lawyers. There is no reason to believe that people who count in society will, as a general rule, and in the long run, put up with a legal system which is, from their standpoint, perverse.[1]

1. In some societies, theocratic or feudal, for example, the legal system might be more autonomous than in the modern world. It is likely that the top strata of any society will always make sure, perhaps without knowing it, that the law is not too far out of line with their interests. After all, law is administered by human beings, who live in society and have the ideas of their times. But styles will differ, and the process will be more or less extreme, more or less self-conscious, depending on the society.

The point seems obvious. Indeed, evidence for the social theory, or at least *some* social theory, seems constantly at hand. The most casual glance at any newspaper, in any modern country, will suggest rather powerfully how social forces are at work making law. Interest groups besiege the legislatures. Government agencies plan and regulate in response to social forces. Every day we read about the pressures of social force on government, on law, and about how the system responds.

Yet things are not always what they seem. Every part of the legal system has its own special procedures; its own way of making rules and decisions. Each part may respond to social forces in a different way. The role of social forces is least clear for the work of the courts. In western societies, ancient traditions surround the judges. Their robes and paraphernalia make them seem majestic and aloof. Even socialist Poland, after 1956, clothed its judges in robes, with purple piping and great gold seals and chains of office.[2] The style of judges' work is formal and autonomous. One sees in court nothing as obvious as the lobbyists, who, in the United States, buttonhole representatives on the very floor of Congress; meanwhile, constituents phone, write, and visit their legislators, demanding action on this or that matter. The judge's cool autonomy may, of course, be nothing but an optical illusion. Every judicial decision, after all, arises out of a *case;* every case is brought by a litigant who has some axe to grind. Hence in at least one sense, social forces (demands) determine the work-load of the courts. And social theories have dominated scientific study of judges.

It is easy to see that some form of social theory will occupy a central place in any modern science of law. The dispute is over details. Social theories are theories about the way law is made, unmade, and remade as a general rule. It does not purport to explain every tiny particular. It will not tell why the Supreme Court of Michigan turned down an appeal, in a will contest, in Spring, 1976. A legal concept, a doctrine, a precedent, a rule of jurisdiction, a work-habit of these individual judges, may explain *this* legal act well and accurately enough. But the outside society makes the general drift, the long run trend. In the main, medieval law fit medieval society as a glove fits a hand; modern law clings to the contours of its society, and does its work. The same is true of each field of law. The world of factories, railroads and mines made the law of industrial accidents. Environmental law emerged in an age of rampant technology and shrinking resources. Not that iron laws of history dictated precise rules and practices. One can always find an inappropriate event or decision here and there, one that went against the tide, and which is best explained by "internal" (traditional legal) rules. But the idiosyncratic, individual

2. John Hazard, "Furniture Arrangement as a Symbol of Judicial Roles," *Etc.*, **19**: 2, p. 181 (1962).

case does not last. In the end, the flow of law, the great historical movements, glacial, relentless, sweep them away.

How could it be otherwise? The cases in court surge up out of life situations; the legislatures debate living issues of their day. Solutions must fit dominant opinion; if not, dominant opinion and dominant force will have their way, by hook or by crook, if not immediately, then eventually. Hence, social theories are best suited to explain whole fields of law and rather long time periods. In modern legal systems, they fit the law-making process (in legislatures and administrative bodies) more snugly than they fit the work of the courts. An "internal" theory may work reasonably well in explaining minor, short-run legal events. As we rise higher and higher above the plains, so to speak, social theories fit better and better, while internal theories fade into insignificance.

There are, of course, many varieties of "social theory." Marxist legal thought puts its emphasis on economic forces. Law is defined as those rules of conduct which express the will of the ruling class, the class that owns the means of production. Law is guaranteed "by the coercive force of the state." It has the function of "safeguarding, making secure, and developing social relationships and arrangements agreeable and advantageous to the dominant class."[3] Other social theorists, too (Willard Hurst, for example,[4]) put primary emphasis on the power of economic forces, but reject strict Marxist thought. The historical school of the nineteenth century, and many sociologists (William Graham Summer), stressed *cultural* elements in the background of law: law emerges from the moral ideas, traditions, and habits of a community. *This* form of social theory is the very opposite of Marxism in its political implications. Law is an organic growth, a product of deeply held traditions, rooted in the national consciousness. Its nature implies the futility of too much "social engineering." Attempts to restructure law radically, and quickly, are doomed to fail, perhaps causing great harm in the process.

The Basic Proposition of Social Theory. All social theorists might agree, perhaps, on one basic proposition implicit in their work. This can be roughly put as follows: *any legal act[5] results from, and is determined by, the preponderance of social force actually brought to bear on the subject.*

---

3. S. A. Golunskii and M. S. Strogovich, "The Theory of the State and Law," in *Soviet Legal Philosophy,* trans. Hugh W. Babb, Cambridge, Mass.: Harvard University Press, 1951, pp. 351, 369, 370.

4. See, for example, J. Willard Hurst, *Law and the Conditions of Freedom in the Nineteenth Century United States,* Madison: University of Wisconsin Press, 1956.

5. By "legal act" we mean any conduct in the legal system by a person or entity with authority—a judge's decision, a police officer's arrest of a thief, the enactment of a statute.

Law and Public Opinion.   It is important to note what this proposition does *not* say, as well as what it says. It does *not* say that the will of the majority makes law. After all, most societies make no pretense of majority rule, so that any such proposition would be completely absurd. Even in "democratic" societies, which insist that "the people" are sovereign, and where law supposedly "reflects public opinion," the will of the majority (in the sense of a head count) does not and cannot make law. Assume a perfect democracy, with complete equality of income. Assume we can take a public opinion poll and find out "what the people want." The poll does not, and cannot, tell us how much social force is *actually exerted* on a particular question of law. In the first place, polls measure what people say, not what they do. A poll picks people at random, people who may or may not have had any previous interest or concern with the question. The questions are asked one by one; they are not linked together, as part of a system of behavior. We can ask whether drug laws should be stronger or weaker; whether we need socialized medicine; whether taxes are too high. In real life, issues are intertwined. People interact, trading off behavior for behavior. They bargain and compromise. Moreover, polls often ignore intensity of feeling. They count every yes or no the same, whether loud or soft, whether hesitant or certain, whether shouted or whispered.[6]

Pure "public opinion" (in the polster's sense) is a feeble predicter of law for two strong reasons. First, in every society, wealth and power are unevenly distributed, so that some people's wishes count more than others. Second, people differ in their interests, wishes, and wants, in their intensity of feeling, in their activism—even when their power and wealth are the same. Imagine two people identical in income and social status, both opposed to nuclear power plants. One uses her talents to further the cause, spending time, money, and skill. The other keeps his opinion to himself, and spends his time selling insurance. The first one will have much more impact than the second.

Public opinion does have an impact on law, but "public opinion" must be understood in a precise and special sense. First of all, some people—but only some—actually take an interest in any given subject. Those that do not cannot be counted, whether they have an "opinion" or not. In the second place, some people have more power and wealth than other people. On almost any subject, at any given level of intensity, the chairman of the board of Royal Dutch Shell will have more impact than an old man in a hospital for veterans, an unwed mother on welfare, or a Turkish laborer in Munich. Legislators are, of course, well aware of

---

6.   On public opinion and the law, see Julius Cohen, Reginald A. H. Robson, and Alan Bates, *Parental Authority: The Community and the Law*, New Brunswick, N.J.: Rutgers University Press, 1958, and the critique in Lawrence M. Friedman, *The Legal System: A Social Science Perspective*, New York: Russell Sage Foundation, 1975, pp. 162–65.

these facts. They know that some people and groups are more active politically than others. They know that some people and groups have the time, the money, and the will to support or oppose them in important ways. The behavior of lawmakers reflects this awareness.

LAW AND POWER

What makes law, then, is not "public opinion" in the abstract, but public opinion in the sense of *exerted social force*. This depends on power and intensity. Of course, the concept of "power" is not easy to pin down. Power is elusive, hard to see, hard to measure, hard to define. Power, according to Max Weber, is "the probability that one actor within a social relationship will be in a position to carry out his own will despite resistance."[7] But how can we tell which actors are in this position? We can tell who has *had* power by seeing who won a particular struggle, but even this can be misleading.

Power, after all, can be silently exercised; when it is most overwhelming, it needs to do least to maintain itself. Silences are not very measurable. We read in the paper that a group of citizens has banded together and (successfully) fought plans to build an airport near their neighborhood. This was a use of power. We might imagine that if we observed enough incidents and read enough newspapers we could discover who cracked the whip in this particular community. And yet we might be badly mistaken. We might miss the subtler forms of power. Power molds the very shape of the community's "agenda"; it determines which matters are even discussable, and which are not.[8] In Switzerland, for example, no one seriously suggests federal ownership of food stores; in China, no one seriously suggests selling steel mills back to private owners. Such ideas do not reach the level of debate. Power does not—need not—lift a finger to prevent the issues from arising. Interests, proposals and hopes become real demands only as they pass through a system of filters. One such filter is the socioeconomic structure of the community. Proposals possible in theory become impossible in practice after passing through this filter. If they are impossible enough, they become literally unthinkable.

Interests and Demands.   Let us look once more at our basic proposition, that is, that legal acts are determined by the preponderance of social force brought to bear on the subject. It is not social force, in the abstract, that makes law, but social force acting *on the subject*. There is a world of difference between an *interest* and a *demand*. An interest is a

7.   Max Weber, *The Theory of Social and Economic Organization*, Talcott Parsons, ed., New York: Free Press, 1964, p. 152.

8.   On this point, see Robert Alford, *Bureaucracy and Participation: Political Cultures in Four Wisconsin Cities*, New York: Random House, 1969, p. 194.

feeling that a course of action will be advantageous to a person or group. (Sometimes the word is used in the sense that the course of action will be advantageous in fact.) Those things that people in general want, need, or like are, objectively speaking, their interests. But a *demand* begins with a subjective sense of interest. Suppose we were visitors from another planet and observed thousands of hungry, landless workers huddled in shacks in Mexico City, surrounded by great opulence. We could calculate a set of interests: the poor need, want, and like more money and food, and better housing and medical care. We could also roughly compute how much *power* poor people have or could muster in Mexican society. The equation—objective interest plus power—tells us more or less how much social force *could be* exerted on the legal system, wtih regard to this or that question, and in what general direction.

But our equation, of course, could not predict what is *actually* going to happen, whether revolution is imminent, or not, or what changes are bound to take place. We could not predict even if we could make similar computations for all classes and groups in Mexican society. What *could be* is not the same as what *is*. Law is not the product of (objective) interests and power; it is the product of demands, and these come from *subjective* interests. Subjective interests are what people see as their interests. People may be, and often are, ignorant, frightened, or misguided. And even subjective interests do not lead inexorably to demands, that is, to exerted social force. Another filter—a cultural one—intervenes. A person must believe that it makes sense to pose demands; that recourse to the legal system will be morally right, will be good strategy, and will bring net gains.

Let us take a simple example: a husband and wife quarrel incessantly. The husband leaves, and the wife shuts the door on her marriage. Will she ask for a divorce? Not if she is a practicing Catholic, even though the state law allows divorce, and even though she has "power" to demand a divorce from a court and an objective "interest" in freeing herself from her husband. She will not do so because her objective interest is blocked by a screen of values and beliefs. What is true of an individual person is also true of aggregates. In some countries—Italy until very recently—there was no right to divorce. The Vatican, with power of its own, was opposed. But the resistance of the Vatican would have come to nothing if the ideas, values, and perceptions of enough voters had not induced them to vote as the Vatican wished.

To restate the point: "forces" or "interests" do not make law directly. As far as the law is concerned, power, influence, and wealth are of no concern unless they turn into actual demands on the legal system. Demands flow first from subjective perceptions of interest, and second from attitudes of willingness to express and press demands. To put it another way, social forces must be converted into demands on the legal system, in order to produce legal acts (rules, statutes, doctrines, practices). Attitudes, ideologies and values act as chemical agents, so to speak; they change interests into demands (or block such changes). This is the role of the element we call the *legal culture*.

We can see, then, how and why ideology makes a difference to a system of law. There is nothing (in theory) to prevent the majority from voting to redistribute income from the rich to the less rich. For many reasons this does not happen, but surely *one* reason is the system of beliefs in most nonsocialist societies. People have ideas about the limits of legitimate demands. (Some of these are written into constitutions.) They respect the social order, and they feel radical change would be morally wrong, or that any change would be for the worse. Similarly, those who form a ruling class, or an elite, do not necessarily extract all the advantage they might from the worker-bees of their society. The very myths and ideals which sustain their position may curb the use of the power.[9]

A CATALOGUE OF INTERESTS[10]

So far, we have spoken about "interests" without discussing what that word entails. We will now try to talk of interests in a somewhat more precise way. Not all interests are the same; some are *direct* and some are *indirect*. John Smith has a direct interest in a proposed (private) bill to award him $10,000, in settlement of a claim. People have a direct *positive* interest in any legal act that promises to put money in their pocket; they have a direct *negative* interest in one that will take money out. Suppose a law proposes to raise old age pensions 15 percent, and to finance this increase with a 1 percent tax on sales of beer and wine. A particular old pensioner stands to gain $150 from the law; he will lose too, about $1, since he drinks some beer and wine. On balance, he will gain $149. As a general rule, we expect people to favor proposals which directly promise a net gain and to oppose those that threaten net loss.

Direct interests need not be money interests. A bill to prevent hunting and fishing on a tract of wooded land directly affects those who hunt and fish there. People tend to favor whatever adds directly to their power, prestige, or sense of well being. Institutional or bureaucratic interests are important; officials want their agencies to grow in size and influence. There are also moral and aesthetic interests. People favor measures that express or approve their points of view, or that give a dominant place to their ethical principles. Devout Catholics oppose abortion laws; people

9.   See Chap. 6, supra, p. 67.

10.   See Lawrence M. Friedman, *Government and Slum Housing: A Century of Frustration*, Chicago: Rand McNally & Co., 1968, pp. 184–86.

who do not drink often favored prohibition. One can also speak of status-group interests. Doctors, blacks, actors, Catholics—members of any particular group—will tend to support measures which, they feel, will raise the income, power, prestige, or happiness of the group as a whole, even if they themselves do not have much to gain.

Other interests are much less direct. No sharp line divides direct and indirect interests. They shade insensibly into each other. A long-run or contingent interest can be considered indirect. A city announces plans to tear down rotting buildings in the old part of town and put up a convention hall, a parking ramp, luxury apartments. Merchants in or near the site feel they have an indirect interest. They believe the new buildings will improve the city's tax base, or create an atmosphere of growth. All this will raise the value of their land, and possibly, in the future, bring them more business. Of course, the scheme will cost money. Taxes may rise. The project will tear up the streets and displace populations—at least for a while. This may hurt business. Also, downtown growth may cut sales in a merchant's suburban branches. Do the merchants stand, on balance, to gain? The positive interests are distant, indirect. They are hard to calculate. Even the most rational actor is reduced to an educated guess.

THE DISINTERESTED: INTERESTS AND REFORM

Not all action is the product of direct or indirect interests. There is a residue of action that is hard to explain in these terms. We can lump this behavior together and call it "reform," for want of a better word. Reformers are people who spend time, money, or energy on an issue in which they have no interest, direct or indirect; or as to which their activity is out of all proportion to the size of their interest.[11] No calculus of benefits and burdens can predict the size or type of reform activity. Yet reform is a fact of life; indeed, reform activity is everywhere in modern life. People are no longer locked into traditional frames of mind; they believe in progress and change, and they believe in working toward these goals.

As a rough general rule, for most people and on most issues, direct interests are more powerful than indirect interests, and reform motives are weaker than strong direct interests, perhaps weaker than strong indirect interests too. These propositions hold *generally* true. For the normal run of humanity, reform is a luxury. Experience tells us that

---

11. This qualification is necessary, because technically speaking, every taxpayer has a direct interest in any measure that spends taxpayers' money in any way, however small.

people who grow or sell tobacco, or smoke, will be against laws to outlaw or tax cigarettes. A worker in a munitions factory, who may lose his job if the government spends less on defense, is not likely to beome a strong pacifist. Even dedicated reformers are highly specialized. They spend energy selectively; on most issues, economic or emotional interests govern. A person working passionately to save whales from extinction is not likely to be head over heels in the battle for tax reform too.

Yet ideas and ideals *do* move people. Attitudes and ideologies monitor interests; they act as a kind of switching device, shunting interests onto the track that leads to demands on the legal system, or holding them sidetracked, or deflecting them onto some other course. And an ideology can turn into a demand, just as an interest can. Most people who lobby for prison reform have never been in prison and have no direct or indirect interest in the matter.

How Demands and Interests Change. Moreover, "interests" are perceptions; they are opinions or guesses, not objective states of reality. As far as legal activity is concerned, real costs and benefits do not matter in themselves; what matters is the way a person or group *perceives* the benefits and costs. People can be radically wrong, even about short-run, direct self-interest; they can be even more wrong about the contingent, the long-term, the indirect. People are constantly making blind guesses about where their interests lie. Often, they base these guesses on poor information. Perceptions are harder to see, and more volatile, than "real" interests, hence, it is difficult to predict how much social force will turn into *pressure* on the legal system, even when the objective interests are known.

On many issues, too, there is no majority with a strong direct interest. Should the state of New York force food stores to close on Sundays? Shall a barge canal be built through southern Florida? Should the United States change to the metric system? There *are* direct interests on either side of these issues: people who own food stores in New York, or work or shop in them; people with businesses or land in southern Florida; manufacturers of crackers and cookies who would be forced to change their packages in a metric world. But many of these direct interests are quite small; and there are indirect and contingent interests, which are hard to assess. The proposed canal could cost money—taxes, in other words. It might affect the Everglades National Park, disturbing the tourists. Food prices might go up (or down) if markets closed on Sundays. Some clerks would lose their jobs, other clerks might enjoy a Sunday at home. A metric system might make American business more competitive in foreign markets. On the other hand, people would find it bothersome to drop their lifetime habits.

In real life, people with small interests ignore all these questions. Still, representatives from Maine, Illinois, and Oregon will vote on

Florida's canal. People who want the canal badly are a tiny minority. To succeed, they must enlist a majority—but the majority has no interest to speak of in the matter. In Congress, vote-trading may take place, openly or implicitly. A representative from Illinois may follow the party line on the issue (if there is one). He may bargain with the Florida delegation, promising support in exchange for help on a measure that benefits *his* state. Or he may simply vote in such a way as to store up credit for the future.

At all times, great stocks of political force lie dormant, unused— underground, so to speak. It is this latent force that gives reformers and partisans their opportunity. They try to enlist the neutrals in their cause. "Neutrals" are people who see their interests as evenly balanced, or who have no idea where their interests really lie. Reformers often appeal to inner motives—civic-mindedness, patriotism, morality. Just as often, their artillery is based on interests. They try to show people what the law will mean to them. They try to show how the barge canal will upset the balance of nature in Florida, and hurt the tourist trade. Partisans on the other side will argue that the canal will raise land values and give people jobs. People opposed to the Sunday law will argue that it will raise prices and inconvenience working people. We may also hear about Sunday traffic and noise—issues, in short, that listeners might translate into personal terms. In other words, reformers will try to rouse the sleeping giant—the dormant perceptions, the latent interests. Efforts to draw out dormant force go on constantly. They are common, even normal, as it were, in the life cycle of law.

Perceptions of interests, of course, change constantly. Reformers are catalysts only. They preach and instruct and exhort. Once a law or rule is in effect, a new situation arises. The practical impact will be better or worse than people thought. Merchants who backed urban renewal see costs rising, business falling, and they learn, to their horror, that their homes or their businesses are in the bulldozer's path. They become, overnight, bitter opponents of the plan.

The opposite process also occurs. A group fights tooth and nail against some proposal, thinking it will bring them annoyance or harm. When they lose, the sky does not fall in. Sweden changed from left to right hand driving. More than 80 percent of the voters had opposed the change in a referendum. Once the change was made, people adjusted; opposition faded away. In the United States, the organized doctors fought bitterly against Medicare, a plan to provide medical care for the old. When medicare became law, they learned to live with it—even to get rich from it—and their attitudes softened.[12]

---

12. The Swedish case is described in Britt-Mari P. Blegvad and Jette Moller Nielsen, "Recht als Mittel des sozialen Wandels," in *Zur Effektivität des Rechts,*

JUDICIAL BEHAVIOR AND THE SOCIAL THEORY

Most of our discussion has been drawn from the world of legislation. Legislative bodies consciously make law. In a way, then, legislative examples tilt the scales in favor of an extreme form of the social theory. As we mentioned, it is easy to see social forces at work among the Parliaments of the West. The representatives are men and women who have run for office; they, or their party, have made promises to the voters about changes in programs and laws. In some countries, people can and do approach their representatives directly, asking for lower taxes, cheaper food prices, controls on the import of oranges, and so on. Parliamentary debate is often frank and free. Legislators battle and argue point of views, in plain sight of the world.

In these very countries, the courtroom world seems light-years away. Litigants do not promise to support or threaten to defeat the judge—even where, as in the United States, the judge is an elected official. Everyone who enters the courtroom—lawyers, litigants, officials—observes the elaborate and formal rules of the game. In most places, the atmosphere is hushed and reverent, the language technical and stiff. As a general rule, people hide their real interests and emotions behind legal words and phrases.

Does the social theory apply to this austere, rational world? In individual cases, and in the short run, it is hard to see social forces at work. Instead, one is almost blinded by the great sunburst of law: legal terms, procedures, doctrines, craftsmanship. The skill of lawyers and judges, the structure of courts, and the judicial tradition cannot be entirely discounted. Judges *are* different from legislators. Panels of judges do not vote in the open. They are not representatives who try to guess or follow what their constituents want. Every trial lawyer is sure he or she has sometimes persuaded a judge through sound legal argument. Every trial lawyer is sure cases have been lost because of some whim, quirk, or habit of a judge. No doubt these lawyers are right for some cases, some of the time.

Still, in the long run, and for the mass of litigation, it would be strange if the courts were immune to social forces. The basic argument is familiar. *If* the judicial system were highly autonomous, it would produce many "wrong" results, that is, results which went against what major social, economic, and political forces saw as their interests. This would

Vol. 3, *Jahrbuch für Rechtssozioligie und Rechtstheorie*, Bielefeld: Bertelsmann Universitätsverlag, 1972, p. 429. The case of medicare is described in John Colombotos, "Physicians and Medicare: A Before-After Study of the Effects of Legislation on Attitudes," *American Sociological Review*, Vol. 34, p. 318 (1969).

necessarily happen, since "autonomous" means that the courts march to their own drummer. In the long run, why would society or its rulers tolerate such a system—especially if most people believe that most of the law is man-made and treat it as a means to an end. People with wealth and power would challenge the work of a judicial system if it refused to do as they wished; or they would try to neutralize it, or find some way around it. Litigants might hammer away in court, seeking change. Or legislatures would sweep away offending doctrines. Or society would set up rival agencies and bypass the courts. For an example of *challenge*, consider how civil rights litigants in the United States hammered away at race segregation until the courts began to accede. For an example of legislative supremacy, consider the fate of the appeal court in South Africa; it was about to review a statute which stripped the "Cape Colored" of their right to a meaningful vote, when Parliament cracked down and prevented the court from acting.[13] For an example of *bypass*, common in administrative law, consider the Veterans' Administration in the United States, whose decisions are "final and conclusive," and cannot be appealed or reviewed by any court.[14]

The ideology of an objective, classless legal system might affect these incursions, but probably only within narrow bounds. Even if courts are nothing worse than stiff and technical and resistant to change, they will in all likelihood be bypassed. That this occurs, we have already seen, when we discussed the decline in litigation.[15]

Of course, courts have not by any means lost all function. They still do an immense volume of work, and fill real needs. Hence, we expect to find that courts, in the long run, move in the direction they are pushed by social forces. After all, courts cannot budge without litigants, and litigants represent the outside world in the flesh, rather than the world of legal concepts. In the nineteenth and twentieth centuries, the major industrial countries, whatever their legal starting point, whatever their judicial structure, whatever the prevailing philosophy of the judges, have moved along paths that were strikingly parallel in a number of areas: rules about industrial accidents or the interpretation of business agreements. Why and how did this happen? The most obvious way to explain this convergence is to point to parallels in background social forces. Even legal structures and concepts are not immune to social force. Mao's philosophy of law, or Jefferson's, is not the same as that of St.

13. Albie Sachs, *Justice in South Africa*, Berkeley, Cal.: University of California Press, 1973, pp. 143–45.

14. See Robert L. Rabin, "Preclusion of Judicial Review in the Processing of Claims for Veterans' Benefits: A Preliminary Analysis," *Stanford Law Review*, **27:** 905 (1975).

15. Supra, p. 30.

Thomas Aquinas or Julius Caesar. Legal thought is appropriate to its epoch. In the long run, society molds legal thought in its image.

We can assume, then, that the work of the judges is socially determined, in whole or in part. But it is not easy to study the subject rigorously. Modern political science has bravely tried, especially in the United States, and especially with regard to the Supreme Court. In general, political scientists have accepted social theories, rather than what lawyers and judges say about how decisions are reached. Social scientists feel that the key to decision-making is not to be found in "the law," but in the judge as a human and social being.

The work on courts and judges has been of various types. Some studies have tried to "scale" the justices, that is, they arrange the justices in line from (say) liberal to conservative, according to the way they vote in cases on a single general issue. The hope is that one can explain and predict judges' decisions from their position on the scale.[16] Some scholars have also looked at *structural* factors. Appellate courts are made up of sets of judges who interact with each other and with other courts. Judges like to get along with their colleagues. They also use short cuts, strategies to get the work done, rules of thumb. In other words much of their behavior can be expained in organizational terms.[17]

Judicial Decision-Making and the Background of Judges. Some scholars have also looked at the social background of judges, or their membership in political parties. This, they feel, might be the key to understanding how judges work. They have looked, too, for attitudes and values. They have combed judges' speeches off-the-bench, or tried to use interviews or questionnaires. This research faces severe technical problems, and when all is said and done, what it has turned up is far from startling.

One can certainly show that judges are not drawn from the ranks of the ordinary folk. They are not John and Jane Everyman. An extreme case is the British judiciary; the judges of the two highest courts (the House of Lords and the Court of Appeals) overwhelmingly represent the tiny upper class. Of 72 judges of the Court of Appeal who served between 1876 and 1972, almost a third were children of knights or noblemen.[18]

16. See, in general, Glendon Schubert, *The Judicial Mind, the Attitudes and Ideologies of Supreme Court Justices, 1946–1963*, Evanston, Illinois: Northwestern U. Press, 1965.

17. See Walter Murphy, *Elements of Judicial Strategy*, Chicago: University of Chicago Press, 1964. For Germany, see Rüdiger Lautmann, *Justiz—die Stille Gewalt*, Frankfurt/Main: Athenäum, 1972.

18. C. Neal Tate, "Paths to the Bench in Britain: A Quasi-Experimental Study of the Recruitment of a Judicial Elite," *Western Political Quarterly*, Vol. 28, pp. 108, 118 (1975).

Spanish judges, by and large, are the children of other judges, or of bureaucrats, doctors, or lawyers. In West Germany, where 5 percent of the population could be classified as upper class or upper middle class, 46 percent of the judges come from this background. The lower class makes up 55 percent of the population, but supplies only 6 percent of the judges.[19]

The question remains, whether background connects with actual behavior on the bench. Is a judge from a "good family" more conservative than a judge from a working class background? Perhaps the rules and procedures themselves are tilted toward the interests of the haves, rather than the have-nots. If so, one does not need class background to explain (in Galanter's terms) "why the 'haves' come out ahead."[20] In general, decision-making seems to be a complex process. Background explains a little, attitudes a little. But a lot remains unexplained.

Role-Playing, "The Law," and Judicial Behavior. Disappointed with the results of the studies of judicial behavior, some scholars have begun to rethink the whole issue. They are, to some extent, beating a tactical retreat from the more austere forms of social theory. Judges, they now feel, accept the "role" of judge. They play the game of "law;" and the rules of the game are an important influence on their work. The judges themselves, when they speak, emphatically agree. They do play the game, they insist, by (legal) rules. [21]

Still, it is clear that not all judges play the law game; even those that do, do not play it every time. Probably, in routine cases, judges, particularly lower court judges, consciously follow rules as best they can. This means that "law" prevails in these cases. To decide such cases—routine commercial cases, uncontested divorces, misdemeanors with a guilty plea—is to do a job more or less like the job of a marriage license clerk. A judge's work, then, is of two sorts. One is routine, administrative, predetermined. Here "the law" *does* rule. A smaller number of issues and cases—rare in the lower courts, more common in appellate courts, most common (in the United States) in the Supreme Court—are novel, exciting, hotly contested, fraught with great consequence. Here role playing and "the law" are less decisive.

Judges, in other words, do not react to cases in a uniform way. Passion, conscience, or social force control the big cases. When the United

---

19.　Theo Rasehorn, *Recht und Klassen, Zur Klassenjustiz in der Bundesrepublik*, Darmstadt: Luchterhand, 1974, p. 42. For the Spanish data, see José Juan Toharia, *El Juez Español, Un Analisis Sociologico*, Madrid: Editorial Tecnos, 1973.

20.　Marc Galanter, "Why the 'Haves' Come out Ahead," *Law and Society Review*, Vol. 9, p. 95 (1974).

21.　See Joel B. Grossman, "Role-Playing and the Analysis of Judicial Behavior: The Case of Mr. Justice Frankfurter," *Journal of Public Law*, Vol. 11, p. 285 (1962).

States Supreme Court had to decide whether to force President Nixon to give up his tapes, when the German Constitutional Court was called on in 1975 to decide whether abortion law conflicted with the "right to life," when Israeli courts had to pass on the guilt of Adolph Eichman, judges were well aware what was at stake; this awareness must have made a difference. A minor tax case, on the other hand, might puzzle or bore a judge. The judges might see such a case as technical only; in either event they might well decide to let "the law" govern. But it is no accident that some issues look boring, trivial, and technical, while others seem important, novel, earthshaking; this is the very stuff of culture. In brief, the crucial decision may be the decision (rarely articulated) whether or not to follow "the law." A case where the judge so chooses appears to be mechanically decided; but the essential decision was the decision to *act* mechanically, and that decision is not truly mechanical. Yet it seems to judges that they are bound by the law, in most cases, and they act accordingly.

Scholars who study how judges decide cases have spent enormous amounts of time and energy studying legal variables, role variables, attitude variables, value variables, background variables, socioeconomic variables, and so on. They have spent surprisingly little time and effort on another factor, which may be the strongest of all: the pressure of outside force, of public opinion, in short, of the world in which the judges live.[22] Part of the fault lies in the methods of research. Many researchers have, for one reason or another spent their time and effort in mapping out and explaining differences *among* judges on a panel. They have worked mostly on appellate cases, and on cases which are not unanimous, since unanimous cases cannot be "scaled." This misses the possibility that social forces are pushing *all* judges in a certain direction. If the time-span is long enough, and if one concentrates on trends, the effect of social forces on judges as a group stands out more clearly against its background. To study social forces, we might study lower court cases, the humdrum invisible cases. And when we come to look at appellate cases, we should not neglect the unanimous decisions. Indeed, these might be the most important—the cases where judges all see eye to eye. Such a study would look most closely at cases in the aggregate—typical cases—rather than at big, dramatic cases, or cases picked apart one by one. All Supreme Court judges, no matter where they hang on the scale, have been sensitive to

---

22. One notable exception is Beverly Blair Cook's study, "Sentencing Behavior of Federal Judges: Draft Cases—1972," *University of Cincinnati Law Review*, **42:** 597 (1973); this study found that outside "systemic support," or "public opinion" was the single best variable for explaining sentencing behavior. She suggests, however, that this variable works best at explaining areas of "broad judicial discretion . . . where by definition the judge must exercise his own judgment," such as sentencing, ibid., p. 604.

black aspirations, since the Second World War. All have been concerned with fairness in criminal justice. Despite many ups and downs, there have been clear trends in state courts, too. In the nineteenth century, every single state court, without exception, adopted the fellow-servant rule, which made it impossible for an injured worker to sue the employer, in most cases of industrial accident.[23] Today, every single state is expanding products liability. The trend is strong and universal. No one can doubt that some silent, invisible force is at work.

23. Lawrence M. Friedman and Jack Ladinsky, "Social Change and the Law of Industrial Accidents," *Columbia Law Review*, **67:** 50 (1967).

CHAPTER 9
THE MEDIUM
AND
THE MESSAGE

In the last chapter, we dealt with the way in which social forces make law, that is, how pressures from the outside world generate demands on the legal system. These result in specific legal acts: statutes, executive orders, rules and regulations, judicial doctrines, and decisions. Each of these is an "output," a response. But the story of legal process by no means ends there. Each output is a directive, addressed *to* someone: the public, litigants, officials. For example, a "rule" is a general statement, telling some part of the public how to behave, what it can or cannot. When the legal system produces a rule, who listens and who obeys? That is the subject of this and the following chapter.

First, we take up the question of the *communication* of the legal act to its audience. Then we turn to the question of compliance. This leads to a discussion of sanctions and deterrents, enforcement and nonenforcement, and related questions.

COMMUNICATION OF LEGAL ACTS

A legal act (rule, doctrine, practice), whatever functions it serves, is a message. It must be transmitted to an audience, or it can have no effect on behavior. There are many ways to transmit a message. We can transmit directly—face-to-face, for example, or by telephone. Or we can transmit indirectly, by putting an ad in the newspaper, sending a message out over radio, posting a notice on a bulletin board, or shouting at a crowd. Senders, in other words, can talk to their audience one at a time, or they can broadcast their message diffusely. Other things being equal, direct, personal messages have a better chance to reach their goal than diffuse messages, broadcast over the air. When we speak to a person directly, face to face, we *know* that our audience has gotten the word. An ad in the paper, giving the same message to the same audience, runs a greater risk of going astray. Sometimes it is just as cheap and as quick to give a message in person. But if the message has to reach thousands of people, it will be too slow and expensive to deliver it one at a time. Some wholesale method, some form of broadcasting, will have to be chosen.

The *size* of the audience, then, real or potential, is an important variable. Some legal acts apply to a class, some apply to one or more individuals, considered as such. A legal act which, in its terms, is addressed to a class, and which applies or can apply to an indefinite series of acts, over time, and which contains a statement of legal consequences following on some form of action or behavior is called a *rule*. (The law against wrecking trains, quoted earlier,[1] is a rule. It is not addressed to specific people or times but is a general prescription. It tells its audience what can happen, legally speaking, after certain behavior, that is, the wrecking of a train.) It is easy to describe the formal differences between an order (or decision) and a rule. Orders and decisions are not general, as rules are. But in practice, they fade into one another. Rules tend to be more important than orders, because they are more general. But a single decision or order may have tremendous impact; the order to drop the first atomic bomb had an effect on the lives of millions. A general rule, on the other hand, may be very narrow (if it applied to "all quintuplets" or "all living ex-Presidents"); and some rules, moreover, are simply unenforced.

On Effective Communication of Rules

An important aspect of a rule is its vagueness or specificity. The degree of specificity affects the chance that a rule will reach its audience. When a police officer, standing a foot away, shouts, "Stop or I'll shoot," a message is being delivered that is highly specific both as to audience and terms. When a wife says to her husband, "be reasonable," the audience is specific, but he may not know what she means. Messages that are doubly specific (as to audience and terms) are the most likely to hit their target. Much depends on whether the audience tunes in. Specificity helps; so does the content of the message. If it has personal meaning, or engages the hearer, it is more likely to get across. Some people, reading their newspaper, find foreign news boring; some skip the sports page. A person who sees her own name is almost certain to stop and read. Her mind will

---

1. See pp. 90–91.

also be alerted by any mention of her husband, her children, or her friends, her neighbors, her group; news about her town catches her attention far quicker than news about far-off places.

There are, in other words, clues to effective communication. Pinpointing the audience is one. Clarity of language is another. If a message is vague and general, it will not have much impact, other things being equal, even if it reaches its audience. Listeners can misunderstand easily; they may wonder: was that intended for me? Or they may simply not know what to do.

Let us take, for example, the well-known New York case, *Riggs v. Palmer*.[2] A sixteen year old boy poisoned his grandfather. Could he inherit under the dead man's will? The court said no. In its opinion, the court quoted the "fundamental maxim" that no one "shall be permitted to profit from his own fraud, or take advantage of his own wrong." The decision itself, and the ensuing command, were precise and specific. Young Palmer forfeited the inheritance; his aunts, Mrs. Riggs and Mrs. Preston, were to take the estate. This message went to a small audience, which could be pinpointed exactly, and the content of the message was clear. The broader "principle" (no one should "profit from his . . . wrong") was also a message. But in what way could this message reach any audience, or affect any behavior? First of all, it was simply broadcast in the air, so to speak; people who picked it up on their receivers by chance could not really know what to do with it. Art. 1134 of the French Civil Code announces that "Contracts . . . must be carried out in good faith." Here, too, the casual reader has not the vaguest notion what behavior is called for.

This is the problem with beautiful and flexible "principles" of law. Professional jurists love them, but they are poor communicators, whatever their other virtues. The homely speed limit—stiff, nonconceptual, unlovely—does much better; it is in plain English and sits in big letters at the side of the road. Every motorist driving by can understand it at a glance.

Specificity, we have said, makes a message easy to grasp. But exactly what does specificity mean? At the heart of the speed limit is a number term: 55 m.p.h. The opposite would be a vague, qualitative "principle" such as "drive at a reasonable speed." In other words, the more quantitative the message, the more specific it is. But quantitative terms are only a special case of a larger category: words, phrases, and ideas, about whose meaning people do not disagree. One person's "55" is the same as every other person's. One person's "ugly" is not; or one person's "reasonable." If these terms were universally agreed upon, they could be as specific as "55" or "63.9." In fact, they are not. But social consensus may attach to words and ideas, which are not quantitative, not inherently specific. In

2.   115 N.Y. 506, 22 N.E. 188 (1889).

1400 in Ireland or France, it was blasphemy to deny the existence of God. There was simply no questioning this point. Similarly, in 1850, in England or Denmark or Peru, it was plainly lewd and plainly illegal, to appear on the stage in the nude. In 1975, one is not so sure. The messages conveyed by the words "blasphemy" and "lewd" have changed. When a term is quantitative, this rarely happens. But the *number* is not magic; what is (relatively) unchanging are ideas about what numbers mean.

Legal Complexity and Knowledge of the Law

As we have seen, there are good reasons why some legal messages— statutes, contracts—are left deliberately vague.[3] In addition, some areas of business or life are so complicated, so technical, that it is unrealistic to try to write rules that the ordinary person can understand. Imagine writing a cartel code or a building code for the average citizen.

In many fields, then, the texture of rules is so dense that they can hardly be communicated. Here middlemen, information brokers, spring up who collect, digest, store, and pass on rules, orders, and decisions in usable form. Lawyers are among the most prominent of these middlemen. The federal tax law—the Internal Revenue Code—is the most complicated statute in the United States. It is hundreds of pages long, and utterly unreadable. In addition, there are thousands of rulings and regulations, which are as much a part of the law as the statute itself. No layman can cope with this legal hippopotamus. Tax lawyers and accountants, however, know their way through the maze. They also collect tax laws and materials, so that the answers to questions lie at their finger tips. The tax laws are not only complex: they are also diffuse, messages broadcast (so to speak) into the air. The government does not—and cannot—send them directly to those who will use them. The government may not know who these people are; they may not know themselves. For example, marriage, divorce, and death affect tax status. If we changed the tax rules on these subjects, who should we inform and when? People do not know if and when they will need these rules.

Knowledge of law, as one might expect, is not spread evenly in society.[4] There are class differences, age differences, group differences. Societies, too, are very variable in this regard. In a small, tight community, without professional lawyers, most people will probably know the main

3. See p. 90.

4. See Adam Podgorecki et al., *Knowledge and Opinion About Law*, London: M. Robertson, 1973; Berl Kutschinsky, "Knowledge and Attitudes Regarding Legal Phenomena in Denmark," in *Scandinavian Studies in Criminology*, Vol. 2, 1968, p. 125.

working rules. This cannot be literally true in a modern industrial society. In fact, druggists know something about the law relating to drug stores, drivers know some traffic laws, big companies hire people who know antitrust law and the law of the stock market. The general public knows next to nothing about these subjects. People know about *relevant* aspects of law—not every fine detail, but enough to get by. Everybody knows, for example, that it is a crime to rob a gas station, or embezzle from a bank; only experts know the technical details. The average woman has never heard of a "negotiable instrument," but she knows enough to endorse and cash her checks.[5]

LEGAL BEHAVIOR

Communication of a rule or an order is essential to its impact. Otherwise, there can be no response. But communication is only a beginning. When the message is received, how do people respond, and why? We will call any response to a legal act, *legal behavior*. We mean by this any piece of voluntary conduct, which is influenced in any way by a norm, rule, decision, or order. For these purposes, anything is voluntary that is not strictly involuntary. It is involuntary to blink, to secrete hormones, to be dragged to the gallows and hung. But if a law officer shouts, "stop or I'll shoot," and a man stops dead in his tracks, his conduct is voluntary, and hence it is legal behavior. Of course, the behavior was coerced, to put it mildly. Nevertheless, the man *could* have kept on running; some people do. A great deal of legal behavior is in some sense coerced. The state, through rewards and punishments, tries to manipulate behavior. But there are degrees of coercion; students of the social aspects of law are interested in any act where choice is an element, however slight, because of their interest in legal behavior, that is, the response of populations to legal acts.

The question is, when an order is given, or a rule announced, what will follow: compliance, noncompliance, evasion; use, nonuse, misuse; by whom, when, and how? For the sake of simplicity, we will focus on compliance and noncompliance. Take any rule in effect in a community, and assume that the rule is announced, in some way, to some audience. The audience may now choose to obey or disobey. What factors, in the end, determine this choice?

Since legal behavior is a matter of choice, we are necessarily dealing with people's ideas and motives. They seem to be complex, but we can divide them into four general categories. The first is *self-interest*. I often

5. See Daniel J. Gifford, "Communication of Legal Standards, Policy Development, and Effective Conduct Regulation," *Cornell Law Review,* **56:** 409, 410–418 (1971), distinguishing between "official" and "popular" versions of law.

choose to obey the speed limit, because I am afraid of an accident. Self-preservation, pure and simple, keeps me within the letter of the law. Even without any speed limits, many people would drive at a reasonable speed, to avoid an accident.

Strictly speaking, behavior motivated by pure self-interest is not *legal* behavior at all. A second form of rational calculation, however, does take into account law and legal process. Many people drive carefully and slowly, because they are afraid of the police; their behavior, in other words, is sensitive to *sanctions*. Reaction to *sanctions*—threats and promises, punishments and rewards—forms the second motive for legal behavior.

A third motive we can call, for want of a better term, response to *social* influence. People behave in this or that way because of what family, friends, or some other group does, thinks, or says—in other words, they are sensitive to the thoughts and actions of significant others. So, a person may observe the speed limit because his wife, sitting next to him in the car, may nag, joke, entice, praise, or support him; because, if the police arrest him, his name will appear in the newspapers, and his neighbors may react; or perhaps because he may lose his job if he gets in trouble. Notice that in these cases too, our subject is reacting to threats or promises of sanctions, just as real as those of the law but from different sources.

Lastly, there is the *conscience* factor in legal behavior. People may keep within the law because they think speeding is immoral or illegal; their sense of right tells them what to do. As we shall see, each of these factors of legal behavior is itself complex. We take up each of them in turn.

ON SANCTIONS

We first discuss what is in some ways the most basic factor in legal behavior: response to *sanctions*. People try to avoid *punishment* and seek out *reward,* like a plant that bends toward the light.

Exactly what is meant by "reward" and "punishment?" To begin with, mere words on paper do not, in themselves, influence anybody's conduct. An effect on behavior is produced when some subject perceives a *threat* of punishment. The threat, of course, has a greater range than its effect on people actually punished. Few people pay fines (except for traffic offenses); fewer still go to jail. But legal threats may affect many people who merely see or hear about punishment, or who simply know it is there. This is so-called *general deterrence*. The effect on the person actually punished is called *specific deterrence*. Zimring and Hawkins point out that special deterrence is, in a sense, just a special case of general deterrence. Thieves sent to jail have already robbed once; if jail is a deterrent (once they get out), it is because they know that jail can happen again.[6] "Punishment," then, really means the *threat* of punishment, and more precisely, the echo of that threat in the mind of the subject: the subject's fear, dread, or expectation of a painful possibility. Similarly, when we say reward, we mean the *promise* of a reward; more precisely, *its* echo in the mind: the pleasant expectation, the smacking of lips, the anticipation of joy.

Types of Sanction

People use the words "reward" and "punishment" quite casually, even loosely. A punishment is anything felt to be costly or painful. Most people would agree that death, whipping, jail, fines, reprimands, and losses of privilege are genuinely painful. But in some cases it is not so easy to tell what is punishment and what is reward. The one who receives may see "punishment" in a different light from the punisher. There are some people who like to be beaten. A hungry, homeless drunk, on a cold winter night, might want to go to jail.[7] More important is the fact that individuals and groups, though they tend to agree on what is reward and what is punishment, may not rank them the same. Some people dread jail more than others. Prison is a more powerful deterrent, it is said, for white collar criminals, than for the ordinary thief or delinquent. (Whether this is so or not is hard to say.) A fine of $100 is a fortune to one person, a trifle to another.

In loose, ordinary speech, we are apt to say that the punishment for (say) theft is "a year in prison." But the real punishment is more complicated than mere loss of freedom for a year. First, the thief will be hunted and arrested, may go through a trial, and will be questioned, harassed, and shamed in many ways. The thief may lose a job, and perhaps reputation and spouse. There are prisons and prisons; some may inflict far more punishment (rape, bad food, cruel guards) than others. In any event, prision is not house arrest, not merely a place where people cannot freely come and go. When finally set free, the thief may continue to be punished. Now the thief is a person with a "record" and may find it

---

6. Franklin G. Zimring and Gordon J. Hawkins, *Deterrence, the Legal Threat in Crime Control*, Chicago: University of Chicago Press, 1973, p. 225; see also Herbert L. Packer, *The Limits of the Criminal Sanction*, Stanford, California: Stanford University Press, 1968; Jack P. Gibbs, *Crime, Punishment, and Deterrence*, New York: Elsevier, 1975.

7. Though probably outsiders exaggerate this effect. For a richer picture of "urban nomads," see James P. Spradley, *You Owe Yourself a Drunk*, Boston: Little, Brown & Co., 1970.

hard to get a job or move into "straight" society.[8] All this is part of the "punishment" for theft. How people perceive these side punishments is, of course, also variable.

Stigma and Shame

The deterrent effect of punishment is the aspect of punishment which has been most widely discussed in the literature. But punishment itself is only a technique, a mechanism, for delivering or creating certain effects, notably the prevention of crime. Deterrence—inducing fear of punishment inside a potential deviant, thus causing the person to shy away from the forbidden act—is one of these effects, and a most important one. But there are others; indeed, Jack Gibbs has identified nine "possible ways that punishment may prevent crimes," *besides* deterrence.[9] One of the most important of these nine is *stigmatization*. *Stigma* is a label attached to a person, which stimulates punishing reactions from people in surrounding society.[10] The inner reflection of stigma is *shame*. Shame is awareness and acceptance of stigma. The fruits of stigma are often overt; an employer refuses to give a convict a job; people next door refuse to be be friendly; someone rejects the convict's friendship. In general, fear of stigma deters insofar as it induces a sense of shame, or a fear of shame, or a fear of the overt results of the stigma of punishment.

Legal systems often try to foster stigma and shame. They have good reasons. Stigma and shame make punishment more effective, at no extra cost (in dollars) to the system. A year in jail is (in theory) less powerful a sanction than a year in jail, plus a lifetime of disgrace. The state will have to lay out money for the year in jail, buying food, paying for guards and utility bills. The disgrace is free. (The disgrace, of course, may have terrible side-effects, but these do not cost the state money directly and are therefore easy to overlook.) Stigma and shame are indispensable to the system of sanctions in small societies. Often tribal systems lack jails or the equivalent; the death penalty is rare and extreme. The best way to bring norms home is to enforce them with stigma and shame. In Puritan Massachusetts, the man or woman who was idle, blasphemed, stole a pig, or fornicated, could be put in the stocks, to be seen and derided in public. In small, tight communities, as we have seen, there is no escape from the neighbors; in such places, stigma and shame are effective teachers and

8. Isaac Ehrlich, "The Deterrent Effect of Criminal Law Enforcement," *Journal of Legal Studies*, 1: 259, 264–65 (1972).

9. Jack P. Gibbs, *Crime, Punishment, and Deterrence*, New York: Elsevier, 1975, p. 57. Among the other effects are *incapacitation* (a man in jail cannot rob; a killer put to death cannot kill); *enculturation* (the process of punishing instructs people in society about the norms); *reformation* (punishment teaches a lesson).

10. See Erving Goffman, *Stigma, Notes on the Management of Spoiled Identity*, Englewood Cliffs, New Jersey: Prentice-Hall, 1963.

punishers. Among the Ashanti of Ghana, as reported by R. S. Rattray in the 1920's, ridicule was one of the strongest and most common punishments. A malicious tale-bearer, for example, "had his or her face smeared with charcoal, was compelled to hold a live fowl between the teeth and to parade the town, beating a odawara (gong)."[11]

Many societies use ostracism as a punishment for serious crime; many use banishment. Expulsion from the community is in some ways only a heightened form of ostracism. Psychological banishment (excommunication) has also been a common, and powerful, sanction in many societies. In medieval Jewish communities, the ban was announced in the synagogue, while candles were snuffed out and the ram's horn sounded.[12] Albanian tribesmen punished the killer of a priest with banishment; they also banished any man who murdered his enemy during a public truce. To force the exile out of his home, his house, fruit trees, and livestock were destroyed by fire.[13] In all societies, cultures, and subgroups there are punishments ranging from dirty looks to exile that make use of stigma and shame. And, except perhaps in large modern countries where cities permit anonymous escape, these punishments can be as devastating, and as final, as a sentence of death.

The Effectiveness of Sanctions

There is a growing literature on sanctions and their effect. Much of this literature asks whether punishment deters. At one time, some scholars doubted whether punishment had much deterrent effect. Baldly stated, this cannot be right. Any theory of legal behavior must assume that people, by and large, do not want to be punished and will act so as to avoid fines, jail, whipping, or the electric chair. This means that a threat of real punishment *will* deter, and a real promise of reward will act as an incentive, all other things being equal.[14]

Of course, the mere threat of punishment will not deter everybody. Statements about deterrents are statements about marginal effect. They are like statements about price. If the price of gasoline rises from $.40 to $.70 a gallon, and all other factors remain more or less the same, we expect people to buy less gasoline. This is the law of supply and demand. To

11. Robert S. Rattray, *Ashanti Law and Constitution*, Oxford: Clarendon Press, 1929, p. 327.

12. David M. Shohet, *The Jewish Court in the Middle Ages*, New York: Sepher-Hermon Press, 1974, p. 149.

13. Margaret Hasluck, *The Unwritten Law in Albania*, Cambridge: Cambridge University Press, 1954, pp. 244–45.

14. The literature is summarized in Franklin E. Zimring and Gordon J. Hawkins, *Deterrence, the Legal Threat in Crime Control*, Chicago: University of Chicago Press, 1973; the subject of deterrence is handled with great care and insight in Jack P. Gibbs, *Crime, Punishment, and Deterrence*, New York: Elsevier, 1975.

an economist, then, the basic premise is simple: punishment deters crime, because "demand curves slope downward. If you increase the cost of something, less will be consumed." If you "increase the cost of committing a crime, there will be fewer crimes."[15] But this "law" or rule does not predict what any particular person will do. As the price of gasoline rises, some people continue to buy. They have a great deal of money, love to drive, or must drive for some compelling personal reason; they simply pay the higher price. Other people, whose decision to drive or not drive hangs by a hair, will walk, ride a bicycle, or stay home. In the aggregate, less gasoline will be sold—other things being equal. The argument is the same for punishment and deterrence. A real increase in punishment, if people are aware of it, will make *some* people think twice about committing the act which is punished. It is not necessary to assume that everyone is "rational," that everyone is some sort of cost-benefit computer. Basically, all that is meant is that people, in general, go after what is pleasant and profitable, and avoid what stings, bites, and costs.

We assume then, as a matter of theory, that threats to punish do tend to deter, and that promises of reward encourage the rewarded behavior (which no one ever denied). We assume, too, as a matter of theory, that any *increase* in the level of threat, other things being equal, tends to increase the deterrent effect, and a promise of greater reward, other things being equal, adds to the incentive. In recent years, attempts have been made by economists and sociologists to test these propositions empirically, especially the deterrent effect of punishment. In general, these recent studies tend to find some empirical support for the deterrent effect. In one study, for example, crime rates in various police districts of Los Angeles were compared. These rates varied, it was claimed, according to the likelihood that offenders would be caught and sent to prison.[16] Laurence Ross carefully studied the impact of the British Road Safety Act of 1973, which threatened drunk drivers with serious penalties. Ross found in the early years of the Act, a significant deterrent effect.[17] Deterrence, however, is devilishly difficult to measure, and the statistical pillars of many of the studies (though not all) are rather shaky.

Capital Punishment

The basic propositions about sanctions seem almost intuitively true. Severe punishment should have a strong deterrent effect. Why is the subject controversial? Some of the reason is no doubt due to the debate over capital punishment. Even today, there is considerable controversy on the

15. Gordon Tullock, "Does Punishment Deter Crime?", *The Public Interest*, Vol. 36, pp. 103, 104–5 (Summer, 1974).

16. Ibid, p. 103.

17. The study is H. Laurence Ross, "Law, Science, and Accidents: The British Road Safety Act of 1967," *Journal of Legal Studies*, Vol. 2, p. 1 (1973).

subject. Some studies argue that capital punishment has no effect. Some American states have had a high murder rate, despite capital punishment; others (Wisconsin, for example) have had a low rate, though they had long since given up the death penalty. Other scholars disagree. One of them, Isaac Ehrlich, recently claimed to show, by statistics, that every execution in the United States has a measurable effect, reducing the number of murders. The Justice Department and the newspapers vulgarized his findings into a claim that every execution saves eight lives. Ehrlich's own data and conclusions have been severely attacked. The empirical studies, it is fair to say, do not prove the point one way or the other.[18]

What are we to make of this controversy? First of all, it is certain that capital punishment does deter, at least some people, and some acts. Readers can test this by introspection. They know that they would stop doing many, most, perhaps all of the things they do, to avoid the risk of death. What we can say, however, if we are opposed to capital punishment, is that the death penalty, as it is used today, in Western nations, does not seem to produce enough obvious deterrence, at least as compared to life imprisonment or other heavy penalties, to justify its cost in dollars and in side effects.

What are the side effects? Supposedly, the death penalty inflicts psychic and moral harm on society. According to Barbara Wootton, it "lets loose . . . elements of primitive savagery which civilization may have pushed beneath the surface, but has still failed to exterminate."[19] It is hard to prove or disprove this and other propositions about the evils of capital punishment; a growing number of people in the United States, and perhaps elsewhere too, are eager to retain or restore the penalty of death for certain crimes. There are many gradations of practice and opinion. Many countries do not use capital punishment. The Union of South Africa, on the other hand, uses it frequently. For the year ending June 1971, eighty men were executed in South Africa. Only four of them were white.[20] On June 18, 1975, Saudi Arabia publicly beheaded Prince Faisal Ibn Masaed , who had killed his uncle, the King. Most foreigners found this act disgusting. Until the 1860's, hangings in Great Britain were public too.[21]

18.   Peter Passell, "The Deterrent Effect of the Death Penalty: A Statistical Test," *Stanford Law Review*, **28:** 61 (1975).

19.   Barbara Wootton, "Morality and Mistakes," in *The Hanging Question*, Louis Blom-Cooper, ed., London: Duckworth, 1969, pp. 13, 14.

20.   Six out of ten white residents of Capetown, according to one sample, favored the death penalty; but many of these people were genuinely troubled about its overuse. James Midgley, "Public Opinion and the Death Penalty in South Africa," *British Journal of Criminology*, Vol. 14, p. 345 (1974). Many countries in Europe and Latin America have abolished the death penalty, for example, Colombia, Costa Rica, Finland, and Italy.

21.   See David D. Cooper, *The Lesson of the Scaffold, The Public Execution Controversy in Victorian England*, Athens, Ohio: Ohio University Press, 1974.

In the United States, the use of the death penalty declined steadily until the late 1960's. In 1951, 105 people were executed; in 1961, 42; in 1966, 1.[22] Moreover, the reviewing process became slower and slower, as the penalty lost its grip on public sympathy. Many convicts sat on death row for years, while appeal after appeal dragged on through the courts. Perhaps the most celebrated case was Caryl Chessman of California, sentenced to death on May 21, 1948, executed in May 1960, nearly twelve years later, after endless writs, appeals, reviews, and procedural maneuvers.[23] This was slow torture; yet the fact remains that a rare, slow punishment may add very little to the risk that a potential murderer perceives—compared, say, to life imprisonment. Assume for the sake of argument that a woman is thinking of poisoning her husband, to collect his insurance and to marry her lover. She knows that she runs a risk of getting caught. If caught, she loses money and lover, and she faces a lifetime in jail. These are severe penalties. Suppose she assesses the risk as one out of ten. Suppose she is also aware that a handful of murderers are put to death. In any event, this happens only after ten or twelve years of appeals. Suppose she assesses this added risk as one in 1,000. Obviously, its deterrent effect would be very small—perhaps not measurable at all, just as the effect on demand for a diamond necklace would be undetectable, if the price went up from $40,000 to $40,001.

The Deterrence Curve

The point about the death penalty illustrates one feature of what we might call the *deterrence curve*. An increase in threat, taken seriously by those threatened, leads to a decrease in the threatened behavior. Suppose we make a graph of the relationship between threat and behavior. As threat goes up, behavior goes down. What is the *shape* of the graph? Is it linear? This would mean that, if we double the risk (from one chance in five of a year in jail, to two chances in five, or one chance in five of two years), the deterrent effect (assuming the message gets through) will double

22. William J. Chambliss, "Types of Deviance and the Effectiveness of Legal Sanctions," *Wisconsin Law Review*, 1967: 703, 705.

23. See "The Caryl Chessman Case: A Legal Analysis," *Minnesota Law Review*, **44**: 941 (1960).

   In 1972, the United States Supreme Court declared existing death penalty laws unconstitutional, Furman v. Georgia, 408 U.S. 238 (1972). After 1972, many states passed new statutes, trying to preserve the death penalty in such a way as to avoid the constitutional problems mentioned in the Court's opinion. In 1976, the Court in a series of opinions headed by Gregg v. Georgia, 428 U.S., 96 S. Ct. 2909 (1976), invalidated some of these statutes and upheld others. What the Court actually held, however, was not easy to interpret as of this date (1976).

too. But there is no reason to expect so neat a relationship. The greater the punishment, the more its tendency to deter; as it approaches perfection, there are fewer people left to deter, and the effect gets weaker and weaker, Suppose a hundred drivers a day park overtime on Main Street. The fine is $1, and one violator out of ten is caught and ticketed. We raise the fine to $5. Now only twenty-five violate per day. We double the fine to $10; we go down to ten or so violators. But these ten are tough cases; when we increase the fine to $20, we lose only one or two of them. It takes a fine of $100 and a tow-away system, to bring us down to one or two a day. The curve, in short, flattens out.

What factors influence the shape of the deterrence curve, or the impact of a promise or threat? We have mentioned some of them already. The *actual* risk is one—the severity of the threat, and its certainty (how likely it is to turn into reality). Severity and certainty only operate insofar as they are reflected in *perceptions* of risk. The key factor in a sanction is the way a threat or promise resonates inside the subject. We are less concerned with the "real" threat or promise, than with the perceived threat or promise: what people think are the risks and rewards.

Real sanctions and perceived sanctions, to be sure, may be closely related. But they are by no means identical. On the one hand, actors can be ignorant of risks; they may badly miscalculate. People do not really know how many shoplifters are actually caught in the act, how many are sent to jail. On the other hand, there is the "phantom effect"—people see risks where risks are absent; they imagine the police under every bush.[24] Other things being equal, any increase in *perception* of threat or reward will move behavior. Of course, an increase in real punishment quite commonly brings about a change in perception. Many societies try to make sure that this happens. In Singapore, in 1974, the government announced loudly, publicly, and in graphic detail its plans to punish crimes with open flogging.[25] When hanging was public, performed in front of great crowds of people, its message was hard to ignore.

Speed of sanctions is another important factor, perhaps as important

---

24. The term "phantom effect" is from Jan M. Chaiken, Michael W. Lawless, and Keith A. Stevenson, *The Impact of Police Activity on Crime: Robberies on the New York City Subway System,* New York: New York City—Rand Institute (1974), p. 23. Pouring in more police reduced crime, even during times when the police were not actually there.

The "phantom effect" may wear out if increased enforcement really *is* only a phantom. This apparently took place in England under the Road Safety Act of 1967. The effect of the law declined, as "the public began to learn that they had overestimated the certainty of apprehension and conviction." H. Laurence Ross, "Law, Science and Accidents: The British Road Safety Act of 1967," *Journal of Legal Studies,* Vol. 2, p. 1, 76 (1973).

25. New York Times, Nov. 26, 1974, p. 4, col. 3.

as certainty and severity. An immediate sanction has more wallop than a sanction delayed. A dollar in the hand is worth a dollar; the right to a dollar in ten years must be heavily discounted. Psychologists have tried to show, by experiment, that delay in punishment waters down its effect. These conclusions, however, come from the rarefied world of the laboratory; here one speaks of "delay" when (for example) an electric shock comes 30 seconds after behavior, rather than immediately. But it is logical to assume, as Barry Singer argues, that a six month sentence for a crime, immediately imposed, would be more effective than a longer sentence, beginning sometime in the distant future.[26]

Civil Damages and the Deterrence Curve

This sensible proposition also should apply to civil damages. A person who breaches a contract, or who is negligent, may be (legally) liable for damages. But the threat of damages for breach of contract is a rather weak deterrent. Legal process is slow. In a big case, litigation may drag on for years, before any damages are actually paid. This drastically reduces any possible deterrent effect.

In the law of contracts, too, one recovers only "economic" damages, and not even all of these. Suppose a buyer orders a machine, at a price of $4,000, and the seller fails to deliver. The ordinary rule is that the buyer may recover only the extra cost of buying the machine on the open market. (If the buyer can get one for the same price, that is, $4,000, no legal injury has been suffered.) The buyer *cannot* recover for pain, suffering, inconvenience, disappointment, or loss of profits. On the other hand, in tort cases—actions for personal injury—the winning party *can* recover for pain and suffering, sometimes quite large amounts. Perhaps society is not eager to "stamp out" breach of contract (it is inevitable in a commercial society), but it does wish to discourage accidents and negligent behavior, if it can. Where the legal system is truly serious about deterrence, it tends to punish too much—extract an eye for an eye, or perhaps two eyes for one. It makes the wrongdoer pay, and pay, and pay. If you steal a chicken, or a box of nails, you can go to jail for years. This price is far out of line with the market value of a chicken or a box of nails. But society seems to believe it could not deter the thief with lesser "damages."

The Demand for Deviance

It is obvious that *some* legal rules are obeyed more than others, at any given level of enforcement. In other words, the deterrence curve is

---

26. Barry F. Singer, "Psychological Studies of Punishment," *California Law Review*, **58**: 405, 421 (1970).

different for various types of misbehavior. Or, to put it yet another way, the demand for some kinds of conduct is elastic, for others inelastic. Illegal parking is more sensitive than rape to changes in sanction. William Chambliss divides crimes into two groups, "expressive" and "instrumental."[27] An expressive act is pleasurable in itself. Rape and drug addiction are expressive. An instrumental crime (embezzlement, income tax evasion) is only a means to an end. Punishment, Chambliss feels, can deter instrumental crimes; it has little or no effect on expressive ones.

Other scholars, however, doubt that Chambliss's categories help us understand why the demand for certain acts is elastic or inelastic. Johannes Andenaes points out that "the fear of even mild social sanctions often leads to the suppression of expressive acts (for example, yawning, picking one's nose, or crying out angrily)."[28] Hunting deer (out of season), shooting rare game, and bagging exotic birds are expressive acts; yet threats and sanctions are probably fairly successful, in deterring these crimes. When demand for behavior is elastic, more enforcement effects, or new techniques of enforcement, tend to show excellent results. When demand is inelastic, the return on investment is poor. To say that the demand for rape seems inelastic means that heavier punishment would not deter very much. Perhaps the rapist and the tax evader *are* different sorts in that the rapist is out of control. This may merely mean that the present level of enforcement deters all but the hard core cases. The punishment for rape is severe, and the moral pressures are great. In other words, the curve has reached the point where it has largely flattened out. The deterrence curve often shows, by its shape, that demand for an act is elastic, up to a point; after the deterrent has worked for the vast majority, a "saturation point" is reached,[29] and inelasticity sets in.

As Chambliss himself admits, few crimes are exclusively expressive. Murder is expressive when it is a crime of passion; but there are hired killers, too, and people who kill for insurance, or to inherit money. Each "crime"—indeed, each type of legal behavior—is actually a cluster of types; each has its own deterrence cure, its own degree of elasticity. We can arrange types of legal behavior along a line, with overtime parking at one end and drug addiction, perhaps, at the other, according to how elastic (or inelastic) the demand, in the typical case. Undoubtedly, there are patterns and types, but Chambliss' categories are not sufficiently varied or complex.

---

27. William J. Chambliss, "Types of Deviance and the Effectiveness of Legal Sanctions," *Wisconsin Law Review*, **1967**: 703.

28. Johannes Andenaes, "Deterrence and Specific Offenses," *University of Chicago Law Review*, **38**: 537, 538 (1971).

29. William B. Bankston and James A. Cramer, "Toward a Macro-Sociological Interpretation of General Deterrence," *Criminology*, Vol. 12, p. 251, 265 (1974).

Personality also will affect legal behavior. Leonard Berkowitz and Nigel Walker asked a group of college students in England what they thought about a set of propositions (for example, "the individual who sees another person attempting to commit suicide and does not try to stop him is acting immorally"). They then told some of the students that the behavior described was legal (or illegal); others that it was strongly condemned (or approved) by their peers. Afterwards, they measured *changes* in attitude. Attitudes tended to shift, to conform to what the peer group and the law dictated; the results, they found, correlated with scores on personality tests.[30]

Culture, too, affects legal behavior. We have no reason to expect the same deterrence curve for armed robbery or drunkenness in Iran, Argentina, and Nepal. Shifts in reward and punishment will bend legal behavior at the margins. But we cannot predict the *base* on which these changes are rung. In Japan, or Chad, or Portugal, how much theft will occur at a zero enforcement rate, that is, what is the "pure" demand for theft, untouched by sanctions? Obviously, there is no meter that can measure the demand for deviance, but the demand exists, and varies, and its effect can be sensed at least indirectly.

Feedback and Interaction

Up to now, we have talked about legal behavior as if it arose out of a simple, two-person situation. One person (or entity) gives a command. A second person, in the audience, receives the message, calculates benefits and costs, listens to peers, consults the voice of conscience, and decides to act.

But this little picture is in many ways too simple to represent reality. When the police stop drivers on the highway and threaten to give them tickets for speeding, the drivers may accept their fate meekly; then again they may not. They may put up a struggle, argue, plead, or make excuses. In some cities, they may offer bribes. Once in a great while, a driver will strike an officer and try to race away. None of this is itself compliant or noncompliant, as far as speeding is concerned. Rather, these bits of behavior are attempts to modify the sanction. We will call activity of this kind *interaction.* One important form of interaction is *bargaining.* Another is *resistance.*

Let us watch more of our drivers. Occasionally, a driver, after getting a ticket, will call up the mayor, or the chief of police, and complain

---

30.   Leonard Berkowitz and Nigel Walker, "Laws and Moral Judgments," *Sociometry,* Vol. 30, p. 410 (1967).

about the case. Very infrequently, an irate driver will try to persuade City Council to change the traffic laws. In a rare or extreme case, a driver might even try to overthrow the government. We call such reactions *feedback*. We notice, too, that some drivers change their behavior because of the rule. A few may be so frightened or scared by their experience, that they give up driving and ride the bus to work. Taking a bus, of course, is neither "compliance" or "noncompliance" with rules about speeding. But it is legal behavior in our definition; it is behavior causally influenced by a legal order or rule. Changes in behavior of this kind, that is, outside the realm of compliance, noncompliance, use, and nonuse, but causally influenced by a legal act, are the *side-effects* of the act.

We have spoken about the *impact* of a legal act; this is a very general term, referring to all legal behavior (not merely compliance) that is influenced by a legal act, including all side-effects and feedback behavior. A legal act can have substantial impact, even when it is not "effective" or "successful." "Success" (or "effectiveness") refers to *net* impact. When a legal act is followed by behavior which conforms to the expectations, or fulfills the purposes, of the original actor or actors (legislature, judge, administrator), and when the behavior is not offset by countervailing side-effects, the act is *successful*.

The more complicated the legal system, the more occasions for bargaining and other kinds of interaction. This is true both on the civil and the criminal side. Let us look at criminal justice more closely. A section of the penal code states that a thief is liable to be punished with a year or more in jail. Of course, this does not happen automatically. Criminal justice is not an alarm that goes off at the touch. The theft has to be reported, the thief caught, charged, prosecuted, convicted, and sent away. This calls for action by the victim, and by police, prosecutors, lawyers, and judges. In prison there are wardens and guards; later on, a parole board may deal with the prisoner's case. At each step of the way, there are human beings whose behavior is bound to some degree by formal rules, but who have *some* discretion as well; at each step of the way, we may find bargaining, legitimate and illegitimate resistance, not to mention side-effects and feedback.

Plea-Bargaining

In the United States, there are many forms of exchange between a person accused of crime and the authorities. The most notorious is known as plea-bargaining. A person charged with a crime agrees to plead guilty to a lesser offense if the prosecutor drops the greater one, or agrees to ask for a milder sentence. Plea-bargaining is ubiquitous and controversial in the United States and Canada. Most criminal defendants plead guilty, usually in return for a lower charge or lighter penalty. A survey in New York City found that 80 percent of all serious criminal cases (felonies) were settled through plea-bargaining.[31]

David Caplowitz reports court-approved bargaining in civil cases too. Most delinquent debtors never go to court, never contest, and simply lose by default; the few who show up in court tend to be told by the judge to "go out into the hall and work out a settlement with the plaintiff's lawyer." To "settle," the debtor must agree to pay part of the debt, even if the debtor thinks he or she should pay nothing, for whatever reason. This process led Lenny Bruce, the comedian, to say that "in the Halls of Justice, the only justice is in the halls."[32]

Some people defend plea-bargaining; they see it as a sensible way to keep courts from drowning in overwork. Each side gives a little, and each side gets a little. Others argue that plea-bargaining works against the weak, the poor, the black; the accused is hustled quickly through court to conviction; all that is gained is the dubious privilege of escaping an inflated charge. The state is like a merchant in a bazaar, who asks a ridiculous price, and then lets the buyer "bargain" for the normal amount.[33]

Many critics of plea-bargaining, and its civil form, suggest that no *real* bargaining takes place. But this may be slightly misleading. There is bargaining; clearly, official norms are bent and manipulated; there is give and take. The only question is, who gives what and who takes what? Critics of plea-bargaining argue that it is a sham as far as the defendant is concerned. The lawyers bargain, the prosecutor bargains; each gains a bit and gives a bit; the defendant is helpless and has nothing to contribute. The bargaining, however, is a cold hard fact.

How widespread is the process? Plea-bargaining, we are told, does not exist as such in Europe or Latin America. Yet as Vilhelm Aubert describes criminal justice in Norway, one cannot help but see analogies. People accused of minor crimes can agree to pay a fine, instead of submitting to full prosecution. Technically, the accused does not admit any guilt, but the effect is much like a guilty plea to a lesser offense. There

---

31.   New York Times, February 11, 1975, p. 1, col. 5–6, p. 70, col. 1–2. There is a large literature on plea-bargaining; see Donald Newman, *Conviction: The Determination of Guilt or Innocence Without Trial*, Boston: Little, Brown & Co., 1966; and there have been many suggestions for changing the system; see Welsh S. White, "A Proposal for Reform of the Plea-Bargaining Process," *University of Pennsylvania Law Review*, **119:** 439 (1971).

32.   David Caplowitz, *Consumers in Trouble, A Study of Debtors in Default*, New York: Free Press, 1974, pp. 218–19.

33.   Data from an unpublished study of criminal court records in Alameda County, California, 1870–1970, by the author and Robert V. Percival, tends to support this charge. Felony cases with multiple charges increased tremendously after 1950.

are other forms of "tacit bargaining" in Norway, too.[34] Undoubtedly, cultural variations are great. In most countries, the living law has not been carefully studied; hence, it is hard to know which patterns are general and which are unique to this or that society. But *exact* equivalents of plea-bargaining must be rare, especially since in many countries (Germany, for example) there is no guilty plea as such.

The General Bargain: Nonenforcement of Law

A more general kind of "bargain," however, is widespread, and may be almost unavoidable in complicated systems of law. The bargain is simply this: high *formal* punishments are balanced by low levels of enforcement. The legal system as a whole is shot through with nonenforcement, partial enforcement, sporadic enforcement. Hundreds of laws on the books are rarely or never enforced, rarely or never used. Every day, at every level of government, officials make decisions about what to enforce, what not to enforce, and in what proportions. In the United States laws about sexual behavior, generally speaking, fall under the head of unenforced laws, though at one time (in colonial America) violations were vigorously prosecuted. Prohibition was a famous case of partial enforcement. Thousands were arrested, but millions bought liquor and drank. There are innumerable further examples.

Causes of Nonenforcement of Laws

What factors lead to nonenforcement, or sporadic enforcement, of laws? Sometimes, in some societies, nonenforcement is formalized, as Jean Carbonnier reminds us; there are places (asylums) where the law cannot be enforced, and there are times (special festivals, for example) where authority winks at "license." These are times when law is "asleep;" [35] like amnesty, these occasions and places seem to serve some sort of safety-valve function. Formal dispensation of this kind is still to be found in modern society, but nonenforcement is far more general and pervasive.

Bargaining and *interaction* are at the bottom of a certain amount of nonenforcement. *Resource squeeze* is another reason—agencies have limited funds and must use them carefully. The police, we know, do not

---

34. Vilhelm Aubert, "Law as a Way of Resolving Conflicts: The Case of a Small Industrialized Society," in L. Nader, ed., *Law in Culture and Society*, Chicago: Aldine Pub. Co., pp. 282, 297–98 (1969).

35. Jean Carbonnier, *Flexible Droit, Textes pour une Sociologie du Droit Sans Rigueur*, Paris: Librairie Générale du Droit, 1969, pp. 23–24.

arrest everyone who commits a crime.[36] It would cost a fortune to do so. The criminal justice system can be compared to a gigantic filter. Of those who commit crimes, some are not caught; some are caught but not arrested; some are arrested but never tried. At each stage, there is resource pressure, and also bargaining, some of which, in some societies, may be corrupt. Certain decisions are forced on the police by political pressure or public demand; it may be impossible, for example, to get rid of some kinds of gambling (church bingo), for this reason.

In addition, the *values* of the enforcers influence whether enforcement of the rules handed down from above will be vigorous or slack. Local police may see nothing wrong with children playing ball in the streets, or with a little friendly gambling; as a result, they drag their feet on enforcement, regardless of what the higher-ups say. In a study of the Soviet attempt to reform family law in Central Asia, Gregory Massell found that local officials, Moslems themselves, evaded, resisted, and sabotaged the operation.[37]

This is a ubiquitous problem, which we can call *the problem of the cadres*. In the vastness of modern regulation, legal acts travel great distance, and go through many hands, before they reach their destination, the point of ultimate behavior. "Compliance" is like some huge organic molecule, made up of great chains of protein. The United States Supreme Court declared unlawful the practice of reciting prayers and reading the Bible in public schools.[38] This decision, in order to be effective, had to travel a complex circuit, down to state officials, school district officials, principals of schools, and finally to the teachers themselves. At every legal point in the chain, the problem of the cadres can arise. As a legal act

36.   See, in general, Wayne R. LaFave, *Arrest: The Decision to Take a Suspect into Custody*, Boston: Little, Brown & Co., 1965; for a similar picture of German police work, see Johannes Feest and Erhard Blankenburg, *Die Definitionsmacht der Polizei*, Düsseldorf: Bertelsmann Universitätsverlag, 1972.

Recently, scholars have attacked, on ethical grounds, the unequal enforcement of criminal law. A legal system, they say, should strive for full enforcement. If society cannot or will not enforce a rule fairly and completely, it should abolish the rule, and strip the behavior of its criminal label. "Making and retaining criminal laws that can be only sporadically enforced," argues Herbert L. Packer, can "result in actual harm." *The Limits of the Criminal Sanction*, Stanford: Stanford University Press, 1968, p. 287. Law enforcement becomes corrupt and arbitrary; the public sees this, and loses respect for the law. On this last point, to be sure, hard proof is lacking; but the ethical position does not depend on this empirical proposition.

37.   Gregory J. Massell, "Law as an Instrument of Revolutionary Change in a Traditional Milieu: The Case of Soviet Central Asia," *Law and Society Review*, Vol. 2, p. 179 (1968).

38.   The cases were Engel v. Vitale, 370 U.S. 421 (1962); School District of Abington Township v. Schempp, 374 U.S. 203 (1963); a large literature discusses the impact of these cases, including William K. Muir, Jr., *Prayer in the Public Schools, Law and Attitude Change*, Chicago: University of Chicago Press, 1967.

moves down the chain to its destination, it sets off legal behavior at every stage; the behavior can be positive or negative; and it is determined by one or more of the clusters of motives that influence *all* legal behavior— fear of punishment, hope of reward, peer group pressure, and internal values. A "rule," in other words, is not the simple formulation that it seems to be. The "rule" in the school prayer case was really a series of interlocking rules, a chain of firecrackers, each one igniting the next. Each subrule has, implicitly, a form more or less of this type: Tell X, your immediate subordinate, to put Rule A into effect, and see that X does so. A weakness anywhere along the line will break the chain.

Investment in Enforcement

Enforcement obviously depends on how much time, money, and effort is spent on it. Ten inspectors of weights and measures can do more work than four, but they cost more money. We can think of enforcement decisions at two levels or stages. First, a community decides how much it wants to invest, generally speaking, in law enforcement. Once that decision is made, there are subdecisions about how to parcel out these resources. The ten inspectors can look at department stores, grocery stores, or open-air markets. Police can patrol a beat, work on the vice squad, handle traffic, or serve as undercover agents. If there are only so many police, and five are assigned to traffic duty, the question arises, shall it be Fifth Street or First Street or Main Street, school crossings or business districts. Similar two-stage decisions take place on the civil side: how much will be spent on judge's salaries; how many courts will there be; will poor litigants be subsidized; how much effort will be made to expand family courts, as opposed to commercial courts, and so on.

Investment decisions obviously vary from place to place and from time to time. But each decision to invest or not invest is itself a legal act. It comes out of the social background. A decision to invest is a *feedback* decision; the social force actually exerted on the authority system determines the level of investment.

Technology, of course, also has a bearing on enforcement, and on the cost of enforcement. Science has given the law finger-printing, radar, blood typing, and forensic medicine. New technology aids justice, improves crime control, and helps cut down the cost of enforcing the laws. But technology can also alter the delicate balance between the power of subject and state. People do not always *want* efficient enforcement. An obvious case is wiretapping. People also squirm at the thought of computers scanning their tax returns. They may approve of enforcement of tax laws, but enough is enough. They are also uncomfortable when the police catch speeders with radar.

Enforcement and the Nature
of the Conduct Affected

The *nature* of the conduct, which the law is trying to reach, also profoundly affects the effectiveness of law. Legal behavior is very varied. A dollar spent to enforce rule P does not yield the same result as a dollar spent to enforce rules Q and R. This is almost self-evident. Some kinds of deviance are hard to deter, because they are deeply rooted in habit, tradition or desire. Needless to say, it would be impossible to stamp out sex. Prohibition showed that drinking was a tenacious habit. There are stiff penalties for smoking marijuana; but the use of "grass" grows and grows. "Deeply rooted," however, is only another way of saying that the sanction level has to be enormously high to make any difference, that only high voltage can produce any meaningful results.

A law is "unenforceable," in practice, if people have a strong incentive to act in defiance of the law, and if it is impossible to justify or implement a plan to jack up sanctions to the point where they will work. During Prohibition, millions of people still wanted to drink. When "deviants" are as numerous as the sands of the deserts and have reasonable access to power, enforcement becomes more and more difficult. This is so for two reasons: first, the "deviants" themselves exert pressure for non-enforcement; and second, as the cost of enforcement goes up, people begin to question whether all this effort is worthwhile. Many Americans did not mind a nice *little* war in Vietnam, but they backed away as the price went up and up.

There are many laws—drug laws, sex laws, rationing laws—that are like unpopular wars. The state may try to increase rewards and punishments, but its efforts are frustrated at the enforcement level. The "problem of the cadres" defeats the law; sometimes outright corruption sets in. These "unenforceable" laws are like a leaky garden hose. Turn up the pressure at one end, and more water squirts from the holes. It is hard—perhaps impossible—to deliver more water at the business end, no matter how much water flows in.

Some crimes, moreover, are easier than others to detect. Adultery and sodomy are consummated privately, behind closed doors. It is costly to enforce laws against hidden, secret crime, especially if no "victim" steps forward to complain. Other things being equal, a dollar spent to stamp out such crimes produces less return than a dollar spent to enforce obvious deviance, and crimes where the victim cooperates with the police. During the energy crisis of 1973–74, some countries, Norway for one, outlawed driving on Sunday. The point was to cut down the use of gasoline. Many plans could be tried; but none was as easy to enforce. No one could be more conspicuous than a violator, racing along an empty highway, in broad daylight. Hence no rule could have been cheaper to enforce, or more efficient.

Deterrence and Labeling

In this chapter we have talked about sanctions, assuming that they have an effect on behavior, and we have discussed very generally how and why they do, and to what extent. But it is clear that sanctions are not always "effective," or "successful," even when they do have an impact. They may generate bad side-effects; bargaining, resistance, feedback, and non-enforcement may dissipate or neutralize their results.

These facts help explain the controversy in the literature over deterrence. Deterrence is not really in dispute; what is controversial is the criminal justice *system*. This is a complex network of behavior, with many actors, at many levels, not to mention feedback, interaction and side effects; group and moral factors also influence people in the system, and influence the potential deviants too. Sociologists and criminologists who write about deviance and crime tend to look at the system from the bottom up. They see injustices and inefficiencies, which leads them to doubt that sanctions, in reality, are working. Economists, on the other hand, are more likely to abstract away imperfections. They construct theoretical "models" of the system, in which sanctions work rather smoothly and well.

The two approaches run roughly parallel to two strategies of research in the study of deviance and crime. Many scholars are attracted to the so-called labeling theory.[39] These scholars are interested mainly in how and why society comes to label some act as deviant, and what effect the labeling process has on the person labeled, and on the behavior of others toward him or her. Charles Tittle points out that labeling theorists consider punishment self-defeating. It "causes the offender to be labeled a deviant by others"; this "closes out nondeviant options and activates a transformation of self-image." This can only lead to more deviance, because the poor wretch now has fewer choices (honest people will not hire the deviant or associate with the deviant), his self-concept changes (he thinks of himself as a criminal, say), and for company and support he can and must look to birds of his feather. The "control theorists," members of the other camp, stress the way in which sanctions teach and deter. For them, punishment is effective; after all, the burnt child dreads the fire.[40]

39. See Howard S. Becker, *Outsiders, Studies in the Sociology of Deviance*, New York: Free Press, 1963; Edwin M. Schur, *Labeling Deviant Behavior, Its Sociological Implications*, New York: Harper & Row, 1971.

40. Charles R. Tittle, "Deterrence or Labeling?" *Social Forces*, Vol. 53, p. 399 (1975).

Both schools, however, are describing a *process*, and both can be basically correct. There is no reason to doubt that a sanction system can easily affect some behavior; deterrence works for overtime parking. Punishing overtime parkers simply does not touch off the chain reaction of labeling. The labeling perspective is, however, a powerful tool in its place. It helps analyze what happens (say) to a slum teenager, who is repeatedly arrested, and labeled delinquent (perhaps for doing what a middle class boy or girl from the suburbs could easily squirm out of). Essentially, labeling theory argues that side-effects can destroy the deterrent effect of a sanction. It is an empirical question, when and why this is so. The general theory can be correct, without calling into question the assumptions that control theorists make—and vice versa. There is room for both points of view in the study of criminal justice.

CHAPTER 10
SOCIAL AND MORAL ROOTS OF LEGAL BEHAVIOR

THE GROUP FACTOR IN LEGAL BEHAVIOR

In the last chapter, we talked about the effect of sanctions. We pointed out that sanctions were only one of three great clusters of motives that might explain legal behavior. In this chapter, we will briefly discuss two other factors. The first of these is the factor of the surrounding society. We can call this the *group factor* in legal behavior.

All societies, except the very smallest, have dialects of culture. No society of any size is totally homogeneous. Countries usually have within their borders many ethnic and cultural groups. These may speak different languages, and follow different customs; they may differ in race or religion. Each group (or subculture) has its own traditions, and, to a certain degree at least, its own living law. The living law of a subgroup almost certainly will deviate from official or dominant law. It frequently happens that one system punishes behavior that the other rewards, and vice versa. This is one classic source of inelasticity, or unenforceability. Normally, in such a situation we expect behavioral results when the state raises the sanction level—threats of punishment, or promises of reward. But perhaps, at the same time, the subgroup increases *its* sanctions. They may neutralize the effect of "the law." The government's army, let us say, is trying to crush a band of guerrillas living in the hills. The government offers big rewards to informers and threatens to torture and kill whoever gives food or shelter to the rebels. Normally, one would expect the villagers in the hills to give the government what it wants. But if, in response, the rebels sweep in to the village, armed to the teeth, demanding food, threatening informers with death, and taking hostages, we would not know what to predict. This is one type of leaky hose. Or, the government increases penalties for the sale of narcotics. Addicts are desperate; the price goes up, and higher profits offset the greater risk to sellers of narcotics.

In plural societies, it may be nearly impossible to enforce a law when a compact and determined subculture strongly opposes it. We can cite, again, one classic case: Moscow's disastrous attempt to force Soviet family law onto the Moslems of Soviet Central Asia, in the 1920's.[1] But the group factor is influential in every society, and for everyone, whether or not a person is a member of an organized subculture. What a person's family thinks (and does) what friends think and do, what people at work think and do, what the union, the church, even casual passers-by on the street, think and do, all have some impact, more or less, on legal behavior.

The group factor, then, ranges all the way from a kind of shadow government (for example, the Mafia in Sicily at the height of its power) to the influence of almost random actions by total strangers. Between these two extremes, there are some important face-to-face groups. The family is one. It has important sources of power. It lacks some of the weapons in the arsenal of the state (for example, it has no jails), but, like the islanders on Tristan da Cunha, it can deliver rewards and punishments quickly, effectively, and without red tape.

In theory, the group factor can be compared quite closely to the sanction factor, that is, to official state intervention. The same basic propositions should apply to both. An increase in threat from the group will discourage the threatened behavior, all other things being equal; an increase in promise of reward will act as an incentive. The same general remarks—about speed and certainty of delivery, about the problems of enforcement, about the "leaky hose" phenomenon—will equally apply, *mutatis mutandis*.

The literature readily concedes the power of the group in legal behavior; indeed, this factor lies at the root of much of what is written about enforcement and nonenforcement of the law. But actual experiments or studies of this factor, as such, are not terribly common. One study examined pedestrian behavior in New York City. Many people, it was found, walked across the street even when the sign said, "Don't Walk." But when people saw a model clearly abiding by the rule, the violation rate dropped. When the model broke the rule, the violation rate rose.[2] Notice that

1.   Gregory Massel, "Law as an Instrument of Revolutionary Change in a Traditional Milieu, the Case of Soviet Central Asia," *Law and Society Review*, Vol. 2, p. 179 (1968).

2.   Lionel I. Dannick, "Influence of an Anonymous Stranger on a Routine Decision to Act or not to Act: An Experiment in Conformity," *Sociological Quarterly*, Vol. 14,

nothing in the (official) sanction structure changed; shifts in behavior must be explained by some other factor—the influence of the model, as a moral guide, or the risk of embarrassment or shame.

To be sure, the model was a stranger, hence not exactly a member of the pedestrian's "group," but model and subject were members of the same society and were at least temporarily in face-to-face contact. Under these circumstances, disapproval by a stranger is a sanction, even though mild.[3]

The Group as a Positive Factor in Enforcement. Legal literature, in general, tends to treat the group factor as a negative force. People have habits, customs, and traditions, and they take part in group life of one sort or another. Because of this, bureaucrats and planners find it hard to make a dent in their behavior. Culture, in other words, is treated as an obstacle, and as essentially conservative. Of course, a law that goes against the grain is likely to fail in its purpose. The hackneyed example is Prohibition. People liked to drink; the culture of the cities, whether working-class Catholic or educated elite, approved of social drinking. (Most of the "drys" were small-town Protestants), But the opposite case is also true: that is, laws that make use of the culture, which draw on its power, can multiply their strength. Force—even the threat of force—costs money. If a rule can tap some hidden source of compliance or favor, it gets more for each dollar spent on enforcement.

"Tapping the culture" does not mean telling people to do what they want to do anyway. It means contriving new regulations in such a way as to cut with, not against, the grain. Mostly, law does this so automatically that we take it for granted; for example, it uses money as a reward. People have gotten used to filing income tax returns; this makes the idea of a "negative" income tax, as a way of distributing welfare, more attractive. Labor law picks Sunday, not Tuesday or Friday, as the day of rest. Every law in some respect evokes old habits or symbols. No other way of running the system can work.

We have discussed the peer group as a kind of rival state. But, as the last point makes clear, the group factor is also a powerful tool of enforcement and reenforcement. Without cooperation, nothing moves in the legal system. Many laws depend on informers or complainants. The

---

p. 127 (1973); compare Johannes Feest, "Compliance with Legal Regulations, Observation of Stop Sign Behavior," *Law and Society Review,* Vol. 2, pp. 447, 453 (1968).

3. In an interesting variation, one researcher studied the effect of the presence of a *child* on street-crossing behavior. When a child stood at the crossing, adults obeyed the rules far more often than when there was no child present. Apparently, when children are around, some adults become conscious that they are models, that *they* have to "set a good example;" they behave accordingly. Ann Stanton, "A Study of Adult Pedestrian Behavior at Traffic Signals in the Presence of a Child," unpublished seminar paper, Law School, Stanford University, 1975.

police, as a rule, arrest only on demand. There are administrative agencies that follow what has been called the "mailbag approach." They react when people send letters of complaint; otherwise they do nothing.[4] Criminal cases, says Donald Black, often "pass through a moral filter in the citizen population before the state assumes its enforcement role."[5] This is another fact that blurs the line between criminal law on the one hand, and contract, tort and "private law" in general on the other. Many norms of criminal law lie dormant, until some private party brings them to life. And many norms, officially in force, lapse in practice because the demand for enforcement dies out.

MORALITY AND LEGAL BEHAVIOR

The third, and last major factor in legal behavior is the inner voice. This voice is called by a variety of names—conscience, the sense of right, legitimacy—and it covers, in fact, a variety of motives. Under this general heading, we classify all those motives and reactions that we cannot trace to signals about sanctions, either from the state or from people around us. (The word *sanctions* is important, because the state and the peer group both use other techniques as well. They can and do try to appeal to our inner sense, conscience, patriotism, loyalty, and so on).

We can distinguish between a number of these inner motives.

1. First of all, there is *civic mindedness*. This is the idea that we ought to obey some rule, because it is good for other people (or for people as a whole), even though it is not in our personal interest. It is "civic-minded" or "patriotic" to risk death in the service of one's country, or for a cause. Many people will obey a sign that says "Keep Off the Grass," out of civic motives, even though compliance adds steps to their journey. People may try to conserve energy, file prompt and honest tax returns, and, in general, obey the law "for the good of the country," quite apart from the threat of punishment.

2. *Morality* refers to a somewhat different motive. People often follow norms for religious or ethical reasons, rather than reasons of personal or social utility. Morality can be a powerful motive. It keeps people from stealing and killing. It is the reason why Moslems and Mormons do not drink; why most people do not cheat at cards; why some students follow an "Honor Code."

3. Still another motive is the *sense of fairness*. When a rule is "fair," it deserves support not because of its content, but because of some *formal*

---

4. Edward F. Cox et al., *The Nader Report on the Federal Trade Commission*, New York: Grove Press, Inc., 1969, pp. 39–40.

5. Donald J. Black, "The Social Organization of Arrest," *Stanford Law Review*, **23**: 1087, 1104 (1971).

quality, for example, the fact that it applies to everyone alike. I may not think the rule is sensible, but I recognize that it is intended to apply to everyone in a given situation, not only to me. If others obey it, or have obeyed it, or seem about to obey it, I might decide to obey the rule myself, because it would be "unfair" to make an exception of myself. This is another reason why a person obeys rules about saving gas and oil in times of shortage. Fairness—especially in the form of "equality before the law"—is a powerful ideal in modern societies. It admonishes us to treat equals alike. Stuart A. Scheingold quotes a curious example of the ideal at work: a New York City health official, he reports, "discovered excessive concentrations of poisonous lead in several samples of paint marketed in the New York area." But he refused to expose the names of these paints, because, he said, "he had not tested all the paint on sale . . . and it would be unfair to name some companies while others that might also have excess lead were not included in the sample."[6]

4. So far, we have mentioned motives that do not depend on general faith in institutions. Civic mindedness, fairness, and morality relate to the form or content of rules. *Trust* is a rather different motive. *Trust* is faith in authority, faith that they know what they are doing, because they are wise, because they are experts, or because they have inside information. People read in the paper that the Food and Drug Administration has banned Red Dye No. 2 from all food products. Many will assume at once that the agency knows what it is doing. The lady-slipper, a type of orchid, is listed as an endangered species. The nature lover accepts the decision of the experts and will never more pick or disturb this flower.

5. *The Concept of Legitimacy.* Finally, there is another kind of trust— a trust in procedures, structures, or authorities. Strictly speaking, this is what we call *legitimacy*. Many writers use the term, but it is not always carefully defined. According to Max Weber, a rule, custom, order or system is "legitimate" when it is "endowed with the prestige of exemplariness and obligatoriness."[7] Niklas Luhmann has defined legitimacy as a "generalized willingness to accept decisions whose content is as yet undetermined, within certain limits of tolerance."[8] The various definitions revolve around a common core. Sometimes people obey a rule, not out of self-interest or trust in authority, but because it is simply "the law." Rules of law, in other words, are for them *legitimate*. The *content* of a rule does not make it legitimate, nor does it matter (within limits) whether the rule is right or wrong. A feeling of legitimacy is a feeling about the *source* of a rule, or the *form* of a rule, or the *procedure* for adopting it. It is a judgment about the way the rule came about, or the authority of the persons who made it. Legitimacy is quite unlike trust. Trust depends on facts. You can impair or destroy trust by showing that the facts are wrong and that the fact-finders know not what they do. In the short run, legitimacy does not depend on facts; it cannot be disproved.

6.   Stuart A. Scheingold, *The Politics of Rights: Lawyers, Public Policy, and Political Change,* New Haven, Conn.: Yale University Press, 1974, p. 54.

7.   Max Rheinstein, ed., *Max Weber on Law in Economy and Society,* Cambridge: Harvard University Press, 1954, p. 4.

8.   Niklas Luhmann, *Legitimation durch Verfahren,* Darmstadt: Luchterhand, 1975, p. 28.

Max Weber described three "ultimate principles" of legitimacy or, in other words, three types of valid authority. One was the *traditional*—the authority of a patriarch or a chief. A second kind he called *charismatic*. Charismatic authority is based "neither upon rational rules nor upon tradition." The follower of a charismatic leader "surrenders" to "the extraordinary." Charisma flows from "actual revelation or grace resting in . . . a person as a savior, a prophet or a hero." It is the authority of a Moses, a Christ—a dramatic, personal magic; it carries its own stamp of validity. Christ claimed the right to supersede the law of Moses —without lobbying, without rational argument. *Rational* authority is Weber's third category. It stems from respect for the underlying process. People look to and obey the norms, not the personal magic or traditional claims of the one who makes the norms. Belief in majority rule or in due process is a form of legitimacy. In general, legitimacy is a belief in legality, or, as Weber puts it, an "acquiescence in enactments which are formally correct and which have been made in the accustomed manner."[9]

In most societies, most people probably do have respect for the rules, whatever their content (and within limits). They feel some sort of duty to obey, whenever a law or a rule is duly enacted, or a judge makes a decision, or an administrative agency gives out an order in the usual way, or a police officer tells them to stop, or turn, or drive to the right. No doubt, most people do not closely examine what they feel and think on the subject. They would find it hard to explain *why* legal acts are legitimate. An obstinate interviewer might elicit a comment or two about majority rule, elections, or procedures. Some people would say that law must be obeyed, otherwise order would collapse, and society would perish. People probably believe that law, on the whole, is just and fair; in any event, its rules have been properly made, and should not be lightly disregarded. There are rules of bridge, rules of soccer, rules of chess; these rules tell us if a bid or a move or a play is valid or not. Rules of process or procedure—rules about how *laws* or *decisions* may be made—and rules which identify authority, have a similar quality in people's minds. The game cannot be played without such a guide.

Moral Factors: the Negative Side

We have listed five motives comprising the moral factor. Each was described in positive terms, but each one has its negative side as well. The opposite of legitimacy is illegitimacy; the opposite of trust is distrust; of fairness, unfairness; of morality, immorality. A Catholic may feel that laws allowing abortion are desperately immoral, and also bad for society, though less obviously so. In the literature, illegitimacy, in particular,

---

9.   Weber, op. cit., p. 9.

plays a prominent role. After all, what does *not* conform to legitimate procedures is not worthy of respect. Hence it is quite as important, in studying legal behavior, to have some measure of the *negative* side of these attitudes, the instances in which there are feelings of illegitimacy, or unfairness, immorality, and the like.

On Measuring Legitimacy

The question of the strength of the inner motive (and especially the concept of legitimacy) has fascinated many scholars. The importance of the whole cluster of inner motives seems indisputable. But actually, we have very little hard data *about* these attitudes. Only recently has there been much research on the subject.

It is vital to know, for example, how strong these feelings are, how stable or unstable, how much they are subject to change and manipulation. Legitimacy, as we defined it, is basically a matter of procedures, faith in law, in processes and institutions, not in results. We do not need a theory of legitimacy to explain why people obey a person with a gun, or adhere to an order that brings them personal honor or gain; or obey their religions or their moral codes. Legitimacy means an attitude (and behavior) about institutions and processes. That the attitude exists seems certain. People do accept the law as law; they feel that they must go along with rules, if (they think) the rules were legitimately made. They grumble about outcomes, but in the same breath, they concede that society would fall apart without respect for legitimate authority. Yet some institutions deserve (and get) more respect—more of a sense of legitimacy—than others. The public makes many fine distinctions. People may believe that the Prime Minister is honorable, but that local officials are thieves, whose acts do not deserve respect. No doubt, in many cases, these judgments rest on reality.

Respect for law also varies from culture to culture. Population samples, in a number of countries, were asked to react to a statement that "the law should be observed regardless of whether it is a fair or unfair law," or some variation. In Canada, 40 percent agreed, in Poland, 45 percent, in Holland, 47 percent, in the United States, 51 percent, in West Germany, 66 percent, in Japan, 73.4 percent.[10]

These are striking differences. But they are not easy to interpret. Small differences in wording or tone, nuances in translation, may make big differences in the answers given; age and social status surely bend

---

10. Adam Podgorecki, "Law and Justice—Central Concepts and Issues," *Polish Sociological Bulletin*, No. 1–2, 1973, p. 9, 23–24. Research on public attitudes toward law is spotty; for most countries there is none at all. A major exception is Italy; see Renato Treves, *Giustizia e Giudici nella Società Italiani*, Bari: Editori Laterza (1972), pp. 71–79.

the responses. It is suspicious that the results of a second study seem so different. This study sampled two groups: young people (between 18 and 24), and older people (roughly the generation of the first group's parents) in three countries, Germany, Japan, and the United States. The respondents were asked to choose between two statements: "One should always obey the law, whatever the circumstances," and "Sometimes one must violate the law, in the interests of a cause." Young people over-whelmingly agreed with the second statement: 61 percent in Japan, 66.8 percent in the United States, and 70.7 percent in Germany. For the older people, the law was more sacrosanct: only 34.9 percent in Japan, 38 per-cent in the United States, and 55.7 percent in Germany chose the second statement.[11]

The Strength and Stability of Legitimacy

We can well ask: how strong *is* the feeling of legitimacy, the feeling that law validly made is worthy of every respect? Suppose an institution is consistently "wrong," that is, consistently produces results that go against a person's values, interests, or feelings? How long will it take to tarnish the legitimacy of such an institution? Perhaps citizens begin to lose faith when there is even *one* "wrong" result, provided it is wrong enough, and sharply affects their way of life, their ideology, or their creature comforts. The United States Supreme Court always did well in the polls; but after a series of bold decisions on racial equality, Southern whites began to turn against it. Another body of opinion was offended by cases increasing the rights of people accused of crime.

It is reasonable to guess that, in the long run, people will withdraw their feelings of legitimacy from any institution that always produces "wrong" results. Perhaps the King can do no wrong; but an evil, dissolute King has trouble with his public. Liberals believe in freedom of speech as a "principle," even (they say), for those whose ideas they detest. Deep down, however, they know that liberal speech is most likely to suffer from a tyrant. If they were absolutely sure that only fascists and racists would be muzzled, would some liberals change their minds, at least subcon-sciously? In fact, people hold selective attitudes toward basic rights. They agree with all sorts of glittering statements, in the abstract, but they make many concrete exceptions. Freedom of speech, yes; atheists in the public schools, no. In other words, what bolsters legitimacy—whatever people

11. Survey conducted by the Youth Bureau, Prime Minister's Office, Japanese Government, under the direction of Tamotsu Sengoku. About three quarters of a group of over 500 white and black adolescents in the southern United States agreed with the statement that people "should always obey laws." Harrell Rodgers and Edward B. Lewis, "Political Support and Compliance Attitudes: A Study of Adoles-cents," *American Politics Quarterly*, Vol. 2, pp. 61, 66–67 (1974).

say—is the smug conviction that legitimate institutions do the right thing, that is, what people who feel this way want. A suggestive little study, carried out in three German cities, underscores this point. The subject was cases between landlord and tenant. The researchers interviewed winners and losers. Naturally, most winners (78 percent) went away quite satisfied; most losers (82 percent) were dissatisfied. The litigants were asked if the experience had strengthened or weakened their faith in the system of justice. Not a single loser felt more confidence; two-thirds reported a weakening of confidence; the rest were indifferent.

This finding seems obvious, even trivial. But what happened to legitimacy? Why did the losers lose confidence, when the procedures were valid, and the results legitimate? The feeling of legitimacy, it seems, had a certain fragility. Not that the losers became revolutionaries, but their faith in the system went down a notch or two. Oddly enough, the winners were much less affected. They gained confidence, but only a little —much less than the losers lost.[12] People probably feel their cause is just. They expect to win. It is the "unjust" loss that hurts.

The Moral Factor and Legal Behavior

So far we have spoken only of attitudes, not of behavior, and the studies mentioned (the German housing study, for example), were studies of attitudes. There is a hypothesis (and it is certainly not proven) that people are more likely to comply with rules they feel are legitimate, than those they feel are not.[13] A similar hypothesis could be framed about the other four types of inner motivation, civic mindedness, morality, fairness, and trust. We would also expect to apply to these motives the same general principles that apply to fear of punishment, hope of reward, and the group factor. People are more likely to obey a system or order, if, for some reason, there is an increase in the intensity of their feelings that the order or system is legitimate, other things being equal; and the same goes for civic-mindedness, morality, fairness and trust. Similarly, on the negative side, when a rule lacks or loses legitimacy, incentive toward compliance declines. Other things being equal, a *decrease* in legitimacy, or an *increase* in illegitimacy will impair the urge to comply, or, in an aggravated case, actually push a person down the road to disobedience or rebellion. This would hold true for unfairness, immorality, and

12.   Hartmut Koch and Gisela Zenz, "Erfahrungen and Einstellungen von Klägern in Mietprozessen," in *Zur Effectivität des Rechts*, Vol. 3, *Jahrbuch für Rechtssoziologie und Rechtstheorie*, Düsseldorf: Bertelsmann Universitätsverlag, 1972, pp. 509, 527–28; for a similar finding, see Herbert Jacob, "Black and White Perceptions of Justice in the City." *Law and Society Review*, Vol. 6, pp. 69, 78 (1971).

13.   See Harry V. Ball, "Social Structure and Rent-Control Violations," *Am. Journal of Sociology*, Vol. 65, p. 598 (1960).

distrust as well; and for the feeling that a rule is against the common good.

How attitudes *actually* translate into behavior is another question, and a serious one. Suppose a person sees or feels unfairness, or illegitimacy, or unworthiness of trust, operating in one situation. He or she may be disgusted and disillusioned. But how far does this cancer spread? Is there a "spill-over" effect? It is often said that weak, uncertain, hypocritical enforcement—of modern drug laws, for example—undermines respect for justice and erodes the rule of law. This is an empirical statement, of course. It may be true in part, but how much? And where? And for whom? Compliance is a selective process. As Harry Jones puts it, "There are bank robbers who obey traffic laws and burglars who pay their debts."[14] People disgusted with police brutality, or the enforcement of sex laws, or political corruption, do not necessarily lose faith in the courts, or in the Ministry of Transport; it is doubtful that they incline toward jaywalking, embezzlement, or rape. The facts are still to be established.

Each era, and each society, has its own set of theories of legitimacy. Legal systems rely heavily—and *must* rely heavily—on voluntary compliance. Force is monstrously inefficient, often immoral, and, perhaps, in the long run self-defeating. Hence insofar as they translate into behavior, attitudes about legitimacy, about obedience to law, may be the very glue that binds a society together. This is of more than philosophical interest; in some sense, despite all our skepticism, attitudes of legitimacy must be treated as indispensable. Theories of legitimacy, then, may be soldiers, patrolling society with silent but efficient power, enforcing, and protecting the system of laws and the structure of the state.

There is no reason to assume, however, that theories of legitimacy have equal strength in every society. In traditional societies, for example, trust and legitimacy may be far more mighty than in modern, urban, industrial societies, which are rapidly changing, which have large, restless populations, and which have learned to question many values. In some traditional societies, perhaps, the idea that the laws (or customs) are holy and right is drilled into people's minds during childhood. Such deep-rooted notions cannot be overcome except through powerful, exceptional experiences. Modern society is much looser, much more "rational." It is also more skeptical. This may make trust and legitimacy more brittle than in older societies—more dependent on actual outcomes. If so, then the little German study is quite understandable; perhaps we would get different results in a tribal society.

Yet we assume, generally speaking, that legitimacy, even in our

14. Harry W. Jones, *The Efficacy of Law*, Evanston, Ill.: Northwestern U. Press, 1969, p. 81.

societies, is a mighty pillar of compliance. Hence, if legitmacy in the United States (or other Western countries) is truly volatile, then so too is legal behavior, and the society is in danger of gross instability. In fact, studies show a sharp decline in trust in government, in recent years, in the United States.[15] Many Western countries share a "law and order" problem, or a problem of civil disobedience and criminal terror. The subject, however, is vast and slippery. Not enough is known about causes and effects to make safe generalizations.

Questions of obedience and legitimacy are quite complex. There are all sorts of authorities (that is, people and institutions entitled to give orders) and all sorts of authority *situations:* a teacher in front of a class, a police officer directing traffic, the Internal Revenue Service issuing a regulation, the Supreme Court handing down a ruling. Some are situations of great immediacy: the "authority" stands in our very presence, giving orders. In others, authority is quite remote.

Obedience to Authority: The Eichmann Experiments

Oddly enough, despite the "law and order" crisis, and the frailty of legitimacy, one can also find evidence that modern men and women are *too* obedient to authority. Such a conclusion might be drawn, for example, from the famous experiments conducted in the 1960's by Stanley Milgram. Milgram's subjects were told they were taking part in a study of memory and learning. The "learner" (actually an actor) was strapped into a chair. The "teacher" sat at a shock generator, with a panel of thirty switches, running from 15 to 450 volts, and labeled accordingly: "slight shock" at one end, "danger—severe shock" at the other. (Actually, the machine was not wired to the "learner" at all.) The "teacher" was told to give shocks to the "learner," if he gave wrong answers to the questions. At each error, the "teacher" was ordered to increase the level of shocks. An astonishing percentage did so, till the bitter end, even though the "learner" screamed with simulated agony, and finally lapsed into total silence (some subjects even thought he was dead).[16] What caused this strange, excessive obedience? It was not the sheer love of inflicting pain: many subjects were terribly distressed at what they were doing and begged for permission to stop. But the experimenter coldly ordered them to proceed, and most people did, driven by an urge to obey, an acceptance of authority, of amazing strength.

Milgram's studies are often called the "Eichmann" experiments;

---

15. Arthur H. Miller, "Political Issues and Trust in Government, 1964–1970," *American Political Science Review*, Vol. 68, p. 951 (1974).

16. The experiments are described in Stanley Milgram, *Obedience to Authority, An Experimental View*, New York: Harper & Row, 1974.

it is said that they show how ordinary people can be brought to perform the most monstrous acts.[17] Clearly, many people in Hitler's Germany—and in many other societies—have committed atrocities, on orders from above. Is any society immune? In one recent study, 144 Canadian adults were asked this question:

> Assume for the moment that you are a Canadian soldier fighting in a war in a far away foreign country. A commanding officer orders you to shoot the inhabitants of a small village including old men, women, and children, which is suspected of aiding the enemy. In this situation do you think you would follow orders and shoot them, or refuse to shoot them?

Thirty percent said they would shoot; 70 percent said they would refuse. Of course, the Canadians did not know how they would really react. Most people, if we take them at their word, will resist such orders; but enough will be left over, and to spare, to do the devil's work.[18]

Factors in Harmony and Conflict

Various factors and motives, then, influence legal behavior. It is easy to see that they can lend each other great strength, *if* they coincide, that is, push in the same directions. If a person's conscience, family, church, friends and neighbors, all advance the same norm, and so does the law, it is safe to predict that the person will comply, except under extreme provocation. To take a simple example: there is no problem at all for most people in complying with rules against murder. They themselves feel strongly about murder; so does everyone around them; so does the state. When only *one* factor operates, and the others are silent, the single factor should have unusual weight. A city can reduce parking violations dramatically, by raising fines or putting in a policy of towing away cars illegally parked. Parking does not exactly cut to the moral bone; and all the peer groups are indifferent. Illegal parking, then, is unusually sensitive to sanctions. The converse, of course, is also true; if the city lowers the fine or (more likely) relaxes enforcement, it can expect a jump in violations.

So much is simple, and obvious. More interesting is the question: what happens when factors conflict? Which ones are weak and which are strong? Is the sense of fairness more powerful than the influence of friends? There is little in the literature that even suggests any answer.

17. Adolph Eichmann was an official of the Nazi Government, who bore heavy responsibility for the slaughter of the Jews; at his trial, he defended himself on the grounds that he merely carried out his superiors' orders.

18. The study is Neil Vidmar, "Retributive and Utilitarian Motives and Other Correlates of Canadian Attitudes toward the Death Penalty," *Canadian Psychologist*, Vol. 15, pp. 337, 347 (1974).

Probably there is no *general* answer, only partial answers, depending on the deterrence curve for the behavior in question, the character of the behaving population, and the particular sanction and motive. There is much talk about delinquent subcultures, for example—the influence of gangs and similar groups on people who belong to them. But it is not easy to tell how much influence a gang has on its members, compared to family or police. Many boys and girls in slum areas never join a gang, but grow up to be model citizens. What equation explains their legal behavior?

The situation is even more complicated than has been so far suggested. We have grouped motives for compliance under three general headings. But each heading contains many subfactors, and these, too, may conflict with each other. A woman who lives in Sydney, Australia, is subject to local and federal law. She may be a Catholic, of Irish descent, a clerk in a department store, a union member, a householder, and a member of a family; each of her "groups" asserts at least a slightly different claim on her mind and behavior. Some groups are weak, some strong. Some may agree with one or more official norms. Some will be able to threaten or promise real sanctions; some will not. She may be more or less strongly attached to this or that group—only mildly a Catholic, but a fervent mother and sister, a strong trade unionist, an indifferent neighbor. Her feelings of civic mindedness, morality, legitimacy, fairness, and trust do not necessarily coincide. Some rules may seem legitimate, but quite unfair; or moral but illegitimate; or fair but bad for the country. (In Milgram's study, morality and obedience to authority were in hopeless conflict.) Australia presents a mild case of conflict. Where cultural diversity is more severe, the clash between legal cultures may become more aggravated. India is a good example, or Mexico, or Israel.

Studies of the Relative Strength of the Factors

Empirical studies, measuring the relative strength of the factors, have been few and far between. One rather clever study tried to compare moral appeals with threats of sanction. Students in a class in Florida were allowed to grade their own quizzes. The instructor (unknown to the students) knew the true grades; he could measure how much cheating was going on (a great deal, it turned out). Later, certain students were told they had a moral obligation to grade themselves honestly. Others were told that their quizzes had been spot-checked. Cheating seemed to be rife, and they were warned that cheaters would be punished. The moral appeal had no effect on cheating; the threat of sanction did.[19] Richard Schwartz

---

19. The study is Charles R. Tittle and Alan R. Rowe, "Moral Appeal, Sanction Threat, and Deviance: An Experimental Test," *Social Problems*, Vol. 20, p. 488 (1973).

and Sonya Orleans, in another study, studied compliance with income tax rules. They tried to measure the impact of appeals to conscience, compared to threats of punishment. Both factors, they found, made a difference, both led to fuller, more honest tax returns. But appeals to conscience were stronger by far.[20] In an experiment in Denver, Colorado, local judges agreed to vary dispositions in cases of drunk driving. One month, drivers would be fined, the next month put on probation, the next month given "therapeutic probation," that is, treated for alcoholism, or forced to attend courses on alcohol and its problems. These various "treatments" did not produce significant differences in result.[21]

The three studies, taken together, are rather inconclusive. We lack a theory powerful enough to explain their differences, and to make sensible generalizations. All three were studies of Americans. Most subjects were middle-class; in one study all of the subjects were students. There is no reason to assume that what is true of tax law or drunken driving must be true for all or most other laws, or true to the same degree for Eskimos, Danes, or working-class women in Madrid. Nor can we tell how much threat is a "unit" of threat, what level of passion in an appeal to conscience makes one "unit" of appeal to conscience, how much praise from a church group is a "unit" of praise. Nor do we know how much therapeutic probation to equate with a $50 fine, or a day in jail, in order to compare these rather different interventions with some degree of rigor. Moreover, there is no such thing as an "appeal to conscience"; there are many kinds of appeal. One person may be completely unmoved by a patriotic speech, but deeply affected by arguments of honor, mercy, or justice. In the Florida study, the moral appeal had no effect; but its contents may have been weak, or given in a feeble tone of voice, or lacking in meaning for its audience. Yet these factors make a difference.

Studies of Factors in Conflict

The studies did not pit factors *against* each other, but measured instead their relative strength. We know even less about what occurs when the factors work in opposite directions. Suppose a norm is supported by peer group and conscience, but opposed by the state. Will people obey? It is clear that norms strongly opposed by peer group and conscience are hard to enforce. This was the case in the nineteenth century, when the

20. Richard D. Schwartz and Sonya Orleans, "On Legal Sanctions," *University of Chicago Law Review,* **34:** 274 (1967).

21. H. Laurence Ross and Murray Blumenthal, "Sanctions for the Drinking Driver: an Experimental Study," *Journal of Legal Studies,* Vol. 3, p. 53 (1974). The outcomes were somewhat contaminated since the Denver judges, despite their promises, did not faithfully carry out the experiment.

United States government struggled against Mormon polygamy in Utah. Ultimately, the government won, but it took enormous pressure. Another example was the attempt to import new norms of marriage and family law in Moslem Turkey, in the 1920's; at first, this too was a notable failure.[22]

In a study conducted in Poland, people were asked whether they did or did not cross a street against a red light (provided, of course, no cars were coming). Forty percent said never; about a third admitted that they sometimes transgressed. Then the researcher watched how people actually behaved at crossings. He found these proportions were just about right. People were also asked *why* they obeyed. 16.3 percent said they did not want to risk a fine; 19.6 percent said it was a question of habit; 36.5 percent said they liked "order."[23] If we can believe these statements, then in this situation, at least, we have some rough idea of how much sanction and conscience contribute to behavior.

"New" Rules and "Old" Rules.   But, clearly, the mix of motives is different for different kinds of rules. There are "old" rules—such as rules about murder—which the culture sustains, and which are also moral, legitimate, and firmly implanted in conscience. At the other extreme are "new" rules—regulatory laws, technical norms without history or emotion. Here, the moral element is weak, or absent; behavior has to lean on other factors. Threats and promises are particularly important. But no one doubts that the "new" rules are legitimate. Deep moral conviction delivers compliance more effectively than simple legitimacy *without more.*

Legitimacy refers to an attitude; but the theory is that this attitude will affect a person's behavior. Behavior in turn affects attitude. Imagine a "new" rule, backed up by threats of punishment. You must stop your car when the traffic light is red. People comply; this goes on for years, and is repeated hundreds and hundreds of times. The behavior becomes familiar—almost a habit. Now attitudes may begin to attach to this easy

---

22. See below, ch. 11, p. 164.

A study by Michael J. Hindelang tried to compare peer pressure and conscience. He wanted to test the idea that what makes a delinquent delinquent is peer pressure; that delinquents do not have moral ideas any different from nondelinquents; but they feel peer pressure, pushing them in delinquent directions. Hindelang compared attitudes of delinquents and non-delinquents, on a range of behaviors—stealing, using marijuana, getting into fights. Did the delinquents *approve* of these acts, or did they merely think their friends did? He found that delinquents thought their friends had about the same moral evaluations they did. In other words, he could find no evidence that peer group pressure was acting to force delinquents to do acts they secretly disapproved of. Michael J. Hindelang, "Moral Evaluations of Illegal Behaviors," *Social Problems*, Vol. 21, p. 370 (1974).

23. The study is Jerzy Kwasniewski, "Motivation of Declared Conformity of a Legal Norm," *Polish Soc. Bull.*, No. 1, p. 74 (1969).

and usual behavior; it gains moral strength because it is comfortable and customary. People "learn" the behavior, and favorable attitudes follow along. One can speak then of an "intergenerational 'drift' toward increased moral justification of required conduct."[24] A great deal of modern law that was once novel or controversial now seems as natural as breathing. Traffic lights are not very old, as human history goes. Yet in the Polish study, if we believe the respondents, "habit" has become an important element in compliance. People accept traffic rules, almost without question. They carry drivers' licenses, passports, draft cards, social security cards, identity cards in wallet or purse, as their local law requires, and without much thought. A dense network of regulation surrounds us; it sits as lightly on our shoulders as the cushion of air about the earth. In countless ways, law acts as a kind of learning theorist, making robots of us all.

Unlearning also takes place. Most people in the United States are not chronic violators of speed limits. Often, however, there are several or more places in town where "everybody" goes 40, even though the speed limit is plainly marked 25. It is easy to see this happening, but it would be good to know how and why it began, and how and why it spread. What did the first violators feel about breaking the rule? What do people feel now?

On Deviance

Deviance is one kind of legal behavior. Deviance is behavior which is (or is labeled) a departure from the norm, as society defines it. Not all deviance is crime (rudeness can be deviant) and not all crime is deviant (if "everybody" is doing it). *Interaction* is legal behavior oriented toward legal actors, rather than toward rules. It is interaction to argue with a policeman, or to offer him a bribe. Interaction can be perfectly lawful, even praiseworthy; but it can be deviant, too.

In an interesting essay on deviance, Joseph Gusfield has noted that society attaches different labels to deviants, depending on how society reads the deviant's attitude.[25] Some deviants do not question the norm itself. Gusfield calls these *repentant* deviants. Many a reckless driver knows perfectly well that traffic laws are necessary; and is sorry he broke the rules. Some deviants are *sick*. They cannot help themselves. If a deviant accepts this label, he is like a repentant deviant, in one important

24. Harry V. Ball and Lawrence M. Friedman, "The Use of Criminal Sanctions in the Enforcement of Economic Legislation: A Sociological View," *Stanford Law Review,* **17:** 197, 221 (1965).

25. Joseph Gusfield, "Moral Passage: The Symbolic Process in Public Designations of Deviance," *Social Problems,* Vol. 15, p. 175 (1967).

way: neither in word or deed does he attack the strength or legitimacy of the very norms he breaks. Sick people are usually in favor of health. A third type, which Gusfield calls the *cynical* deviant—a professional thief, for example—violates without regret or feeling. Finally, the *enemy* deviant does not accept the deviant label—or the norms. Unlike the others, these deviants think the norms they break are wrong or illegitimate; they are in open rebellion against these norms.

As Gusfield points out, these labels are not static; for various forms of deviance, they change over time. A drunk can be a cynical, repentant, sick, or enemy deviant. Homosexuals, once (perhaps) mainly repentant deviants, were next treated as sick deviants; then some of them turned militant, rejected the old labels, fought the old norms, became, in short, *enemy* deviants.

Enemy deviants are not typical, but their case is important. Enemy deviance is deviant feedback or interaction. It tends to be supported by a subculture or movement; otherwise, the enemy deviant would be an isolated hero, martyr, or fool. Enemy deviance flourishes where two sets of norms conflict, one official, and one unofficial. The Mormon polygamists of the nineteenth century were enemy deviants.

When deviance changes from one class to another, we have what Gusfield calls "moral passage." Repentant deviants are, typically, unorganized and oppressed. How do they turn into enemy deviants? Information plays an essential role. Deviants cannot easily break out of isolation, unless they know they are not alone. Until they formed communities, and began to talk to each other, the so-called "sexual minorities" could not constitute much of a movement. But communication is only one prerequisite. Something must trigger a frame of mind and help to build an organization. The subgroup must also provide its own rewards and punishments; it must be able to mobilize group opinion, or evoke inner feelings among adherents. Without the right mix, the movement will die.

In a sense, every existing norm is part of a *status quo,* just as any attack on a norm is an attack on society. Yet modern societies are never static. They expect norms to change; it is good, not bad, to be flexible, adaptive, and responsive to change. At any given time, only *some* norms are so sacrosanct that they must not be questioned. The *status quo,* in other words, is not a monolith. Some parts are flabbier than others, more easily changed, because they mean less to the people who count in society. We will return to this point in the following chapter.

For now, we observe that, other things being equal, societies can tolerate less enemy deviance than deviance of other kinds. Speeding is an example of ordinary norm-violation. It is dangerous, it causes accidents. It is hard to control. It is definitely a problem, but on the whole, society lives with it. Yet enemy deviance must be resisted and repressed, or it will ultimately alter the norms. Indeed, this happens constantly. "Weak" norms disappear; "strong" norms—norms vital to people in power—hold on tenaciously. But for any given norm, social reaction to enemy deviance tends to be harsher than reaction to other kinds of deviance. A juvenile who begs for mercy and confesses sin (sincerely or not) gets lighter treatment than a defiant young tough; a robber who accepts a plea bargain gets lighter treatment than the "hard head" who demands a jury trial.[26] (Of course, those who cooperate save time and money for the authorities; for this, too, they are appreciated.) Bank robbers who simply want money are less dangerous than bank robbers who want to destroy the capitalist order. Society resists most bitterly those "enemies" who attack not only peace, safety, and property, but also the authority of the governors, their monopoly of respectability. Still, some crimes are so dangerous that motive hardly matters. Society cannot tolerate much murder, much kidnapping of leaders and executives, much skyjacking, whether by madmen, rebels, or simple criminals.

Most people assume that crime and deviance are inherent evils; that one must strive to wipe them out, like poverty or disease. But can there be such a thing as a society without deviance? In any social group, there are rules or norms. People, on the average, conform. Some people overconform; and some conform far less than average. Behavior, in other words, follows the normal bell-shaped curve. Deviance, after all, means conduct that deviates; it does not mean evil behavior. There will be deviance (subpar behavior) even in a monastery, in a "society of saints, a perfect cloister of exemplary individuals."[27] These deviant acts will be the merest bagatelles; but they fall short of what is expected within the walls.

This line of argument, rooted in the thought of Emile Durkheim, suggests that no society can rid itself of deviance as such. Deviance may, in fact, be a constant. A certain percentage of behavior will always stray from the social norm. Deviance is not entirely useless. It has an important function: it defines the moral borders of the group. Some way of deciding what is deviant, some process of defining and punishing bad conduct, is essential for any form of group life. As Kai Erikson puts it, "morality and immorality meet at the public scaffold, and it is during this meeting that the line between them is drawn."[28]

The thesis is interesting, but hard to confirm or disprove in detail. One problem is the double meaning of deviance. Deviance means be-

26. See, for example, Lynn M. Mather, "The Outsider in the Courtroom: An Alternative Role for Defense," in Herbert Jacob, ed., *The Potential for Reform of Criminal Justice*, Beverly Hills: Sage Publications, 1974, pp. 263, 281–82.

27. The phrase is Durkheim's, quoted in Kai Erikson, *Wayward Puritans*, New York: John Wiley & Sons, 1966, p. 26.

28. Erikson, *op. cit.*, p. 12.

havior that deviates *relatively;* but it also means behavior which (so people think) is absolutely bad. The rate of murder, theft, or rape is decidedly not the same in every culture. *Enemy* deviance does not follow any probability curve. Enemy deviance is the intrusive, the unpredictable element. A monastery may be, and probably is, completely free of it. Russia in 1917, Chile in 1970, the United States in 1776, were hotbeds of revolutionary feeling; Switzerland and Holland in 1976 are much more content with the way things are.

A Footnote on Civil Litigation

Most examples in this chapter were drawn from the world of crime and punishment. This is, in part, because there has been more social research on criminal justice than on civil justice. But the basic ideas and propositions about legal behavior apply to both domains. If we ask, when will people *use* a rule of contract law, or sue in tort, or make out a will, the answers, in general, can be framed in terms of punishment and reward, moral feelings, and group pressures. If we raise benefits, we should produce more use of a rule, other things being equal. Higher price supports for cotton encourage the planting of cotton; not everyone, of course, will drop what they are doing and grow cotton. When divorce becomes cheaper and easier, the divorce rate rises, but happy marriages remain intact. Changes in benefits and costs affect the marginal user, the one who could go either way.

Civil and criminal litigation may have very different cost structures, however. The state foots the bill in criminal cases. In civil cases, the litigants pay. In the United States, in a civil suit, the winning party must absorb the lawyer's fees and other expenses. If it costs $300 to carry through a case, win or lose, one can hardly afford to sue on a $250 claim. Tribal courts and "peoples' courts" can be cheap, or free, but the formal courts of Western society are costly.

Of course, high costs are a *selective* barrier. Societies encourage use of some rules, and discourage others. Many parts of the legal system are made deliberately cheap. It is a bargain to probate a will, file a deed, or buy a marriage license. In general, it is *litigation* that is expensive. Litigation is not socially approved or publicly encouraged. This message is reinforced by high costs. To be sure, society does not try to discourage all use of the courts. Many countries use legal aid schemes, small claim courts, "social" courts, and similar devices, to ease the cost burden, if it has tilted too far in one direction.[29] In American law, the contingent fee

---

29. See Mauro Cappelletti, James Gordley and Earl Johnson, Jr., *Toward Equal Justice: A Comparative Study of Legal Aid in Modern Societies,* Dobbs Ferry, N.Y.: Oceana Pub. Co., 1975.

is widespread. Lawyers (in an auto accident case, for example), only get paid if they win. This shifts the risks from litigants to lawyers, who can spread the risks among many clients. The lawyer, in a sense, lends money to the client. In many accident cases, victims could not afford to sue, if they had to pay their own costs; and many victims could not take the risk of losing everything. Partly because of the contingent fee, malpractice suits (against doctors) are very common in the United States; they are rare in England, which does not allow the contingent fee.[30]

Any effective change in a rule of law alters the balance of costs and benefits for any one whose life is touched by the rule. Rules announce: this is allowed, this is forbidden, this or that conduct has legal consequences. The law does not—and cannot—*stop* behavior, in the literal sense.[31] The law makes murder illegal, but not impossible; it attaches a price to this crime. One may, so to speak, decide to pay the price, despite the law. We can look at legal rules as attempts to fix prices in such a way as to drive some conduct out of the market, and to encourage other conduct. This way of looking at law once again blurs the distinction between civil and criminal sanctions. To be careless on the road, causing damage to somebody's fenders, is not considered a crime; the careless driver, however, may have to pay, or face a lawsuit. Breach of contract also exposes a person to the risk of "'damages." These risks, in theory, raise the price of careless driving, or of breach of contract. Civil rules, then, presuppose a cost-benefit model of behavior, just as much as criminal law—if not more so. The same is true of rules that merely channel behavior. To leave your property to charity, instead of to blood relatives, is possible; but you must make use of the law of wills. This is, at the least, a slight nuisance. Any rule that makes the use of wills trickier or costlier—or easier or cheaper—should affect the rate of use.

Moral Aspects of Noncriminal Law

Civil law does not live by sanctions alone. It too relies on inner feelings, and on public sentiment. The curve of use rises when incentives rise, but the state is not the only source of incentives. Bankers and druggists have codes of morality; they are sensitive to the opinion of other bankers or druggists. We have noted how the use of divorce law depends on the surrounding culture: on what mother, or the church, or the

---

30. Note that in most tort cases, the parties are strangers, who meet in a screech of brakes on the highway. A lawsuit does not disrupt any ongoing economic or social relationship.

31. Except, of course, as to those currently "incapacitated" by prison or the death penalty.

neighbors think. Legal culture, in general, is a civil as well as a criminal force.

Civil law as a whole, compared to criminal justice, seems somewhat impersonal and cold-blooded, at least in Western societies. This is even true in tort law, where the law allows punitive damages, and damages for emotional injuries. On the other hand, not every "crime" is an act that offends the common conscience; nor does criminal law hold a monopoly on moral indignation. Civil law usually means law that is privately pursued. A rule becomes criminal when the state takes over enforcement. If a grocer sells ten five-pound bags of rotten tomatoes, no single buyer is likely to sue; even for all ten buyers, a lawsuit is not worthwhile. If we want control over grocers, we must move collectively. This means administrative process—or criminal law.

On the other hand, some parts of the civil law can be stigmatizing, embarrassing, personally destructive: bankruptcy, divorce, defamation, paternity suits. On the whole, stigma and shame are less salient in civil than in criminal litigation, at least in modern societies. Bankruptcy was once highly stigmatized. It has now lost much of its element of shame; this is also true of divorce. On the whole, a fine of $1,000 is *not* the same price for an act, as $1,000 in civil damages. The criminal penalty, like a toxic drug, has many more side-effects, and is more potent than a civil sanction, dollar for dollar, unit for unit, pain for pain.

CHAPTER 11
SOCIAL
CHANGE
THROUGH LAW

The social study of law, as we have seen, starts with the assumption that social forces in some sense produce or influence law. At many points in this survey, we have touched on the relationship between law and social change—how through the ages law has altered, following changes in social structure, for example. Usually the question was how social change affects the law, not the other way around.

This chapter will take a brief look at the role of law as an instrument of change. It looks, as it were, through the other end of the telescope. In question here is the deliberate use of law to affect social change. More narrowly, we ask whether future social change can, and will, take place through the orderly process of law. This chapter defines the phrase "social change through law," and discusses the relationship between state structure and sociolegal change. Two kinds of state-centered change, planning and veto, are mentioned, and there is also a brief discussion of law and revolution.

We must constantly remind ourselves that the word "law" is tricky, prismatic. One can use the word in a very broad sense, to refer to a vast system of instruments, institutions, processes, and forms, including courts, the legislature, the executive, police, private attorneys, and the whole army of clerks, bureaucrats, administrators, civil servants, and their agencies, that serve the modern state. When we use the word this way, "law" becomes a synonym for government. And it is almost self-evident that every major social change (and probably every minor one) works through the law. Nothing significant goes on in a modern nation, in which the state plays no role at all, for which we cannot find a decree, order, rule, direction, or activity, *somewhere* in the chain of cause and effect. Taxes are "law"; declarations of war are "law"; arrests of opponents are "law." Of course, many trends, processes, and events in the modern world concern intensely private behavior. What could be more subterranean than the inner thoughts and private behaviors that have gone to create the so-called sexual revolution? But even *these* thoughts and behaviors interact with others, in such a way as to make new law. The sexual revolution has left its mark on the criminal code, on family law, on laws about abortion, pornography, and divorce. Perhaps these laws, and the forces they set in motion, in turn will influence sexual behavior. In an age of active government, it is only to be expected that government is everywhere, and that law has its hand in every process.

SOCIAL CHANGE THROUGH LAW: A DEFINITION

But people usually have in mind a more modest meaning of "law" when they speak of social change through law. They are thinking of a few institutions which (to them) are "legal" at the core; they are thinking of orderly, formal change, change which makes use of the "rule of law." So, for example, a Latin American country may decide to pursue a policy of land reform. One way is to enact a law limiting how much land a family can own, set up a formula to compensate those whose land is expropriated, and create a tribunal to settle disputes—in short, provide for orderly transfer of land from one class to another. This would be seen by most people (if it worked) as "social change through law." But if the government simply seized the land, or let the peasants seize the land, or connived at these results, or condoned them, as perhaps took place during the Allende regime in Chile, this would not be "social change through law," even though state and government were deeply involved, and even if, by some criterion, the actions were justified.

In other words, people tend to use the phrase "social change through law" to mean public or state action that preserves certain forms of legality. The concept, then, is fairly time-bound and culture-bound. And the outer forms of legality can be stretched pretty much out of shape. The Nazi regime, in Germany, committed terrible atrocities under cover of laws that gave the regime a smattering of legality, legitimizing the exercise of what was really naked terror and raw force, in thin disguise.[1] Vigilantes, in the American West, often held "trials" before they hung a horse-thief or

---

1. See, for example, Ilse Staff, ed., *Justiz in Dritten Reich*, Frankfurt/Main: Fischer Bücherei, 1964, pp. 50–67.

murderer. Dictators of all sorts convene puppet parliaments, and seem to put some store on a legislative rubber stamp.

We take, however, the ordinary meaning of the phrase, and look briefly at its place in the modern world.

SOCIAL CHANGE AND THE SOCIAL THEORY

First, we observe that *social theories* of law, carried to an extreme, treat the legal system (including the state) as a kind of conduit, membrane, or medium, that itself has little or no effect on inputs or outputs. Social forces create demands; demands flow in and through the legal system; they come out the other side in the form of legal acts. But the system itself, basically does not create the demands, does not change them, and, except in form, cannot in the long run shape the outputs. The legal system stands in the middle, mostly passive, mostly inert: it serves, it follows; it does not lead.

This position is obviously far too extreme; some qualifications are certainly needed. The statement is least true for "law" in the narrowest sense (that is, for strictly "legal" institutions, such as the courts), and most true for "law" in the broadest sense. Also, the more active the role of the state, the more the statement has to be qualified. And the state is *very* active in the modern world. Social theories embody propositions about the way the legal system relates to its society. The propositions are not laws of nature. They are empirical statements. The usual equations best fit "open" societies—societies in which political institutions are more or less exposed to public pressure (where people can vote, lobby, coax, cajole, exert influence), and in which people have a more or less instrumental conception of law, which justifies pressures and demands on law and state.

STATE AND LAW
AS INDEPENDENT POWERS

The social propositions, then, best suit parliamentary democracies. Each kind of society will generate its own variety of social proposition. For example, *wealth* does not play the same role in all societies. In some one-party states, wealthy people have tremendous influence; they run the country completely. In countries like France or the United States, wealth has great power, but not without limits. In still other countries, there are few restraints on political power, and the power of wealth is precarious; it is held at the pleasure of the government. The rich, like medieval Jews, can be periodically fleeced. Political influence, too, can be precarious, in states with no normal, orderly way of changing regimes; it is risky to be a big man in Russia, or in General Amin's Uganda. To be a member of the opposition in the Parliament of Britain or Norway is honorable, and may lead to high office; in other countries, it can lead to the firing squad.

In an open society, the law (at least in the broad sense) tends to be *reactive* rather than *proactive;* it initiates less than it responds. In very totalitarian states, the powerful—those with maximum influence on law— are identical, or almost identical, with those who formally run the state. The king of France said, "I am the state," and Hitler could have said, "I am the law." If a single absolute monarch held all political power, he would be able to "make law" without interference. In a sense, one could still say that "social forces" made law in that society, but "social forces" had been concentrated within one person. No such society is (fortunately) possible, but despotisms are common enough in history. Nearly absolute power can be lodged in a charismatic leader, or in a tyrant. In the Zulu state, in the early nineteenth century, Shaka, the king, had fearful power; he could and did order the slaughter of innocents, at will: "caprice, taken seriously, was at the heart of the state."[2]

In terror states, and in socialist states run strongly from the center, government is very much a "leading sector." Power is not widely spread about; wealth plays less of a role than it does in bourgeois society. Shaka could and did terrorize and control the traditional elders. Hitler robbed and slaughtered the Jews, even wealthy and famous ones. The Soviet government crushed the bourgeoisie and land-owners, who were dispossessed as well in Eastern Europe, Cuba, and China. General Amin drove the middle-class Asians out of Uganda.

In all modern societies, however, the power of the state seems to be growing and growing. It grows steadily and, as far as we can tell, irreversibly. The state mixes in, influences, controls every part of the economy (with more or less success). It regulates, taxes, redistributes; it governs social relations; it makes policy and carries it out (if it can). The state, then, is a "leading sector" and it is no longer accurate to think of the social force that makes law as a force exclusively *outside,* to which government responds; it is also a force *inside,* because government is so mammoth, so mighty, so all-embracing. And because government is everywhere, private power is precarious. No single business, no single interest group, no single rival can withstand the government, when government makes full use of *its* weapons, even legitimate ones. This awesome strength, including the power to do evil, leads the citizen to look for some counter-

2. E. V. Walter, *Terror and Resistance, A Study of Political Violence,* New York: Oxford University Press, 1969, p. 192.

vailing force. One likely candidate is "law," in the sense of an independent center of power, honest and neutral, an ancient rival which does not seem to dance to Leviathan's tune. The task of law, people feel, is not merely to do justice between citizen and citizen; law has the right, the duty, the imperative to control the state, to keep bureaucrat and politician within reasonable bounds. Ever since political and legal thought first awoke to consciousness, they have wrestled with issues of law and power. But the problem seems very severe, very concrete, very ominous in the age of "Big Brother."

ON PUBLIC REFORM

Tyranny and red tape are negative aspects of active government. The other side, the positive side, we might call *public reform*. Much social and legal change is engineered, that is it seems to begin inside government and work through or by government. In other words, there are "reforms" that come out of government, which cannot be explained in terms of pressure groups, lobbies, or the ordinary dynamics of bureaucracy. No doubt interest groups, lobbies, and bureaucratic dynamics account for most examples of "reform," even those which seem to bubble up spontaneously from government. Government itself is a vast pressure group. It employs people in the millions; bureaucracy constantly tries to preserve (or build) jobs and power, and it needs to show constant vitality and growth. All this produces a lot of "reform." Still, when we subtract all explainable "reform," we are left with a genuine residue. This is *public reform*.

The Economic Opportunity Act of 1964, has been used as an example. This law was part of the "war against poverty," which President Lyndon Johnson launched in that year. There was no real pressure for the program from the very poor; the public at large was indifferent, or at best mildly in favor. The program was hatched inside the Administration, partly for its own political purposes, but partly because reform-minded people were working there.[3]

Japan, Turkey, and, more recently, other countries of the Third World, have imported large chunks of European or American law. In a sense, this borrowing too can be called public reform. Experts and professionals within the government decide that it would be good to "modernize" the law. In most cases, neither the public at large nor the business community has demanded such a change; the center of gravity

3. On this point see Byron G. Lander, "Group Theory and Individuals: the Origin of Poverty as a Political Issue in 1964," *Western Political Quarterly*, Vol. 24, p. 514 (1971).

lies within the bureaucracy. Japan, in the late nineteenth century, wanted to catch up with the world—to modernize law, following European models, seemed like an important part of the program.[4] In modern society, the articulate public seems, vaguely, to exert a kind of general pressure for reform. In other words, there is a demand for change, rising like a faint smoke from the population; no interest group in particular is its source, and the demand, paradoxically, does not pose the usual sort of interest-group claims; it may even be a demand to help out the weak and the powerless. What is the source of this vague, misty demand? In modern legal culture, people expect active government. Tradition is in bad odor. Stagnant government cannot be good government. Government means policy and programs. Hence, people want their leaders to struggle to solve problems. They want them to work in the public interest; they want progress. This creates diffuse support for public reform.

Public reform follows lines of ideology. In a totalitarian government, it is not easy to tell where public reform begins, and "social forces" end; private and public power are interlaced beyond analysis. Once again, we can refer to Massell's study of the Soviet attack on traditional Moslem culture.[5] Who devised this campaign, and why? Certainly, no pressure group demanded it. The Moslems themselves were against it. The women of Central Asia were docile in their roles. Surely the public in Moscow and Leningrad was totally indifferent. But the government has enormous power in the Soviet Union; the people in command believe in a single mighty state, strongly controlled from the center, and Marxist to the core. Pockets of feudalism, of alien culture, pose a vague threat to the center (the state might fall apart); more important, they offend against Soviet socialist ideals.

Lawyers are themselves a powerful pressure group. They agitate for or against reforms that affect their pocketbooks (for example, no-fault accident law.) They have also inherited a tradition, a culture; they cast their weight—it is not insubstantial—on the side of order, process, restraint. For this reason, people often think of lawyers as a conservative force. But liberal and conservative are relative terms; there are many societies in which it is radical, even heroic, to stand up for orderly, neutral process. Many leaders of the left, and many anti-colonial heroes, were lawyers by training—India's Nehru, and Fidel Castro, for example. And lawyers are often in the vanguard of public reform.

4.   See, in general Zentaro Kitagawa, *Rezeption und Fortbildung des Europäischen Zivilrechts in Japan*, Frankfurt/Main: A. Metzner, 1970.

5.   Gregory J. Massell, "Law as an Instrument of Revolutionary Change in a Traditional Milieu: the Case of Soviet Central Asia," *Law and Society Review*, Vol. 2, p. 179 (1968).

MAJOR LEGAL CHANGE:
ON PLANNING AND VETO

Major legal change through law may be divided into two broad types, one positive and one negative. We will call them *planning* and *veto,* respectively. *Veto* means change that comes about through blocking some proposal or action, or by destroying or undoing some established arrangement, legal or social. *Planning* means change that comes about through *new* legal or social arrangements; to plan means to devise these arrangements and to put them into effect. Social upheaval usually combines planning and veto. In the great revolutions an old order is destroyed, but in the name of a new, revolutionary order.

Planning, as a matter of policy, is found in every country today, revolution or no. Socialist countries—the Soviet Union, Poland, Cuba, and others—are deeply committed to pervasive central planning of economic life. They exercise tight control over the arts, the media, and, to an extent, over social behavior as well. But the rest of the world is also committed to planning. This was even true during the nineteenth century, when, in many "advanced" countries, intellectuals took seriously the ideal of *laissez-faire*. Codification itself is a mild form of planning. The instrumental theory means, in practice, that every group in society *believes* in some sort of planning. People believe, in other words, that it is right and proper to steer and guide the ship of state. They believe that it is right and proper to engineer change through law. In every country today, big and small, regardless of ideology or economic system, the bulk of the population seems to believe in direction from the center. Of course, people disagree about how much, and how (if at all) to control the rulers.

REVOLUTIONARY LAW

Revolution is the extreme form of *veto*. It is interesting to follow the fate of an old legal order, during violent revolution. The Russian revolution was strongly ideological. It was committed to deep change in social structure. The Soviet dogma called for the State (and its law) to wither away. The leaders, moreover, despised existing law, which they (correctly) assumed to be tied to the Czarist regime. They tried to abolish the law, and destroy the authority of lawyers. A "lawless" phase is common in the early stages of major revolutions. The old law is deposed, and replaced by a looser system; lay people, guided by revolutionary principles, seize the reins of justice. In Russia, at the beginning of the period of "war-communism" (1917–18), the court system and the legal profession were abolished; the Czarist codes of law were declared null and void. The regime set up new People's Courts; these were supposed to decide cases in acord with "revolutionary legal consciousness," except where some government decree explicitly covered the matter. Any Soviet citizen, in good standing, was allowed to practice law. Special revolutionary tribunals enforced the "Red Terror." They decided questions "exclusively by the circumstances of the case and by revolutionary conscience."[6]

But it is no law of nature that a revolution must devour existing law. There are revolutions and revolutions. Some revolutions want to stress continuity; some see propaganda value in keeping old legal institutions more or less alive, to show a commitment to legality. The German civil code remained in force throughout the Nazi period. It had little or no political importance; but it was a sign of stability and order—false, but convenient.

In the Soviet Union, too, the brashness of "war-communism" soon came to an end. When the regime won its *military* war, it turned to the task of rebuilding a shattered economy. New legal codes were enacted. Less and less was heard of the withering away of the state. Under Stalin the regime made massive use of terror. But there was a conscious effort to color the state with legality. Terror in the 1930's was secret and underground. The famous "purge" trials were conducted in the open, but they stressed "voluntary" confessions of guilt, and the trappings of fair trial.[7]

LESS TOTAL REVOLUTIONS

"Revolutions" of course, do not always succeed in revolutionizing. Many "revolutions" run up against the leaky hose phenomenon. Revolutions need great force, or (successful) moral mobilization. Many modern "revolutions" do not go very deep—certainly not as deep as their rhetoric. Indonesia's leaders, for example, replaced the very symbol of Western or colonial justice; instead of "the blindfolded lady with scales," they used a native symbol, a stylized banyan tree; there was constant talk of "the law of revolution." But a careful student of the subject concluded, in 1965, that the change was only skin-deep; partly because "the social class in control" was "neither new nor radically inspired," partly because the legal profession had been trained in "the world of colonial law" and remained "immersed" in that world.[8] An old equilibrium often proves to

6. Harold J. Berman, *Justice in the USSR*, New York: Vintage Books, 1963, p. 31.

7. On the court systems of revolutionary socialist countries, see above, p. 31.

8. Daniel S. Lev, "The Lady and the Banyan Tree: Civil-Law Change in Indonesia," *Am J. Comp. Law*, Vol. 14, pp. 282, 306–7 (1965).

be uncommonly tough. The new order exists only on paper; in practice it is largely ignored.[9]

Some "revolutions," then, are ineffective, usually for the same general reasons that make other legal interventions ineffective. Others simply need time to take over the reins, or to percolate into the national consciousness. The course of reform in Turkey is instructive. Ataturk's regime imposed revolutionary changes on this Moslem people, in the 1920's, including vast change (on paper) in an area of law (family law), which is exceptionally durable and tough. At first, it seemed as though little real change in behavior took place. Yet the legal revolution now, fifty years later, is finally taking hold. Many Turkish soldiers fought in World War II and the Korean war; their wives were eligible for financial aid; but they had to prove a valid marriage—that is, a marriage in accordance with the codes. This brought about a wave of civil marriages. And, in the 1970's Turks are beginning to make more and more use of the civil courts; even women are litigating, in some ways "more efficaciously than men."[10] No longer can one point to Turkey as an example of still-born legal change. Many of the "disastrous" Soviet reforms, too, gradually turned into successes.

SOCIAL CHANGE THROUGH LAW: THE ROLE OF THE COURTS

In modern legal culture, we have remarked, it is hard to conceive of major changes in social life, which do not take place in and through law, or produce some *major* legal change. "Law" means, mostly, statute law. It means, secondarily, administrative rules and (in some countries) executive decree. These are the vehicles of planning and regulation, in the modern state. The courts have played, on the whole, a minor and declining role in socio-legal change.

This is to be expected. Judges in civil law countries, in England, and even in the United States, are not supposed to change the law. They are supposed to apply rules laid down by others. They have, in many ways, been gradually stripped of power. Yet in the United States the courts have struck out boldly for social change in a few dramatic

9. See John H. Beckstrom, "Transplantation of Legal Systems: An Early Report on the Reception of Western Laws in Ethiopia," *Am J. Comp. Law*, Vol. 21, p. 557 (1973), for the fate of the Ethiopian codes.

10. H. Timur, "Civil Marriage in Turkey: Difficulties, Causes and Remedies," *International Social Science Bulletin*, Vol. 9, p. 34 (1957). June Starr and Jonathan Pool, "The Impact of a Legal Revolution in Rural Turkey," *Law and Society Review*, Vol. 8, p. 533, 554 (1974).

cases—for example, school desegregation (1954). The Supreme Court abolished the death penalty (though it later partially recanted), revolutionized the law of abortion, and ordered a President (Nixon) to give up evidence which led to his resignation. The federal courts have handed down many striking decisions, in cases arising under the federal Constitution. Here a kind of natural law tradition is still strong, and the Supreme Court and some lower courts feel more or less free to translate into law ideas about due process and the basic rights of man. The high court has been caught up in sensitive issues for over 150 years, and it possesses a store-house of great prestige. This cushions it against the criticism that inevitably follows the more flamboyant decisions. Judicial review is the power of courts to judge whether other branches of government have overstepped their legal powers. In the United States, the courts can declare a solemn act of Congress unconstitutional. The power of judicial review is also found in some countries in Latin America and Europe. Nowhere, perhaps, is it so boldly used as in the United States, but courts have been getting bolder in a number of countries. The West German constitutional court declared void an abortion law adopted in 1974.[11] This dramatic step would have been unthinkable in the past—and also illegal. In 1975, a lower court judge in India ruled that Indira Gandhi, the Prime Minister, had been illegally elected. Here the result was not, however, acquiescence; but rather a seizure of power by Mrs. Gandhi.

SOCIAL CHANGE THROUGH LAW IN A NONREVOLUTIONARY STATE

Most of us, of course, do not live in societies that are undergoing revolution; in many societies revolution is an unlikely dream (or nightmare, as the case may be). Yet we all live in restless times. Many people—highly articulate, active people—feel that social change has not gone far and fast enough. They feel that society cannot long survive, unless it solves some basic problems—maldistribution of wealth or power, crime and unrest, destruction of resources, world overcrowding, racism, hunger, oppression, and so on. Of course, people do not agree on the causes, or cures, of these problems. And among those convinced of the need for massive change, some (a minority) feel that the only path to change is through violent revolution; others feel, or hope, that change can come

11. *Juristenzeitung*, 1975, No. 7, p. 205. The law allowed women to procure abortions legally, up to the twelfth week of pregnancy. The statute, according to the court, could not be reconciled with the Fundamental Law of the republic, which contains the phrase: "Everyone has a right to life."

about within the framework of the system as it is. They hope, in other words, for social change through law—deep, far-reaching social change.

Is this hope in any way realistic? Arguably not: if we took the social theory of law too literally, we might feel that, at any given time, the legal system stands, necessarily, in equilibrium. It reflects, quite accurately, the pattern of effective demands made on the law, in society. But power and wealth give people extra "votes," and the demands of the mighty are the ones which in fact become law. To alter the system in a significant way, without changing its basic structure, is therefore impossible. Only revolution can work such change.

Social structure is indeed tenacious; and it is certainly true that interest groups tend to insist on keeping their share of society's goods. If one's goal was to exterminate capitalism in Switzerland, or Canada, for example, only an army (and a foreign one at that) could achieve the result, in the predictable future. But the lesson of recent history is also a lesson of change. Real change does not take place in society, far-reaching change, and without violent revolution. How do we explain this paradox?

First of all, in modern society, change is considered quite normal. The legal culture, we have seen, expects it. The truly reactionary state— Portugal under Salazar—is rare, and barely viable. Even Saudi Arabia, committed to Moslem orthodoxy, a country where women are forbidden to drive cars, lurches forward into social change. In parliamentary societies, social institutions, however "conservative," are constructed not to stifle change, but to control it, smooth it out, see to it that it moves in an orderly way. Every time a legislature sits, it is committed to make *some* changes; every new government must have change on its agenda.

Secondly, even in a society which is wholly inert, completely tied to tradition, outside forces break in, and coerce some changes in process or substance. The climate alters, an earthquake levels the capital, an enemy invades. In modern societies, technological change can upset long-standing arrangements. Modern medicine cures malaria and helps set off a population explosion. There are unpredictable ebbs and flows in the economy. It is oil wealth which is so fundamentally changing the countries of the Persian Gulf—a situation they hardly anticipated and are hardly responsible for. Society must cope with a kaleidoscope of new situations. A society today is considered "stable," not when it is changeless, but when it is flexible, when it adapts well to change and handles it skillfully.

The Concept of "Slack"

In addition, every system has rich reserves of *slack*—nodes of real leeway and choice. These, however, are not always obvious to the naked eye. Suppose we slice through a legal system in cross-section, and look at it closely. As a matter of theory, we assume that what we see—the state of affairs—is a rough map of what the legally active social forces want. But a "state of affairs" is made up of hundreds of little bits of behavior and structure. They look the same on the surface; but they are in different sorts of equilibrium. If we set children loose in a candy store and tell them to take whatever candy they choose, they will pick candy almost at random—chocolate, jelly beans, sourballs, gum. If we limit them to two dollars worth or to only five kinds of candy, they will work more slowly, discarding what they do not "really" want. The more we press them, the more hard choices they will have to make. At the end, they will keep only that which they absolutely love.

Yet before we imposed the limits, we did not know if, in a pinch, they would give up jelly beans and keep chocolate, or whether the gum would go before the sourballs. We did not know what they liked best and liked least. On the surface all candies were the same; no candy was labeled "essential" or "expendable." Demands, interests, and outputs in the real world do not carry labels either. Some, however, are vital and will be guarded to the end; only revolution can disturb them. Others are weak, teetering on the brink; they will be abandoned at the first whiff of gunsmoke.

Let us take a concrete example. In the 1960s, in many countries, including the United States, students began to demand reforms in university life. They wanted more personal freedom—the right to come and go as they pleased in their dormitories. They also wanted a share in running universities, in hiring and firing. As it turned out, there was considerable slack in the system—room, that is, for change. Some rules gave way, on very slight pressure. Faculty and staff cared little about dormitory rules. They gave them up at the first rumblings of discontent. But they defended their jobs and their status with savage tenacity.

In every society, some rules and institutions, though they serve the interests of the people on top, do so only slightly; some are supported by the barest majority of social force. These are the places where *slack* can be found. These rules are not worth defending. A system has *slack* when support for rules, processes or institutions is so weak that small shifts in force or opinion will move them. This is the case where social forces on either side are neatly balanced. It is also the case where the vast majority of social force is indifferent. If 99% of the people are bored, unaware, or asleep, with regard to some issue, the 1% who care will have their way. But the situation will be rich in slack. If only slightly more than 1 percent of the indifferents rouse themselves, the situation can be overturned. This is likely to occur after a crisis, incident, or scandal, or if a new pressure group forms, or if a reformer like Ralph Nader begins to make noise.

In other words, a status quo consists of two distinct zones. One is the zone of *slack;* the other is the zone of deep defense. Common experience often tells us which is which. The private property system in the United States is in the zone of deep defense. But for many areas of law, it is hard to be sure. How easy would it be to reform the copyright law? or establish divorce in Paraguay? Moreover, situations change. The death penalty, in a number of countries, has shown radical shifts in the depths of its defense.

THE FUTURE OF LEGALITY

What can we say, then, about the future of social change, through law? Can we expect orderly, patterned change, working through traditional legal institutions? In any country, the rate and kind of change will depend heavily on outside events, on culture, and on slack. Prediction, then, is quite impossible. Law, in the broad sense of the word, is a permanent part of human society, and will always be. But whether this or that institution—courts or legislatures—will survive, in any particular form, and play any special role, is certainly not to be taken for granted. Whether any particular *process* survives is likewise uncertain. There are societies—such as Maoist China—in which the leaders are striving to make "law" (in the narrow sense) almost obsolete. In the broader sense, there is as much "law" in Maoist China as is in the United States— perhaps more, because the state seriously tries to control many areas of life which we leave alone. But that sense, as we have said, is not what people usually mean by "law." Law as a tool of social change means old, traditional legal institutions. These change, to be sure, but slowly enough so that we recognize them as familiar all the while, like a human face as it ages day by day. The role of courts in social change, for example, may or may not continue as it is. The courts in the United States may keep on their activist course—or shift direction. The special role of courts may grow stronger in Japan, Germany, Italy, and in the new nations; or it may not. The use of law depends on legal culture—on social attitudes toward law. This in turn is inseparably linked with the traditions of society, with its social structure, with its history. The future of law in any state must remain an open question.

SELECTED
REFERENCES

Of the making of books, according to Ecclesiastes, there is no end; and this includes books about law. Of course, the list is much shorter for books about law and society, but nonetheless the literature has grown exponentially in the last generation. General treatments of the subject are still in fairly short supply, at least in the English language. A few such books are listed here, for the student who may want to explore the subject further.

First, there are a number of collections of materials that provide a general survey. One such is Richard D. Schwartz and Jerome H. Skolnick, *Society and the Legal Order, Cases and Materials in the Sociology of Law* (New York: Basic Books, Inc., 1970). Lawrence M. Friedman and Stewart Macaulay, *Law and the Behavioral Sciences*, 2nd edition (Indianapolis: Bobbs-Merrill and Co., 1977) has more of the style of a law school "casebook." Vilhelm Aubert, *Sociology of Law* (Harmondsworth, England: Penguin books, 1969) and Donald Black and Maureen Mileski, *The Social Organization of Law* (New York: Seminar Press, 1973) are also convenient collections of materials. A survey of some parts of the field is Lawrence M. Friedman, *The Legal System, A Social Science Perspective* (New York: Russell Sage Foundation, 1975). Max Weber's great and seminal work on law, still full of wisdom if not wit, has been translated and published, under the title, *Max Weber on Law in Economy and Society*, ed., Max Rheinstein (Boston: Harvard University Press, 1954). Weber is tough reading; the introduction by Professor Rheinstein is a model of clarity and I suspect that many readers will "cheat" by reading the introduction only, without wading into the involute text.

The anthropology of law is represented by a number of collections, including Laura Nader, *Law in Culture and Society* (Chicago: Aldine Press, 1969). Leopold Pospisil, *Anthropology of Law: A Comparative Theory* (1971) is a stimulating volume; and E. Adamson Hoebel, *The Law of Primitive Man, A Study in Comparative Legal Dynamics* (Cambridge: Harvard University Press, 1954) is a lively and readable account of the legal systems of preliterate societies. The reader who wants a survey of the work of political scientists can look at Herbert Jacob, *Justice in America; Courts, Lawyers, and the Judicial Process,* 2nd ed. (Boston: Little, Brown & Co., 1972). Another survey is James Eisenstein, *Politics and the Legal Process* (New York: Harper & Row, 1973). Despite the title, the book deals exclusively with the United States of America; it should be supplemented with Henry W. Ehrmann, *Comparative Legal Cultures* (Englewood Cliffs, New Jersey: Prentice-Hall, 1976). John H. Merryman, *The Civil Law Tradition* (Stanford, California: Stanford University Press, 1969), is a concise, readable introduction to European and Latin-American legal systems.

The history of law is a rapidly growing field. On American law, the work of J. Willard Hurst is fundamental. *The Growth of American Law: The Lawmakers* (Boston: Little, Brown and Co., 1950) traces the development and impact of legal institutions; Lawrence M. Friedman, *A History of American Law* (New York: Simon & Schuster, 1973), is a narrative account of the development of the legal system, up to the end of the 19th century, with a brief sketch of more recent developments. Richard Posner, *Economic Analysis of Law* (Boston: Little, Brown and Co., 1972) is a general attempt to apply classical economic theory to the understanding of the common law; and a handy collection of readings is Henry G. Manne, *The Economics of Legal Relationships, Readings in the Theory of Property Rights* (St. Paul, Minn.: West Publishing Co., 1975).

There have been a number of studies of the American legal profession, including Erwin O. Smigel, *The Wall Street Lawyer: Professional Organization Man?* (New York: Free Press of Glencoe, 1964), dealing with the big law firm, perhaps a shade too starry-eyed. Smigel might be supplemented with Joel F. Handler, *The Lawyer and His Community; the Practicing Bar in a Middle-Sized City* (Madison: University of Wisconsin Press, 1967), a study of lawyers in a midwestern community, and Jerome E. Carlin, *Lawyers on Their Own* (New Brunswick, New Jersey: Rutgers University Press, 1962), a study of solo practitioners in Chicago. An interesting comparative essay is Dietrich Rueschemeyer, *Lawyers and Their Society: A Comparative Study of the Legal Profession in Germany and in the United States* (Cambridge: Harvard University Press, 1973). Lawyers spend a good deal of their time negotiating; and most claims and disputes never get to court. The literature tends to underplay this part of the system, but we have now one good study, H. Laurence Ross, *Settled*

Out of Court, the Social Process of Insurance Claims Adjustment (Chicago: Aldine Publishing Co., 1970), which helps fill part of this gap.

It would be hard to compile a list of books (in English, at any rate) on the sociology of judges, comparable to the list of books about lawyers. On courts and procedures, one might look at John A. Robertson, *Rough Justice, Perspectives on Lower Criminal Courts* (Boston: Little, Brown and Co., 1974); Harry Kalven, Jr., and Hans Zeisel, *The American Jury* (Boston: Little, Brown and Co., 1966) is the most noted product of an enormous study of one of our most distinctive legal institutions. John Thibaut and Laurens Walker, *Procedural Justice, a Psychological Analysis* (New York: John Wiley & Sons, 1975), reports on a series of experiments designed to test some assumptions and hypotheses underlying the procedural rules of legal systems. Philip Selznick, in *Law, Society and Industrial Justice* (New York: Russell Sage Foundation, 1969) deals with due process and legality outside the courtroom setting. On law and public opinion, see Julius Cohen, Reginald Robson and Alan Bates, *Parental Authority, the Community and the Law* (New Brunswick, New Jersey: Rutgers University Press, 1958); and Adam Podgorecki et al., *Knowledge and Opinion about Law* (London: M. Robertson, 1973).

One of the most hotly debated topics of recent years is deterrence; the literature is well covered and discussed in Franklin E. Zimring and Gordon J. Hawkins, *Deterrence: the Legal Threat in Crime Control* (Chicago: University of Chicago Press, 1973); a recent analysis, quite comprehensive and very thought-provoking, is Jack P. Gibbs, *Crime, Punishment and Deterrence* (New York: Elsevier, 1975).

Finally, one can get something of an overview of the field, as well as a sample of the kinds of work being done, through looking at the various issues of the *Law and Society Review* and, recently, the *Journal of Legal Studies* as well.

INDEX

Abortion cases, in German constitutional court, 109, in United States, 165
Adjudication, 28
Administrative Agencies, 56
Administrative function, of legal system, 13–14
Administrative law, 105
Administrator, defined, 12
Afghanistan, and Islamic law, 74
Africa, colonial law, 46; customary law, 75
Albania, use of banishment, 119
Appellate courts, style of, 86–88
Aquinas, St. Thomas, 41
Arbitration, 28, 31–32
Ascriptive allocative systems, 18
Ashanti, 119
Athens, use of "attorneys," 20; see also Greece
Attitudes, effect on behavior, 149–50; toward law, research on, 77
Aubert, Vilhelm, 128
Australia, 147
Authority, legitimate, Weber's theories of, 78

Banishment, as punishment, 119
Bargaining, 126; and nonenforcement of laws, 129
Barotse, law of, 28–29
Bentham, Jeremy, 53
Bias, in legal systems, 56–66
Biblical law, 49; and legitimacy, 80; see also Jewish law
Bickel, Alexander, 69
Blackstone, classification of law, 50–51
Brazil, use of despachantes, 23
British Road Safety Act of 1967, 120

Canada, as federal system, 71

Capital punishment, debate over, 120–22
Carbonnier, Jean, 129
Chambliss, William, 129
Chance, as allocative method, 17, 18, 19
Chessman, Caryl, 122
Child development, legal consciousness and, 43–44
Chile, 157
China, legal profession, 24
Civic-mindedness, defined, 138
Civil damages, and deterrence, 124
Civil disobedience, 69
Civil law family, 73; attitude toward codes, 91, and third world, 47
Civil liberties, opinion about, 142
Civil litigation, and legal behavior, 153–55; moral aspects, 154–55
Civil rights, 106
Claims of right, 13
Classification, of legal systems, 72–76
Code Napoleon, 42, 51, 73; style of, 90
Codes, Ancient, 38–39; European, underlying ideas of, 42; Germanic, 41
Codification, 162
Codification movement, 42
Colonial legal systems, 71–72
Common law, 73–74; attitudes of judges toward statutes, 91; as closed system, 82; legal reasoning, 82; personality and reality distinguished, 49; style of courts, 87; and third world, 47
Communication, as element in "moral passage," 151, of legal acts, 111–14
Compliance, motives for, 15–16; and "problem of the cadres," 130
Conceptual jurisprudence, 54
Conflict resolution, as function of legal system, 12
Conscience, appeals to, 147–48;

Conscience *(cont.)*
    contribution to legal behavior, 149;
    see also Legitimacy; Morality
Contingent fee, 153–54
Contract law, and civil damages, 124
Corporations, law of 51–52
Costa Rica, judges' concept of role, 88
Costs, and civil litigation, 153
Cour de Cassation, style of, 86–87
Courts, 12, 27–34; functions of, 29–30;
    future of, 168; in socialist countries,
    31; role in social change, 164–65; and
    social theory, 106; in tribal societies,
    29; in twentieth century, 106–7; in
    Western societies, 29; *see also* Judges
Crimes, classification of, 125
Criminal Justice, costs compared to civil,
    154–55; deterrent effect, 133;
    enforcement, 129–30; side effects, 155
Criminal law, distinguished from civil
    law, 50; and group factor, 138
Culture, and legal behavior, 126; legal,
    see also Legal culture
Customary law, in Africa, 74, 75; and
    legal reasoning, 83–84

Death penalty, *see* Capital punishment
Demands, change in, 103–4; defined,
    99–100; for deviance, 124–26; on
    government, 59–60
Denmark, role of lawyers in politics, 27
Denver, Colorado, study of drunk driving
    sanctions, 148
Despachantes, in Brazil, 23
Deterrence, and capital punishment,
    121–22; and civil damages, 124; and
    labeling, 133–34; and legal behavior,
    147; and sanctions, 119–20; studies of,
    120; theories of, 118
Deuteronomy, book of, 38
Deviants and deviance, 11, 133–34; enemy
    deviants, 151, 152, 153; repentant,
    sick, and cynical deviants, 150–51;
    theories of deviance, 133–34; types of
    deviant, 150–51
Dispute settlement, as function of legal
    system, 12
Divorce, and costs of litigation, 153
Dred Scott case, 87
Durkheim, Emile, 43, 44, 152

Economic Opportunity Act, 160
"Effectiveness," of legal acts, 127
Ehrlich, Eugen, and "living law," 55
Eichman, Adolph, 109, 146
"Eichmann" experiments, 145–46
Enforcement, of laws, 129–31; influence
    of peer group, 137–38; investment in,
    131; and nature of conduct affected,
    132–33
England, background of judges, 107;
    country courts, 31; divided bar, 26;
    judiciary, 33, 34, 54, 107; legal
    profession, size, of, 31; public
    hangings, 121; resists reception of
    Roman law, 73; *see also* Great Britain

Erikson, Kai, 152
Eskimos, treatment of murder, 50
Ethiopia, codification of law, 46
Excommunication, as punishment, 119

Facilitative function, of legal system, 13
Fairness, defined, 139; of legal systems,
    62–63
Far East, legal systems, 74
Federalism, 71
"Federal questions," 71
Feedback, 127; and decision to invest in
    enforcement, 131
Fictions, legal 81, 82
France, corporation law, 52; divided bar,
    26; legal reasoning, 80–81; popular
    view of courts, 29; regulation of
    banks, 80
Freedom, and regulation in the 20th
    century, 57–59
Freedom to travel, 58–59
Functions, of legal system, 10–16; manifest
    and latent, 10

Gaius, 40, 41
Gandhi, Indira, 2, 165
Germany, abortion case, 165; background
    of judges, 108; civil code, 42, 163;
    constitutional court, 165;
    conceptualism, 54; corporation law,
    52; "free law" school, 54; Hitler
    regime, 68, 157; judiciary, 34, 85, 87;
    legal ideology, 68; legal profession,
    23–24; legal science, 83; litigation in
    housing matters, 143; respect for law,
    142; size of bench, 34; study of law,
    24; style of courts, 87
Gluckman, Max, and law of Barotse,
    28–29
Government, demands on, 59–60, 161; as
    leading sector, 159–60; as pressure
    group, 160; role in modern law, 56–60
Great Britain, *see* England
Great Yasa, 49
Greece, absence of formal legal thought,
    39; absence of legal profession, 20
Group factor, in legal behavior, 135–38;
    positive aspects of, 137–38
Gusfield, Joseph, on deviance, 150–51

Habit, as element in legal behavior, 150
Hammurabi, code of, 38, 39
Hart, H.L.A., 49–50
Harvard Law School, 25
Hebrew law; *see* Biblical law, Jewish law
Hindu law, 74
Historical school, of legal thought, 53
Holmes, Oliver Wendell, Jr., 54–55, 89
Hurst, J. Willard, 52–97

Ideology, and demands on law, 101, 102;
    and public reform, 161
Impact, of legal acts, 127
India, 2, 165; Hindu law, 74; impact of
    British law, 37–38; litigation, 15–16;
    "sea lawyers," 23

Indonesia, "bush lawyers," 23; legal revolution, 163
Industrial Revolution, impact on law, 51–52
Instrumental theory of law, 53, 59, 62, 68, 78, 162
Interaction, 126, 150
Interests, classified, 101–2; defined, 99–100; as perceptions, 103; and "slack," 167
Internal Revenue Code, 114
Internal theories of law, 92, 93; compared to social theories, 95–96
Islamic law, 45, 74; legal reasoning, 81–82
Israel, 36–37; legal pluralism, 71
Italy, lack of divorce law, 100
Ivory Coast, abolition of customary law, 75

Japan, borrows European law, 46, 160–61; legal profession, 24; respect for law, 142
Jewish law, 38, 74; legal fictions, 82; legal logic, 86; legal reasoning, 81–82; use of excommunication, 119
Judges, as active or passive, 33–34; background of, 107–8; concept of role, 88; decision-making, 105–10; European, 34; role-playing, 34, 108–9; selection, in United States, 33; style of dress and behavior, 96; see also Courts; Judiciary.
Judicial decision-making, and social theory, 105–10
Judicial review, 165
Judiciary, lay, 33; professional, 32–33
Juris prudentes, 20
Justice, and legal ideology, 67–69; two meanings of, 67
Justinian, 40, 41

Knowledge of law, 114–15
Kuba, norms among, 84

Labeling theory, 133–34
Land reform, 157
Language, of law, 88–91
Law, definition of, 1–5, 156–57; future of, 168; origin of, 35; and public opinion, 97–99; as reactive or proactive, 159; and revolution, 162–64; twentieth-century characteristics, 56; see also Legal system
Lawyers, as information brokers, 114; as pressure group, 161; see also Legal profession
Learning, of legal behavior, 150
Legal acts, 6; communication of, 111–14
Legal aid, 153
Legal behavior, 115, 146–50; conflict of factors, 147–50; definition, 115; group factor in, 135–38; influence of model, 136–37; learning and unlearning, 150; moral factor, 138–45; motives for, 115–16; and personality, 126
Legal change, 162–68
Legal consciousness, among children, 43–44
Legal culture, 7–8, 76, 168; and

classification of legal systems, 75–77; and demands on law, 101, 161; and legal reasoning, 78–79; modern, 164; research on, 77
Legal development, concept of, 45–47
Legal education, 24–25
Legal evolution, theories of, 42–45
Legal fictions, 81–82
Legal language, 85, 88–91
Legal logic, 86
Legal norms, distinguished from non-legal, 61–62
Legal pluralism, 135–36, 145
Legal positivism, 53
Legal profession, 19–27; in ancient Rome, 21–22; and legal reasoning, 85–86; rise of, 20; role in politics, 26–27; in Scandinavia, 24; size, 23–24; in Soviet Union, 22; stratification, 26; substitutes for, 23; in United States, 25–26
Legal realism, 54–55
Legal reasoning, 78–86; types of, 80–86
Legal science, 83, 93
Legal system, administrative function, 13–14; as allocative, 16–19; classification of types, 72–76; components of, 6–7; contents of, 48–52; facilitative role, 13; functions of, 10–16; and government, 70; and justice, 63–69; as pluralistic, 71–72; see also law
Legal thought, development of, 38–42; in modern world, 53–56
Legalism, in bureaucracies, 85
Legality, 62–63, 157; future of, 168
Legislation, style of, 90–91
Legitimacy, 62–63, 138, 139, 140, 141, 147; and illegitimacy, 140–41; and legal behavior, 143–45, 149–50; and legal reasoning, 79–80; loss of, 142–143; measurement of, 141–42; in modern society, 144; primary and derivative, 79–80; strength and stability, 142–43; theories of, 77–78
Leopard-skin chief (Nuer), 28
Lesotho, role of chief, 32
Litigation, costs of, 153; decline of, 30; pathologies of, 15–16
Llewellyn, Karl, 55
Lottery, use of in legal system, 18
Luhman, Niklas, 139

Maine, Sir Henry, 37, 43, 44, 82
Malinowski, Bronislaw, 55
Marijuana laws, enforcement of, 132
Market, as allocative method, 17
Marxism, 56, 64–65, 97
Massachusetts, colonial, 118
Mechanical jurisprudence, 94
Mediator, 12, 28
Medicare, 104
Merit, as allocative system, 18
Mexico, legal pluralism, 75; use of litigation, 16
Milgram, Stanley, 145–46, 147

Moral factors, and legal behavior, 143–45, 147–48
Morality, and legal behavior, 138–45
"Moral passage," 151
Mormons, 149

Nader, Ralph, 167
Natural law, theories of, 41, 53, 93; challenged, 53, in constitutional law, 165
Need, as allocative system, 18
Nixon, Richard, 109
Nonenforcement of laws, *see* Enforcement of laws
Norway, bargaining in criminal justice system, 128–29; decline of litigation, 30; enforcement of energy laws, 132–33; legal profession, 24
Notaries, 14

Obedience to authority, 145–46, 147; in Canada, 146
Ostracism, as punishment, 119
Ottoman Empire, legal pluralism, 71

Parking, rules of, 146
Perception, of risk of punishment, 123
Personality, and legal behavior, 126
"Phantom effect," 123
Piepowder, 71
Planning, 162
Plea bargaining, 127–29
Pluralism, in legal systems, 71–72, 135–36
Poland, 96, 149
Police, and nonenforcement of laws, 129–30
"Police science," 25
Portugal, 166
Power, and law, 99
Precedent, doctrine of, 73
"Primitive" law, 74–75
"Principles," compared to rules, 113
"Problem of the cadres," 130, 132
Procedural justice, 64
Prohibition, 129, 132, 137
Property, definition, 17
Prussia, code of 1794, 73
Public opinion, and law, 62, 97–99
"Public reform," 160–61
Punishment, functions of, 118; *see also* Sanctions

"Queuing," 18–19

Redistributive function, of legal system, 12
Reform, defined, 102–3; through government, 160–61
Reformers, 104, 167
Regulation, and freedom, 57–59
Resistance, 126
Resources, and nonenforcement, 129
Respect for law, studies of, 141–42
Revolution and revolutionary law, 77–78, 84, 162–64
Rewards and punishments, as allocative methods, 17; *see also* Sanctions

Riggs v. Palmer, 113
Ritual language, in law, 89
Roman law, classification of law, 51; rediscovery and "reception," 41
Rome, arbiters, 31; codes, 39; development of legal thought, 40–41; legal profession, 20–21
Rules, 4, 6–7, 112; communication of, 112–13; and culture, 149; and definition of law, 4; enforcement, 131; quantitative aspects, 113–14; substance and procedure, 6–7; vagueness or specificity, 112

Sacred law systems, 74, 80–82, 86, 93; legal reasoning, 81–82; legal language, 89
San Benito, California, 16
Sanctions, 117, 148–49; compared to moral factors, 147–48; and group factor, 135–36; and legal behavior, 116–20, 123–24; side-effects, 133–34; speed of application, 123–24
Saudi Arabia, 74, 166; execution of Prince Faisal, 121
Savigny, Friedrich Carl von, 53
Scandinavia, arbitration in, 31; classification of legal systems, 73
Secondary social control, 14
Securities and Exchange Commission, 90
Self-interest, and legal behavior, 115–16
Sex laws, lack of enforcement, 129
"Sexual revolution," 157
Shaka, king of the Zulus, 159
Shame, as aspect of punishment, 118–19
Side-effects, of legal acts, 127
Singapore, 123
"Slack," concept of, 166–68
Slavery, law of, 49
Small claims courts, 31
Social change, 165–66; in Parliamentary societies, 166; role of courts, 164–65; through law, 157
Social control, as function of legal system, 11; secondary, 14
Social science, and study of law, 55–56
Social theories of law, 92–93, 158; compared to internal theories, 95–96; and judicial decision-making, 105–10; varieties of, 97
Socialist legal systems, classifications of, 74
Socialist states, courts, 31; government role, 159
Sohm, Rudolph, 83
Sovereignty, and legal systems, 70–71
Soviet Union, 66, 162–63; comrades' courts, 31; legal profession, 22; reform of family law in Central Asia, 130, 136, 149, 161; revolutionary legality, 84; terror, 163
Spain, background of judges, 108; decline of litigation, 30; legal education, 24
"Spill-over" effect, 144
State, *see* Government
Stigma, 118–19, 155
Structure, of legal systems, 6

Students, and reform of universities, 167
Style, of appellate courts, 86–88, 89
Substance, as component of legal systems, 6
Substantive rationality, in Weber's thought, 84
Success, of legal acts, 127
Sumner, William Graham, 97
Supreme Court (United States), 164–65; and public opinion, 142; school prayer decision, 130; style, 87–88
Sweden, rules of road, 104; welfare legality, 85
Switzerland, 24, 54

Talmud, rules of legal logic, 86
Taxation, 57
Technology, effect on enforcement, 131
Terror, 159; in Soviet Union, 163
Threat, as element in sanctions, 117
Torts, 49, 124
Tristan da Cunha, 37, 137
Trust, concept of, defined, 139
Turkey, law reform, 46, 164
Twelve Tables, 39

Uganda, 89, 159
Union of South Africa, courts, 106; death penalty, 121

United States, attitudes toward instrumentalism, 68; capital punishment, 121–22; corporation law, 52; impact of law, 2; judiciary, 33; legal profession, 23, 24–25; legitimacy, 145; litigation, 31–32; regulation of banks, 60; respect for law, 142; social study of law, 55; welfare legality, 84–85
Utilitarians, 53

Vagueness, of legal rules, 112; in legal writing, 90
Verbosity, in legal language, 90–91
Veto, 162
Victimless crimes, 132
Vigilantes, 157–58
Vote-trading, 104

"War-Communism," 162–63
Wealth, role in society, 158–59
Weber, Max, 43, 55, 84; ideas of legitimacy, 78, 139–40
Webster, Daniel, 25
Welfare law, 57
Welfare legality, 85, 87
Western Samoa, 58
Witchcraft, 66

Zulu kingdom, terror in, 159